Revolutionary Theory and Political Reality

Revolutionary Theory and Political Reality

Edited by

Noel O'Sullivan

SENIOR LECTURER IN POLITICS
UNIVERSITY OF HULL

ST. MARTIN'S PRESS · NEW YORK

Printed in Great Britain
First published in the United States of America in 1983

ISBN 0–312–68033–3

Contents

List of Contributors

PETER CALVERT, Reader in Politics, University of Southampton. Author of *Revolution* (1970), *The Study of Revolution* (1970), and *The Concept of Class: An Historical Introduction* (1982); specialises in the politics of the Americas.

JAMES COTTON, Lecturer in Politics, University of Newcastle upon Tyne, formerly Proctor Fellow at Princeton University. Author of articles on political thought and ideology.

C. H. DODD, Professor of Politics, University of Hull. Author of *Democracy and Development in Turkey* (1979), *Crisis of Democracy in Turkey* (1982), and other books and articles mainly on Middle Eastern subjects.

HAMID ENAYAT, Fellow of St Antony's College, Oxford, and Lecturer in the Modern History of the Middle East, formerly Professor of Politics, Teheran University. Author of *Modern Islamic Political Thought* (1982) and of books and articles on cultural and political trends in the Muslim world.

MICHAEL FREEMAN, Lecturer in Government, University of Essex. Author of *Edmund Burke and the Critique of Political Radicalism* (1980), co-editor of *Frontiers of Political Theory* (1980), and author of various topics in political theory, including the theory of revolution.

NORMAN HAMPSON, FBA, Professor of History, University of York. Author of various books on the Enlightenment and the French Revolution, including *A Concise History of the French Revolution* (1975), and *Danton* (1978).

RICHARD JEFFRIES, Lecturer in Politics, School of Oriental and African Studies, University of London. Author of *Class, Power and Ideology in Ghana: the Railwayman of Sekondi* (1978) and of articles on African politics.

TERRY MCNEILL, Lecturer in Politics, University of Hull. Publications include articles on a variety of topics in the fields of Soviet and East European politics.

H. G. NICHOLAS, FBA, formerly Rhodes Professor of American History and Institutions, Oxford University. Author of books and articles on American history and politics including *The Nature of American Politics* (1980) and *Washington Despatches 1941–45* (1981).

JEREMY NOAKES, Reader in European History, University of Exeter. Editor of *Government, Party and People in Nazi Germany* (1980) and author of articles on German history and politics.

NOEL O'SULLIVAN, Senior Lecturer in Politics, University of Hull. Author of *Conservatism* (1976) and *Fascism* (forthcoming, 1983), and of articles on contemporary political thought.

Preface

This collection of essays is devoted to the theme of revolution and seeks in particular to throw more light on the phenomenon by considering its meaning and implications in a variety of quite different contexts. In this way we have tried to avoid the definitional and ideological rigidities which mar much treatment of the subject. At a more general level, however, three contentions provide a conceptual framework which makes the essays more than mere blow by blow accounts of particular revolutions.

The first contention is that all the various revolutions are connected, in spite of the manifold differences between them, by their common membership in one single, over-arching revolution. This over-arching revolution, however, must be understood as a *process*, rather than as a single *event*. There already exist, of course, two important schools of thought which advance a view of this kind. One is Marxism, which conceives of the process in terms of an advance through capitalism to socialism; the other is the currently influential body of non-Marxist literature which conceives of it as a movement along the path to 'modernisation'. In my introductory essay, I reject both these prevalent views, and argue that the process can best be understood in terms of a shift from 'states' to 'movements' as the basic unit of modern political organisation.

The second contention relates more directly to the methodological problems presented by the study of revolution. During the past two centuries many scholars have dreamt of making the study of politics a science. By implication, they believe that it should be possible to construct a science of revolution. In the second essay, Michael Freeman considers recent attempts to carry out this enterprise, and concludes that they suffer from vagueness and inconsequence. In varying degrees this scepticism about the possibility of a science of revolution is shared by all the contributors. Their essays are therefore primarily historical in emphasis and rest, explicitly or implicitly, on the conviction that attempts at generalisation are a recipe for historical over-simplification.

The third and last contention is that the western revolutionary experience is now so thoroughly diffused throughout the world that an adequate treatment of the subject must itself be based upon a global perspective. What has happened, more precisely, is that for the first time in history a single political vocabulary (viz. the vocabulary of western democratic idealism) has come to provide the predominant political vocabulary in every country, with the result that it is now extremely difficult to distinguish indigenous ideas from imported western ones. Before this problem can be properly dealt with, however, it is necessary to consider carefully the original European and American experience of revolution. The starting point is therefore the liberal-democratic tradition in the form in which it emerged at the end of the eighteenth century. In this connection, H. G. Nicholas begins by reopening the question of whether the American Revolution was really a revolution in a sense which would make it separable from the War of Independence. From the American Revolution attention naturally passes to the French Revolution. Norman Hampson ruthlessly exposes the inadequacies of the influential interpretation inspired by Marxist theory – an interpretation so well-established that Hampson believes it can now properly be described as the 'classical' one.

After these studies of the liberal-democratic tradition, three essays are devoted to the ideal of total revolution which has marked the twentieth century. Terry McNeill puts the revolutionary claims of the Bolsheviks under a microscope, whilst Jeremy Noakes assesses Hitler's rival claim that Nazism is the only truly revolutionary movement the world has so far experienced. James Cotton completes the analysis of totalitarianism with an assessment of the impact of western influences upon Chinese political thought.

Cotton's study leads naturally to the final group of essays, which are devoted to the relevance that the European and American experience of revolution has acquired in the Third World. In this wide area, the problem referred to above of determining how the language of revolution borrowed from the West conforms to political reality is especially acute. Peter Calvert suggests that in the Latin American case this problem can best be dealt with by regarding Latin America as a laboratory in relation to Old World political ideas. In the case of Africa, Richard Jeffries argues that the idea of revolution only makes sense within the confines of the Marxist theory of imperialism, upon which he forthwith proceeds to do an exemplary work of demolition. Clement Dodd deals with the problem of continuity and discontinuity in Turkish political life, and in particular with the problem of interpreting it through the categories of western political experience. Finally, Hamid Enayat introduces a highly contemporary note with his study of the revolution in Iran. It was with deep regret that the editor learned of his premature death before arrangements for publication of the book were concluded.

N. K. O'S., Hull, 1982.

Acknowledgements

I am grateful to Professor C. H. Dodd not only for his advice, encouragement and assistance at every stage of this work, but also for help in resolving the many practical problems that inevitably arose.

I am also grateful to the contributors for the patience with which they read a draft version of my own essay and tried, in the light of their different specialities, to use it as a framework for the study of revolution.

N. K. O'S., Hull, 1982.

I

THE STUDY OF REVOLUTION

1 An Introductory Essay: Revolution and Modernity

NOEL O'SULLIVAN

The concept of revolution is the central concept in the vocabulary of modern political thought. It is central, not only because it is the stock-in-trade of all the great radical ideologies of our age, but also because it is the point of convergence for all the ideas which mark off western political development during the past two centuries from the preceding 2½ thousand years of western history. Yet if it is the central concept of our age, it is also the most confusing one. The aim of the present paper is to indicate briefly the principal sources of this confusion and then to propose (in an admittedly sketchy way) a concept of revolution which avoids them.

Of the various sources of confusion, the most obvious is the fact that the concept of revolution has been the favourite receptacle for a series of grandiose ideological dreams ever since it first acquired its current connotations in 1789. It was shaped originally by the radical democratic dreams which inspired the French Revolution; but throughout the subsequent period the concept has remained entwined in elaborate and conflicting ideological constructions. It is for this reason that the voluminous literature which continues to issue from the proponents of these constructions must be set to one side at the outset: any conception of revolution derived from that quarter would be too closely tied to the ideological womb from which it had issued for it to have any independent analytic value. There would be, in particular, the insuperable problem that what is a revolution for one ideologist is not so for another. Thus Fascism, for example, is a revolution for the liberal ideologist but not, of course, for the Marxist. It is confusion of this kind which bedevils, for example, Hannah Arendt's well-known book, *On Revolution*.[1] For Arendt, a true revolution is essentially a movement which aims at the creation of a republic. Arendt's definition of revolution, it will be evident, suffers from the defect of immediately eliminating from the concept the main idea associated with it in the modern world; the idea, that is, that a revolution aims at the creation not just of new political forms, but of a new kind of society, and even of a new kind of man.

It is not only the ideological treatment of the concept of revolution, however, which makes the phenomenon so elusive and confusing when we attempt to analyse it seriously. At the opposite extreme, the detailed work of historians who have analysed the events conventionally described as 'revolutions' immediately casts doubt on the degree of intellectual precision which the concept possesses outside the ideological camps. For example, the conclusion of one notable contemporary historian, Sir Lewis Namier, is that 'most revolutions are filched or deflected: groups or parties with elaborate programmes try to stamp them with their own ideology and, if successful, claim to be their spokesmen or even their makers.'[2] More generally, he observes, 'Revolutions are not made, they occur.' The circumstances under which they occur may perhaps permit certain simple generalisations to be made, but these generalisations serve, at the same time, to indicate how restricted is the scope of conscious revolutionary purpose in altering the structure of a society.

We begin the analysis of revolution, then, with two contrasting approaches. At one extreme, there are the propagandist accounts of the nature of 'true' revolution offered by different ideologists. At the other extreme, there is the sober, sceptical approach of the historian whose stress on the complexity and intricacy of human affairs threatens to dissolve what we think of as the great revolutions of the modern period into a chance conjunction of events and unintended outcomes. In between these two extremes, however, there lie two further manners of approaching the subject which must be briefly considered.

There is, in the first place, the large body of literature on revolution produced by sociologists and political scientists. Of this, I shall consider only the most wide-ranging and ambitious project, which has been the endeavour to develop a concept of revolution by relating it to something called 'the modernisation process'. In literature of this kind attempts are made to correlate political with socio-economic change, with a view to discerning the circumstances under which revolutionary conditions may be expected to occur. The difficulty, in every case, is that it is always possible to point to counter-examples; to political or social situations, that is, which have accompanied revolution in one country, but which were not present in another. The most convenient examples of the absurdities to which political scientists have thereby been reduced are provided by the way in which different writers handle the Fascist revolution. The difficulty experienced by Organsky in relating both Nazism and Italian Fascism to the modernisation process provides one of the most graphic instances. Fascism, Organsky believes, is something which occurs only in the course of the modernisation process and not at the stage when it has been completed. His theory, therefore, seems to fit the Italian form of Fascism, since Italy was not a highly industrialised society at the time of the March on Rome; but in its Nazi form, Organsky has to legislate Fascism out of existence by branding it as an historical aberration, since it does not conform to the requirements of his theory of the stages of economic and political development. According to Organsky, that is to say, Nazism should not have occurred at all, since Germany was a fully modernised society at the time when Hitler came to power.[3]

Cyril E. Black's *The Dynamics of Modernization* (NY, 1966) presents similar difficulties. Italian Fascism is classified by Black as a developmental dictatorship of a kind which fits in with what he thinks is likely to happen in the course of the industrialisation process, whilst Nazism is classified as a 'unique case' (p. 85) which occurred only because a group of anti-modernist villains managed to seize the state at a point when the social integration which modernisation otherwise brings was within Germany's reach. Unfortunately, the story of all the great, wide-ranging theories of contemporary social science is invariably just such a story of 'unique' or 'special' cases. The modern social scientist, it would seem, is generally a died-in-the-wool Lockean who spends his whole life so deeply enveloped in the lingering shadow of Enlightenment optimism that he may well die without ever experiencing the one thing that redeemed Locke's own intellectual career; the fact, that is, that Locke had a neo-Hobbesian early period.

Before setting developmental theory to one side, it is necessary to consider a somewhat different version of it which has been especially influential, but proves on closer inspection to be equally misleading. The second version, which occurs in a relatively simple form in the work of Seymour Lipset, consists of endeavouring to define and classify revolutions in terms of the 'social base' from which they are supposed to proceed. For Lipset, there are three possible social bases, corresponding to the upper class, the middle class, and the working class. Each of these groups possesses a 'normal', non-revolutionary political style to which it subscribes whilst the going is good; but each is prone to adopt, in times of adversity, an extreme or revolutionary political style. Thus the working class tends in normal times towards democratic socialism, but in face of social adversity it gravitates towards revolutionary communism. Again, the middle class in normal times is moderate and liberal, but in adversity tends towards Fascism. Since the theoretical difficulties presented by this mode of analysis are the same in every case, it will be convenient to illustrate them by noting the problems presented by the case of Fascism. This aspect of Lipset's analysis has received considerable critical attention, mainly because of the connection which he purports to establish between liberalism and Fascism. According to Lipset, the crucial thing to be noticed is the common middle-class 'social base' of the two ideologies, liberalism being the normal form of middle-class ideology, and Fascism its extreme form. The two main difficulties presented by this view are familiar, and need hardly detain us. In the first place, support for Fascism is not significantly connected with middle-class status, since factors such as age, sex and religion were at least as important as social class. Age, in particular, is worth stressing in this connection. National Socialism, as the historian Walter Laqueur remarks, came to power, not as the party of the middle class, but 'as the party of youth'; and the sociologist Hans Gerth reminds us, likewise, that the Nazi Party could truthfully boast of being a 'young party'. The statistics, in this case, are especially interesting. According to the Reich's census of 1933, those between the age of eighteen and thirty constituted nearly one-third (31.1 per cent) of the German population as a whole.

The proportion of National Socialist Party members of this age group rose from 37.6 per cent in 1931 to 42.2 per cent a year later, on the eve of power. ... By contrast, the Social Democratic Party, second in size and the strongest democratic force in German politics, had only 19.3 per cent of its members in the eighteen to thirty age group in 1931. In 1930 the Social Democrats reported that less than eight per cent of their membership was under twenty-five, and less than half was under forty.[4]

Correlating revolutionary politics with 'social base' or social class, then, is not in itself, even where the correlation exists, a way of *understanding* or explaining anything. But apart from this difficulty, there is the further point (made for example by the German historian, Ernst Nolte), that 'What needs to be explained is not that the Nazi Party consisted predominantly of members of the middle class . . . but rather that the party attracted so many workers and noteworthy figures from the upper classes.'[5] One is reminded, of course, of the English doctoral dissertations devoted to examining the shop-keepers who supported Sir Oswald Mosley, when the important thing is that the majority of English shop-keepers never did.

Concern with the social bases of revolution, it may be noted, ends by engulfing the concept of revolution in global confusion. Consider, for example, Barrington Moore's ambitious study, *The Social Origins of Dictatorship and Democracy*. The aim of his study, Moore writes, is 'to explain the varied roles played by the landed upper classes and the peasantry in the transformation from agrarian societies (defined simply as states where a large majority of the population lives off the land) to modern industrial ones.'[6] The immediate difficulty is that what Moore means by 'modernisation' is too vague for purposes of historical analysis. This vagueness is especially evident, for example, at the end of the book, when Moore describes modernisation in terms of 'the ancient Western dream of a free and rational society'.[7] Unfortunately, what Moore means by this 'ancient Western dream' remains obscure. Moore himself does not appear to be aware of any problem, but a glance at Sophocles or Euripides, for example, indicates that the Greeks were too deeply imbued with a tragic sense for them to fit easily into a vision of Moore's kind. The Romans, in turn, were far too practical ever to envisage an abstract Utopia of any kind, and the medieval world, concerned as it was with faith and original sin, had little time for dreaming about a free and rational society. The dream Moore refers to, then, is not an ancient one, but derives from the meliorist hopes which have constituted the intellectual orthodoxy of the last two centuries.

It is against this vague and unsatisfactory conceptual background that Moore proceeds to treat the great revolutions of the modern world. In this perspective, Fascism, for example, is defined as 'conservative modernization through a revolution from above', and is identified as one of three distinct paths by which an agricultural society becomes an industrial one (the other two being through middle-class and peasant revolutions.) Specifically, Fascism is the 'capitalist' and 'reactionary' route to modernisation. This definition, however, occurs at such a high level of generalisation that it inevitably makes 'Fasicst revolutions' out of totally disparate situations. It implies, for example, that any form of paternal or authoritarian government which aims at industrialisation is 'Fascist', with the result that even nineteenth-century politicians like Bismarck, and the Meiji oligarchs in Japan, are converted into revolutionary figures comparable to Mussolini and Hitler. Moore's attempt to explain revolution in terms of universally applicable socio-economic categories, then, merely adds confusion to his initial vagueness.

The work of ideologists, historians, and political scientists, in short, leaves the concept of revolution obscure. There remains, however, one last approach to be considered, which is that of political theory. But if we now turn to the political theorists, we are soon disappointed with them as well. On the one hand, there is the work, for example, of A. S. Cohan. After a lengthy survey of the principal theories of revolution, Cohan defines revolution as 'that process by which a radical alteration of a particular society occurs over a given time span'.[8] Since the whole problem about defining the concept of revolution is that liberals, Marxists and Fascists, for example, do not agree about what constitutes 'a radical alteration', Cohan's definition fails even to begin to retrieve the concept from the ideological morass in which it has for long been submerged. On the other hand, there is the lucid and scholarly work of Peter Calvert, who suggests that we can avoid this problem by relying on the ordinary everyday usage of the word. According to this usage, revolution refers to 'events in which physical force (or the convincing threat of it) has actually been used successfully to overturn a government or regime'.[9] The trouble in this case is that we then have no clear way of distinguishing, for example, Caesar from Lenin, or what happened in ancient Egypt (to which Calvert devotes most of his first chapter) from what happened in Russia, Germany, Italy or China in the present century. It is to Calvert's credit, of course, that he forces this problem upon his reader with such compelling vigour.

The present state of the literature, then, is unsatisfactory, and it is therefore necessary to point tentatively in a different direction. What may now be suggested is that the concept of revolution is least problematic when it is used to refer, not to individual *events* in specific countries during the past two centuries, but to a *process* which is illustrated by those events. This process, which constitutes the true revolution of the modern period, may be briefly described as a tendency towards a shift from 'states' to 'movements' as the basic units of twentieth-century political life. But since the terms 'state' and 'movements' are too familiar, and now too vague, to capture the full drama of what has happened (and is still happening today), it will be more convenient to describe the revolution in question as the shift from a limited to an activist style of politics.

Both the structure and the novelty of the new activist style can most readily by appreciated by considering first the older, limited style of politics upon which it has been grafted or superimposed, and which it has, on occasion, subverted altogether.

The older, limited style of politics (which still survives, in a somewhat threadbare form, in the western democracies) had as its focal point the state tradition. As a form of political organisation, the state emerged in Europe at the time of the Renaissance, where its lineaments may first be clearly discerned in the writings of Machiavelli. From that time until the end of the eighteenth century, the state tradition was marked by five characteristics, which together provide the elements of what I refer to as a limited style of politics. The characteristics of the activist style emerge by way of a series of negations of these elements.

The first element in the state tradition consists of the idea of *law* as the bond of community. A state, that is to say, was believed to be held together, not by some shared *purpose* – such as the religious purpose of getting to heaven, or the secular one of increasing material prosperity, or working for the triumph of the proletariat, or for the purification of the Aryan race – but by the formal bond of law. Within the activist style of politics, by contrast, it is always a shared *purpose* which is the basis of community, and never the idea of law. This purpose is expressed in what we now call an ideology.

In the second place, the state, within the framework of a limited style of politics, was regarded as having a specific territorial identity. This identity was recognised as contingent, being the product of war, of dynastic alliances, of tradition, of power and of diplomacy; but the acceptance of a definite territorial identity contributed, nevertheless, some measure of certainty and predictability to the conduct of international affairs. This commitment to a specific territorial identity, however, disappears within the activist style of politics, since what matters there is the shared purpose. There is no reason, therefore, why an activist regime should not expand in any direction in which it feels that participation in its purpose can be secured, either voluntarily or by the use of coercion.

In the third place, a limited style of politics is one in which a distincton is made between public and private life, or between state and society. The state, that is to say, is never conceived of as an all-embracing organisation, and is not even conceived of as the highest object of *allegiance*, although it is conceived of as the highest *authority*. Thus a man whose highest allegiance is to God, for example, may nevertheless acknowledge the state without inconsistency as the highest authority to which he is subject in life.

In the fourth place, the state tradition was generally regarded, within a limited style of politics, as one in which power was an intrinsic object of suspicion. Thus from Machiavelli's *Discourses* down to de Tocqueville's *Democracy in America* we find that the classic question asked about power is not who should exercise it, but how can power be limited, irrespective of who exercises it?

This last point may be made in a slightly different fashion. Since the end of the eighteenth century, nearly all political thought and practice have been based upon the assumption that *somewhere* in society there is *some* group which would never abuse power if power were ever to be transferred to it. Initially, this belief appeared in democratic guise, in the form of the naïve conviction that the sovereign people could never have an interest in ruling itself badly. Bad government, it was thought, occurred only because kings, aristocrats and priests abused the power they held. Once their power had been taken away from bad rulers and conferred upon the people, an era of justice and harmony would begin, for 'self-government' automatically meant (it was thought) 'good government'. Subsequently, this belief has been modified, but never abandoned. It has been modified, most notably, in the course of disagreements about who constitutes 'the sovereign people'.

This question was first raised by the Abbé Sieyès, in 1789, in his famous pamphlet *What is the Third Estate*? In answer to the question, what is the *real* people? Sieyès replied, it is the middle class. He had, however, merely begun a game which other activists could turn to their own purposes, with a little ideological ingenuity. Thus Marx, confronting the same question, answered, the proletariat; and having identified the sovereign people with the proletariat, he followed Sieyès' example and identified the remainder of society as a parasitic entity feeding upon the productive majority of the community. For Sieyès, the parasitic entity was the aristocracy and clergy; for Marx, it was the capitalists. The same game, however, could be played in a way which upstaged both Sieyès and Marx; and this was the achievement, most notably, of Hitler, who identified the true people with the Aryan race. In principle, of course, there is no reason why the game should stop there. An extreme feminist, for example, might identify the people with women, and brand all men as the parasitic class. Such, then, is the logic and structure of activist demagogy.

We have come to believe, in sum, that somewhere in society there is a group (the 'true' people) who would never abuse power, and the great radical ideologies of our age differ mainly about the particular group they favour, and about the programme (or ideology) which that group should implement if ever it were to succeed in acquiring power. A limited style of politics, by contrast, never assumes that political problems would disappear once power was entrusted to some particular group. It is concerned instead with an entirely different question. This question, as has been said, is that of how institutions can be so organised that they always provide impersonal safeguards against the abuse of power, irrespective of who exercises it. That question is always excluded from the activist political style, which is concerned solely with the 'who?' aspect of power.

Finally, a limited style of politics is marked by its tolerance of a variety of constitutional forms. Until 1789, for example, the European world acknowledged no single legitimate form of government. Absolutism, republics, ecclesiastical states, autocracies and mixed forms of government were all considered to be equally legitimate, although they were not, of course, considered to be equally good forms of government. For example, in December 1652, M. de Bordeaux was sent by Louis XIV to address the Parliament of the English Commonwealth. The French emissary did not claim, in his address, that the Englishmen who had despatched their king and changed the constitution from a monarchy into a commonwealth had thereby absolved the French from honouring existing treaties, or from acknowledging the binding character of new ones. 'The accord which ought to exist between neighbouring states', he declared to the Parliament, 'is not affected by the form of their governments. . . . This realm may have changed its complexion, and from a monarchy become a republic, but . . . our peoples still remain neighbours and the treaties which exist between nations are binding . . . since they have as their principal object the common utility.'[10]

Within the modern activist style, however, this tolerant position has changed completely since, in the new style, one form of government has acquired a total monopoly of political legitimacy. This is the democratic form, which alone is legitimate because, it is believed, power must come 'from below'. This principle was established with the appearance in 1789 of the French *Declaration of the Rights of Man and the Citizen*.

The disastrous result of the new democratic doctrine is obvious as soon as its two main implications are noticed. Previously, the word 'democracy' had referred to one specific kind of constitution amongst many others, all of which were considered equally legitimate. Henceforth, it referred in practice to *no* specific type of government at all (with the result that any type could claim to be 'democratic'). In the second place, by directing attention away from *how power is used* to *where it comes from*, the new democratic doctrine legitimated even the most oppressive government – provided only that it claimed to be 'democratic'.

These, then, are the five intellectual ingredients of the new style of politics which has come to dominate the twentieth century: (i) rejection of *law* in favour of a *purpose* (or ideology) as the bond of a community; (ii) rejection of a specific territorial identity; (iii) rejection of the distinction between public and private life; (iv) rejection of any intrinsic suspicion of power; (v) willingness to accept any use of power, no matter how oppressive, provided only that the holder claims that his authority is of 'democratic' origin. This last claim, of course, has been made – with complete plausibility – by everyone from Napoleon III to Hitler and Mao-Tse Tung.

In themselves, however, these five characteristics only provide a negative characterisation of the new activist style. What is now necessary is a more positive portrait of this revolutionary style, in order to point up the contrast between the word 'state', with its relatively precise level, and the term 'movement', with its essentially nebulous and indeterminate one. For purposes of sketching in the outline of this portrait it will be convenient to turn to the first great modern activist dreamer, Rousseau, whose merit it was to have elaborated all the main features of the style long before it found any practitioners.

Rousseau is conventionally considered in the history of political thought in two ways. One is as the man who introduced into the western vocabulary the concept of the general will, a mysterious and elusive entity intended to deal with the nature of liberty and the problem of political obligation. The other is as a theorist of the empirical conditions necessary for achieving a consensus in democratic societies. He may more properly be considered, however, in a third light, as the thinker who laid bare, at the beginning of the modern period, the practical implications of the activist style. Having already examined the theoretical assumptions behind that style, it is in this light – from the practical point of view, that is – that I now want to list quickly the main things which his work has to tell us about what is involved in the shift from states to movements.

Rousseau's point of departure, it will be recalled, was the conviction that modern states fail dismally in the task of creating virtuous citizens. These states, he wrote in the *Discourse on Political Economy*, 'imagine they have done everything when they have raised money'. They are content, in other words, with ensuring peace and tranquillity in society, and to that end seek nothing more than a routine, outward, purely passive compliance with the law. But in order to produce a true citizen, deeply imbued with an active love of his country, states must encourage men not merely to obey the state, but to love it actively.[11] The aim of political activity, then, is to regenerate men by converting them into active lovers of their state, thereby endowing the state itself with the maximum of spiritual unity, and conferring meaning and dignity upon life itself by endowing it with a moral and even heroic stature.

But the crucial problem, of course, is that the mass of mankind are naturally apathetic, having no taste at all for a life which is permeated by constant and unending demands for self-sacrifice in the service of an activist ideology of this kind. What then is to be done with them, in order to jolt them out of their indifference and keep them endlessly mobilised in the way which Rousseau demands? How is the radical political leader to 'foment and satisfy' that 'reserve of grand passions' which lies latent in every heart?[12] How are men to be inflamed into that condition of 'patriotic intoxication'[13] which he favours? The problem is worth dwelling upon, since it is this question – the problem of how the masses are to be aroused and kept in motion – which has preoccupied activist thinkers and leaders from Rousseau's time down to the present day. Marx, for example, relied on the material impoverishment produced by capitalism to activate the masses. Auguste Comte relied on the dissemination of a new 'religion of humanity'. Georges Sorel desired the propagation of a revolutionary myth (the myth of the general strike). Other thinkers have staked everything upon the spread of education, or upon an unbearable amount of sexual repression, or upon messianic leadership, or upon feelings of sheer hopelessness and misery, as the levers which would finally radicalise the inert populace. Amongst all the answers which have been given to Rousseau's problem, however, the most interesting and influential are of course the simple and brutal ones given by the four great *condottieri* of our own century–Lenin, Mussolini, Hitler and Mao-Tse Tung. If we discount for the moment the differences in political rhetoric, both as between the four of them and as between Rousseau and themselves, then all they appear to add to the political style delineated by Rousseau is a greater organisational and tactical ability, combined with an altogether more brutal and ruthless disregard for legality and for the lives of their fellow men.

In the first place, Rousseau is quite explicit about the fact that the new activist style inevitably tends to convert a limited style of politics into a total one. The division between public and private life, that is to say, must necessarily be broken down. This transformation and extension of the scope of politics occur because in order to create virtuous citizens, the state must 'penetrate into a man's inmost being, and concern itself no less with his will than with his actions'.[14] The aim of the state must be 'to arrange things so that every citizen will feel himself to be consciously under the public eye'.[15] The result is what political scientists would now describe as the unceasing 'mobilization of the masses'* in the service of an all-embracing political ideal. Rousseau himself leaves no doubt at all about this outcome. 'I should wish', he wrote, 'that citizens should constantly be kept occupied with the fatherland, that it should be made their principal business, that it should be kept continuously before their eyes. . . . This is the art of turning men into an instrument more powerful than gold'.[16]

In the second place, Rousseau attaches great weight to the fact

---

* Rousseau himself talks about 'the people'. To use the term 'mass', with its connotations of anomie, would be anachronistic. I have ventured to use it, nevertheless, in order to dramatise the continuing relevance of Rousseau's overall vision of the activist style.

that the new activist political style requires a fully polititicised system of education. Only by politicising the education of citizens, from the day they are born until the day they die, can the objectives of total involvement and total commitment to the state be achieved. 'It is education', he wrote

that must give souls a national formation, and direct their opinions and tastes in such a way that they will be patriotic by inclination, by passion, by necessity. When first he opens his eyes, an infant ought to seen the father-land, and up to the day of his death he ought never to see anything else. . . . This love is his whole existence; he sees nothing but the fatherland, he lives for it alone; when he is solitary, he is nothing; when he has ceased to have a fatherland, he no longer exists; and if he is not dead, he is worse than dead.[17]

Within this system of education, children will never be allowed to play alone, but must play together and in public, 'so that there will always be a common goal toward which they aspire'. The content, the order, and the form of their studies will all be regulated by the state, and their teachers will be of their own nationality.[18] In this way, then, they will acquire the most intense sense of national identity that is possible, and will at all costs avoid diluting their sense of distinction by mixing with peoples of different nationalities.[19]

Thirdly, the politicisation of education must be supplemented within the activist style by what Rousseau called a 'civil religion'. This civil religion, it may be noticed, was intended to serve the same function as that which Sorel later ascribed to the revolutionary 'myth' with which he sought to underpin socialist radicalism. Beyond that, it would introduce into political life that passionate, uncompromising and intolerant commitment to the state which Hitler had in mind when he insisted that only a man or party with a *Weltan-schauung*–a faith, that is–could ever hope to create and maintain a new social order. In one form or another, indeed, the notion of a civil religion, a myth or a *Weltanschuung*, has served as the lynchpin of the activist style of mass politics which, ever since Rousseau, has been the principal alternative (and the main threat) to a limited style of politics. What Rousseau has to say about the nature and function of the religion entailed by the new style of politics is therefore of considerable interest.

'It is very important to the state', he wrote in the final chapter of the *Social Contract*, 'that each citizen should have a religion which makes him love his duties.' Without such a religion, he will act only from duty or interest, and hence without any of the passion brought by active love of the state. This religion will in fact be 'a purely civil profession of faith', whose content is laid down by the sovereign. Its primary purpose will be to inculcate 'sentiments of sociability, without which it is impossible to be either a good citizen or a good subject'. Anyone who refuses to accept the civil religion can be banished from the state, 'not for impiety, but for unsociability. . . . And if anyone, after having publicly recognized these same dogmas, behaves as if he did not believe them, he should receive the death penalty.'

· Fourthly, the new activist political style could only retain the support of the masses if politics was given a highly theatrical form. What is especially noteworthy here is Rousseau's insistence upon the need, in an extra-parliamentary style of politics, for constant direct involvement of the masses in public spectacles. In the first chapter of his essay on *The Government of Poland*, he emphasised the aspect of the new style above all others. How, he asked, can the hearts of the masses be reached? How can they be drawn most effectively into the political cause? Neither coercion, nor material rewards, nor just administration, he concluded, will ever catch their imagination in a way which actively engages them. When Rousseau proposed his answer, he began by asking rhetorically, 'Dare I say it?' What he then proposed was simply this: teach them children's games – by institutions, that is, 'which seem idle and frivolous to superficial men, but which form . . . invincible attachments'. Games, ceremonies, festivals, spectacles – any mass ritualistic activity, that is, which reminds the people of national and exclusive identity, increases its pride and self-esteem, and conjures up before it a vision of its own majesty and importance – such was to be the substitute for constitutional forms employed by this new, mass style of politics.[20] In this way the people are continually encouraged, as it were, to worship themselves, as they marvels at the symbols of their own corporate identity. Through the civil religion, the individual is pulled out of his isolation and submerged in the mass. Through the rites and rituals provided by the religion, the mass in turn acquires a spurious sense of warmth and solidarity of a kind which could, of course, never be provided by parliamentary or dynastic institutions.

Fifthly, Rousseau's portrait of the new political style anticipated the lesson which Hitler described as the key to his own success, in the most important chapter of the *Mein Kampf*.[21] This was that an activist movement was unlikely to win mass support so long as it relied upon a purely nationalistic, or alternatively, upon a purely socialist appeal. The people could not be aroused, Rousseau made clear, unless an appeal to them combined both these ideals. Nationalism, in short, had to be infused with a strongly socialist body of rhetoric. Hitler learned the lesson in Vienna; but the same lesson had been equally well understood over a century earlier.

Sixthly, this activist style would only retain its momentum, as Rousseau argued in effect in the *Social Contract*, if all divisive sub-groups (such as interest groups and political parties) were either eliminated from the social order, or else (which is the same thing) in some way brought into line with the general will by being submerged in it. The constant mobilisation of the population, in brief, is incompatible with permitting it any form of organisation outside the confines of the state structure.

In the seventh place, it is of the essence of this style of politics, as all of Rousseau's writings indicate, that disharmony within the social order can only ever be explained in terms of a conspiracy theory. The need for such a theory follows ineluctably from the underlying premiss of the activist style at large, which is that an actively self-governing people, or a people ruled by men who are sufficiently pure to have only the general will as their policy guide, must necessarily create a society which is perfectly harmonious. If conflict or disharmony nevertheless appears, then its existence is only explicable by attributing it to an internal or external 'enemy'. The need to postulate the existence of some 'enemy' or 'villain', then, is an integral part of the activist style, inspired as it is by a vision of perfect social unity. For Rousseau, the enemy was egoism or vanity, which he attributed to inequality. The enemy, in short, need not necessarily be conceived of in personal terms; it may be conceived of, instead, in a relatively abstract and impersonal way, when it will be presented as some aspect of the social order (or of the international order, if an 'external' enemy proves more useful). It may even be conceived of, as we now know, in genetic terms, in which case the enemy will be identified as a particular racial group. In every case, however, the assumption is that once the enemy is removed – irrespective of whether it is a personal or impersonal one – perfect harmony will be achieved within the state. But since the human condition does not provide for this possibility, what also follows is that the need for an enemy is a *permanent* one. Thus, if Hitler had finally dealt with the 'Jewish problem', for example, then some other group would have had to be selected as a new enemy. It was this aspect of the activist style, one may note in passing, which received its most stark and dramatic formulation by the leading Nazi jurist, Carl Schmitt, who redefined the political relationship as essentially a relationship between 'Friend and Foe'. Without a Foe continually before them, the Friends form no bond. The politics of activism, as Schmitt made clear, requires the permanent existence of a Foe. This Foe need not be an actual threat; he may indeed be a purely imaginary enemy; but an imaginary enemy will do perfectly well provided it rallies and unites the Friends, and in that way serves to keep the masses mobilised.

Finally, the activist style of politics proceeds upon the assumption that the only remaining problem, once the seven previous conditions of the style have been satisfied, is to determine who will exercise power. Within this style of politics, as I have already said, there is no room at all for the central problem of classical political thought, as we find that problem formulated by Aristotle, Machiavelli, Burke and de Tocqueville, for example. In the classical tradition, the central problem is not to determine who will exercise power, but to determine how the abuse of power may be limited *irrespective* of who exercises it. From Rousseau onwards, however, the emphasis in the activist tradition falls exclusively upon the 'Who?' question. This emphasis arises directly out of the utopian assumption that somewhere in society there is some individual, or some group, who could safely be entrusted with unrestricted power, since it would never have reason or occasion to abuse it. For Rousseau, the secret lay in transferring sovereign power to the people. For Marx, it lay in transferring it to the proletariat. For the Fascists, it lay, of course, in transferring it to a '*Duce*' or '*Führer*'.

Such, then, is the structure of the new activist style of politics which appeared – in a purely intellectual or ideal form at first, of course – in Europe at the end of the eighteenth century. What remains is to complete this picture of the revolutionary style which now provides the orthodoxy of western progressive thought by indicating briefly the two principal phases through which the style has passed during the last 200 years. The first phase, which spans the period from Rousseau to roughly 1890, may be called the 'spontaneous' phase of activism. The second phase, which dates from the end of the nineteenth century and continues to characterise the present condition of western civilisation, may be called the 'directed' phase. Let me try to explain the distinction between these two phases as shortly as possible.

In the first or 'spontaneous' phase, activism rested upon the belief that it was only necessary to *call* or *beckon* to the masses in order to trigger off a spontaneous popular uprising. Such was the hope of Rousseau and of the French revolutionaries, for example; and such continued to be the hope of men like Mazzini in Italy, of Herzen in Russia, of Marx, and of nineteenth-century radicals at large. The important thing about all the ideological writings that fall within the first or spontaneous phase of activism, however, is that they added nothing of substance to the structure of Rousseau's thought. What is notable in this period is really a problem which remains suppressed and concealed until the end of it. This problem, which finally gave rise to the second or 'directed' phase of activism in which we now live, is the problem of what was to be done if the masses proved to be too inert and apathetic ever to revolt spontaneously.

By 1890 this problem had become the central concern of activists throughout Europe. The revolution still had not occurred, and, what was worse, prosperity made activists suspect that it was unlikely ever to do so. One possible response was that of Robert Michels, who soon abandoned his revolutionary faith and moved into the sphere of élite theory so commonly favoured by disillusioned radicals. A second response was to think of new ways of galvanising the masses into spontaneous revolt. Here, Sorel's theory of the myth is the most instructive creation of the period. The third response, however, was to prove the most enduring in its relevance. This was to insist that the revolution must be promoted 'from above', over the heads of the masses as it were, and imposed upon them whether they wanted it or no. Such was the significance, in 1902, of the step taken by Lenin in the pamphlet *What is to be Done*? Such also was the step taken by Mussolini, in 1915, when he decided that Italian intervention in the war was desirable as the best way of radicalising the Italian masses.

We now have three-quarters of a century of 'directed activism' behind us, yet the history of this second phase has added only two points of interest to what was already clear to a few thoughtful men by the eve of the first world war. One is an awareness of the vast variety of ways in which the basic and otherwise unchanged components of activism may be reassembled to create new political patterns, merely by varying the emphasis as between the different ingredients in the mix. The other is a certain organisational finesse which activists have acquired in establishing and maintaining despotisms. On this latter subject, the work of most enduring significance in our era is undoubtedly *Mein Kampf*; and it is to Hitler, rather than to Max Weber, that the student of activist political structures will therefore tend to look.

It is this second phase of the activist style, then, which marks the century in which we live – an era of organised or directed activism. To examine particular instances of it in detail is not the present concern; the career of Hitler and other activists would take one, of course, into the domain of political history. The present concern has been, instead, to delineate the origins, nature and significance of that over-arching, on-going revolution within which the various specific revolutions of our time are to be located. This broader revolution, it has been argued, consists in the shift from a limited to an activist style of politics. When used to refer to this phenomenon, the concept of revolution acquires relative precision as a tool for the intellectual analysis of modern history. When used in any other sense – as the first part of this paper suggested – it remains elusive. It remains elusive bêcause the concept carries concealed within it the ideological presuppositions of the activist style, and therefore automatically entangles those who use it within some at least of those presuppositions.

It remains now to note briefly one predictable objection to what I have said. This is that the development of activism seems at first sight to be a phenomenon somewhat remote from our own lives, since the western liberal-democracies still retain the rudiments of a limited style of politics. By way of a concluding observation, however, it may be remarked that what has been described above is not the emergence of a totally independent and parallel style of politics, with an independent history of its own in the modern intellectual and political tradition of European life. The reality is more complex. What has been described is rather the pouring of new wine into old bottles. The result has been a systematic ambiguity within the modern political vocabulary which may be traced back to the end of the eighteenth century, when proponents of a limited style of politics became confused about the scope and nature of that style. They became confused because they too accepted (in a dilute form, of course) three of the beliefs upon which activism feeds–the beliefs, that is, that evil is rooted in the structure of society; that human nature is perfectible; and that democratic government is the sole type of legitimate government. Hence, although we still have the vestiges of a limited style of politics, we have long since lost our ability to defend it in coherent ways. Our own position, indeed, is marked principally by the radical character of our confusion; and if we fail to notice this confusion, and complacently contrast our own situation with that of the great activist despotisms of other nations, it is only because we live on an inherited political capital which we no longer know how to conserve. Thus we disapprove of activist practice, on the one hand, and yet we too often approve of the idealism from which the activist style flows, on the other.

This is why I have called my subject 'revolution and modernity' – in order to stress, that is, that even what remains of a limited style of politics has long been infected (in a more or less extreme way) with assumptions which, when pressed to their extreme, yield the activist regimes. The modern world, in short, now knows for the most part only the tenets of activist ideology, and if it avoids (in cases like our own) the monstrous consequences of an outright activist ideological commitment, this owes more to a preference for lukewarm and addled thinking, than to any clear and definite commitment to a limited style of politics.

NOTES

1. London, 1963.
2. *Vanished Supremacies*, London (1958), pp. 21–2.
3. *The Stages of Political Development* (NY, 1965), pp. 170–7.
4. This quotation, and the references from Laqueur and Gerth, are from Peter Lowenberg, 'The Psychohistorical Origins of the Nazi Youth Cohort', in *American Historical Review*, 75 (1971). Parts of this article are reprinted in *The Youth Revolution*, ed. A. Esher (London, 1974). The reference here is to p. 90 of Esher's book.
5. 'The Problem of Fascism in Recent Scholarship', in *Reappraisals of Fascism*, ed. H. A. Turner Jr. (NY, 1975), pp. 29–30.
6. Penguin (London, 1973; first edn, 1966), p. viii.
7. Ibid., p. 508.
8. A. S. Cohan, *Theories of Revolution: An Introduction* (London, 1975), p. 31.

9. P. Calvert, *Revolution* (London, 1970), p. 15.
10. A. Sorel, *Europe and the French Revolution* (London, 1970; first pub. 1885), p. 39.
11. In *The Social Contract and Discourses* (Everyman, Dent, London, 1973), p. 127.
12. 'The Government of Poland', in *Rousseau's Political Writings* (trans. and ed. F. Watkins, London, 1953), p. 227.
13. Ibid., p. 244,
14. *Political Economy*, Dent ed, op. cit.
15. 'Government of Poland', op. cit., p. 244.
16. Ibid., p. 170.
17. Ibid., p. 176.
18. Ibid., p. 177–8.
19. Ibid., p. 169.
20. Ibid., p. 162.
21. Chapter 3: 'Political Reflections arising out of my Sojourn in Vienna.'

2 Revolution as a Subject of Science

MICHAEL FREEMAN

In this paper I shall consider various recent attempts to theorise about revolutions. I shall ask whether such attempts are, in principle, absurd; and, if they are, what do they, in practice, achieve. I shall take 'theory' to mean 'scientific theory'. I shall ask, then, what sorts of scientific theories have been constructed to explain revolutions, to what criticisms they may be subjected, and how far their defects are due to the undertaking of a fundamentally misconceived enterprise, and how far to one which was merely ill-executed.

But, before I examine some would-be scientific theories of revolution, I wish to consider some *a priori* objections to such undertakings. I shall then be in a better position to judge *a posteriori* whether theorists of revolution have overcome or succumbed to these objections.

Alasdair MacIntyre has advanced several grounds for objecting to 'scientific' theories of politics.[1] He assumes that political science entails the attempt to formulate cross-cultural, law-like causal generalisations which may, in turn, be explained by theories. Such generalisations must be distinguished from mere *de facto* generalisations. The former entail a set of corresponding counter-factual conditionals. But the degree to which an instance confirms or refutes a generalisation depends in part upon the kind of environment in which it is found: the more varied the environments in which confirming instances are found, the stronger the confirmation that the generalisation is both true and truly general. But it is also true that the more varied the test environment, the less likely it is that the phenomena will be the same. This is because a different cultural environment will give to the same terms and to apparently similar institutions a different nature. MacIntyre gives as an example the attempt to test a generalisation about political parties in the

USA and Sierra Leone, two countries in which 'political parties' are fundamentally different things.

This objection might be met by narrowing the scope of the theory. In the case of political parties, we might confine ourselves to political cultures similar to those of the USA, and exclude those similar to those of Sierra Leone. The question would then arise as to whether the pressure of this argument from cultural diversity might squeeze the scope of political theories into extremely narrow limits. This appears to be a serious threat to any theory of revolution. Can a theory which is confirmed by revolution in seventeenth-century England be tested by data from late twentieth-century Nicaragua? Perhaps even the Russian and Chinese Revolutions were different 'things' in the sense in which North American and African political parties are different 'things'. What hope then for a theory of revolution?

There is a further consequence to be drawn from the fact that the beliefs of the actors help to define a political situation. Actors may reflect upon a situation, including those elements of the situation constituted by the beliefs of the various actors about putative laws governing such situations. Having reflected upon these laws, the actors may decide to depart from the behaviour predicted by them. It is, therefore, never possible to identify a determinate set of factors which constitute the initial conditions for the production of some outcome in conformity with a law-like regularity.

MacIntyre concedes that political scientists do establish generalisations, but maintains that they are very limited, that the conditions under which they hold necessarily remain unclear, and that they in no way lead towards the construction of a science.

Notwithstanding the problems which arise in identifying institutions in different cultures as 'the same', MacIntyre is at pains to acknowledge that 'the same actions are regularly performed in quite different cultures'. One class of such actions are those that derive from imitation. There are clear cases where the same intention is embodied in two different cultures. What we shall achieve if we study the projects springing from such intentions are two or more histories of these projects. We shall then be able to compare the different outcomes of the same intentions. But this comparative historical method will not lead to the formulation of law-like generalisations. The antecedent conditions in terms of which such outcomes are explained are sometimes necessary, but never sufficient conditions for the occurrence of some specific outcome. This is a result of the causal role played by the actors' beliefs. The most that comparative history can hope to supply us with in the foreseeable future is *de facto* generalisations about what has been an obstacle to or has facilitated certain types of courses of action.

We may now proceed to 'test' MacIntyre's account of what a theory of revolution could possibly achieve against what certain leading theories have actually achieved.

All the writers whose work I shall examine have a commitment, either explicit or implicit, to some notion of scientific method. Several questions are immediately prompted by the very idea of a scientific investigation of revolution. What conception of revolution is involved? What conception of science is involved? What method of investigation is used? What are the aims of this method and what are the achievements of the investigation? Do these inquiries tell us what we wish to know about revolutions? Are the investigations, in conception and in execution, free from ideological bias? These questions have different answers when put to different authors, so that the field delimited by the term 'scientific approaches to revolution' is quite heterogeneous.

I do not intend to present a general survey of the literature. Rather, I shall select a few works which are of exceptional interest because they pioneered new methods, and/or because they reflected self-consciously on the problems of method, and because they constitute an interesting line of development in confronting the problems of theorising about revolution.

The first work I wish to consider is Crane Brinton's *The Anatomy of Revolution*.[2] The aim of his book was to attempt to establish, *as the scientist might*, certain first approximations of uniformities in four 'successful revolutions in modern states': the English Revolution of the 1640s, the American Revolution, the French Revolution and the Russian Revolution. Brinton did not expect that all revolutions would conform to the pattern of these four: these were simply four important revolutions with which to begin the work of systematisation.

Scientific inquiry required a conceptual scheme. Brinton equated a conceptual scheme with a metaphor which would hold together the details of his revolutions. The metaphor he chose was that of fever. The phases of revolution were like those of fever. The task he set himself, then, was to find uniformities in the way the facts fitted into the conceptual scheme.

The four revolutions were chosen because, on the surface, they seemed to have certain resemblances. They all took place in the post-medieval world, were popular or democratic revolutions carried out in the name of freedom for a majority against a privileged minority, and were successful in the sense that the revolutionaries became the legal government. However, even these four were not at all homogeneous, the American being significantly different from the other three in that it was based on territory and nationality rather than social class, and lacked a strong terroristic phase.

Brinton declared his goals to be modest, but, even within these limits, he was not wholly successful, and we must ask whether the goals were worth while. He was forced to admit exceptions to the uniformities he seemed to have discovered in his revolution, and he lacked any method for explaining these exceptions. Also, for lack of a theory underlying the uniformities, he had no criterion for distinguishing significant from trivial similarities.

Having stated that science worked with conceptual schemes, equated conceptual schemes with metaphors, and introduced the metaphor of fever, he made almost no use of it. He divided revolutions into phases, which were said to bear some similarity to the phases of a fever, but the phases he ascribed to revolution – old regimes; first stages; rule of the moderates; accession of the extremists; reign of terror; Thermidors – clearly owed more to history than to pathology. Although he suggested that conceptual schemes helped scientists to frame hypotheses, he framed none. Impatient of all epistemological issues, he swept questions of causation aside. He was content to discover phenomena which were always found in pre-revolutionary situations. Instead of causes, Brinton offered 'signs' and 'symptoms' of revolution. Some of these 'signs', however, were not always found in pre-revolutionary societies, and many of them were found in most modern societies at any time. There were no criteria for identifying a 'sign' as causally (or in any other way) significant.

What did Brinton's 'scientific' method amount to? A certain detachment from the passions of the participants in revolutions; a sketch of phases which did not fit even his four revolutions very well; some uniformities which, together with the exceptions to them, remained unexplained.

This 'science' was, then, comparative, non-causal, non-explanatory natural history. It was to be severely criticised by exponents of a different sort of political science. In 1964 Harry Eckstein addressed himself to the question of how a theory of 'internal war' should be constructed.[3] Before theoretical study was possible, however, certain preliminary operations had to be carried out: one of these was delimitation of the subject.

The criteria for satisfactory delimitation were derived from the conception of theory. Theory entailed testable generalisation. A subject should be so delimited that valid generalisations could be made about it. A generalisation should cover a number of cases large enough for certain rigorous testing procedures like statistical analysis to be used. Revolution, Eckstein declared, was one of the classic themes of social thought. Internal war was 'any resort to violence within a political order to change its constitution, rulers, or policies'. Its relation to revolution was that of genus to species.

Eckstein offered three justifications for his delimitation of 'internal war': (i) all cases of internal war had common features; (ii) internal war combined different types of violence; and (iii) very limited results had been obtained from comparative historical studies of revolution.[4] The first two justifications are very weak, for many political phenomena, including revolutions, have common features and combine different types of violence. Eckstein concluded correctly that Brinton's method of comparative history had produced limited results, but criticised it on the wrong grounds. He complained that it dealt only with the so-called Great Revolutions of history; it ignored the 'vast spectrum of coups, putsches, uprisings, riots, and so forth'; and it drew mammoth inferences from very few cases. These charges are easy to answer. Understanding Great Revolutions is no mean task; the comparative history of revolution is not required to consider the vast spectrum of *coups* and so forth, since they are not revolutions; comparative history did not draw mammoth inferences.

The second of Eckstein's pre-theoretical operations he called *problemation*. A theory must have problems to solve, questions to answer.[5] Eckstein suggested that questions about internal war could best be arranged in relation to the phases through which every internal war must pass. These phases were: (i) pre-revolutionary conditions; (ii) courses; (iii) outcomes; and (iv) longer-run consequences. No questions about internal war had been more thoroughly neglected by social scientists than those raised by their long-run consequences. This was surprising in view of the fact that such questions were clearly raised by what Eckstein called 'the protracted normative argument between pro-revolutionaries and anti-revolutionaries initiated by Paine and Burke'. Yet Eckstein concerned himself with the causes, not the long-run consequences of internal war.

The posing of fruitful theoretical questions was not a simple matter. We have to discover what was really puzzling about a question. Eckstein gave as an example 'Weber's famous question about the origins of modern capitalism in the West'. But, in asking this question, Weber was not primarily concerned with testable generalisations, but with the explanation of phenomena which were at the same time unique and of universal significance. It is plausible to suggest that the Great Revolutions, which Eckstein scorned for their rarity, were great because of their universal significance.

Eckstein's approach to internal war promised generality and rigour; but its results were disappointing. Having identified the long-run effects of internal wars as especially important, Eckstein had nothing to say about them. His principal reason for rejecting Brinton's emphasis on Great Revolutions is cast into doubt by his own discussion of how to determine what puzzles the theory of internal war should seek to solve. Eckstein failed to give a convincing exposition of either the questions or the answers we should expect from a theory of revolution or internal war.

This approach was carried forward by Ted Robert Gurr, who subsumed revolution under political violence, and defined it as 'fundamental sociopolitical change accomplished through violence'.[6] Political violence was classified into three main types: turmoil, conspiracy and internal war. Internal war included revolution, guerrilla and civil wars. Revolution was, then, a sub-type of one type (internal war) of political violence.

Gurr sought to discover not why political violence occurred, but the determinants of the extent and forms of violence. He gave two reasons for thus setting his objectives. First, the extent and forms of violence were relevant to the effects of violence on the political system; and second, the magnitude of political violence was ethically important. Yet, although Gurr appealed to the effects of political violence in order to justify his examination of its extent and forms, he made no attempt to construct a theory of its effects. He developed a large number of hypotheses about the extent and forms of political violence; seven about the determinants of internal war; none about revolution.

'Revolution', Eckstein had written, 'is one of the classic themes of social thought.' He and Gurr had attempted to treat this and related subjects with a new methodological rigour. In the process, the subject of revolution had disappeared. Both delimited their subjects more widely; both implied that revolution was a type or sub-type of their subject; but neither suggested a way to derive a theory of revolution from the more general theory they proposed. Both raised two sets of problems about revolutions – problems relating to their outcomes and to normative disputes – which they did not begin to solve.

A quite different approach has been taken by S. N. Eisenstadt in his book, *Revolution and the Transformation of Societies*.[7] The chief legacy of the great modern revolutions to modern thought has been a certain image of revolutions with three principal components: violence, novelty, and total change. The spell of this image has led to the adoption of the European revolutionary experience as a model for other societies. As a result, various historical situations have been analysed with categories and assumptions inappropriate to them.

Eisenstadt attributes the following faults to the various approaches which take the image of the classical revolution for granted: (i) they fail to distinguish rebellions and political revolutions from far-reaching social transformation; (ii) they neglect those conditions in the social structure which lead movements of protest in revolutionary directions; (iii) they fail to relate revolutionary phenomena systematically to the dynamics of modernity; (iv) there has been little systematic examination of revolutionary outcomes; (v) the historical and sociological uniqueness of the classical revolution as a type of social transformation has been overlooked; (vi) different types of revolution have been confused; and (vii) such approaches are of little use in the analysis of events which transform traditional societies in ways quite different from those of the classical revolution.

The classical revolution did not differ from rebellions, conflicts and social changes in traditional societies, merely in scope and intensity. It was distinctive in the following respects: (i) the relations between various protest movements; (ii) the relations between these movements and the political centre; and (iii) the basic symbolism of these movements and its structural implications and consequences.

The classical revolution was characterised by a very close connection among heterodoxies, rebellions, central political struggle and institution-building. It was carried out by numerous coalitions of primary and secondary economic and political élites, intellectual and religious entrepreneurs, and leaders of various collectivities. It was distinguished from all other movements of protest by the fact that heterodoxy and rebellion combined protest with relatively realistic attitudes towards the reformation of the state and of social institutions. The connections between various protest movements, and their relation to central political struggles, were associated with a new kind of political ideology: the legitimacy of replacing a bad ruler with a good one yielded to the necessity of reconstructing the entire socio-political order by the legitimate representatives of the community.

From this type of revolution developed a new type of civilisation: the civilisation of modernity. These revolutions subverted traditional legitimation of political centres and of social orders. They raised growing demands for the participation of broader groups in the making of social values and public policies. New ideas of distributive justice and of political legitimacy became fundamental to the idea of modernity.

The new ideology underlying these revolutions was secular, rational, progressive, egalitarian, democratic and universalistic. It was committed to the rational mastery of both the natural and social worlds. The search for rational control, the demand for new forms of distributive justice and for wider participation in central decision-making, tied centre and periphery of society closer together, and brought about greater political centralisation. Protest became partially institutionalised through the legitimation of political parties and interest groups and thus became a basic component of modern civilisation.

The civilisation of modernity began in Europe and North America. The political-economic expansion of western European societies spread this civilisation throughout the world. This process was unique in that it combined the most far-reaching subversion of traditional legitimation that has ever occurred with the creation of a new internationl political and economic system. This international system was initiated by commercial capitalism, but has become a complex system of various economic and political forms. Together with the growth of global capitalism arose global political and ideological systems. Thus, revolutionary ideas first became incorporated into modern society and then became one of its chief exports.

The causes of the classical revolution were as follows: first, the emerging international system of capitalism and nation states exerted pressure on the legitimacy of traditional authorities. Secondly, growing socio-economic differentiation produced movements of protest which included numerous groups easy to mobilise and which were led by entrepreneurial élites. As a result of these external and internal pressures, traditional centres experienced a crisis, particularly relating to their structures and forms of access to them. Finally, a major role was played by Protestantism, which carried forward traditions of heterodoxy and rebellion, maintained close relations between secondary élites and broader strata, and was committed to the restructuring of centres and the building of new institutions.

These are the necessary conditions of revolution. Without them, élite weakness and mass grievances may lead to internal war or to regime change, but not to revolution and revolutionary social transformation. The conditions are not sufficient, however. Whether or not a revolution occurs depends on the cohesiveness of revolutionary groups, their relations to broader groups and to ruling groups. Only if revolutionary groups can overpower these other groups or form coalitions with them are the chances of revolutionary transformation good.

The first revolutions took place in Europe and not elsewhere as a result of the special European mixture of imperial and feudal elements. Imperial systems, such as the Russian, Chinese and Ottoman empires, were able to contain movements of rebellion. In Europe, the multiplicity of continually changing centres and collectivities and the concomitant multiplicity of relatively autonomous élites provided the necessary ingredients for revolutionary developments. The expansion of Europe, however, could evoke in some societies copies of the European revolutionary model if the internal conditions were similar to those in revolutionary Europe.

All classical revolutions led to further modernisation, but their outcomes clearly varied. How should these variations be conceptualised and the variability explained? Eisenstadt proposes three general criteria of comparison: scope and intensity of modernisation; degree of discontinuity in social structure; and success in achieving their emancipatory promise. Variations on these dimensions are to be explained by the structure of the centre, the relations between central and secondary élites, and between them and broader strata. Rigidity and closure of centre are highly conducive to revolution. The more rigid the centre, the more violent the ensuing revolution and the stronger its emphasis on breaking with the bases of political legitimation as well as other major aspects of the institutional structure of the old regime. Where élites of the old regime enjoy solitary relations with broader strata, the new regime is likely to be pluralistic. Where they do not, they are likely to be both more radical and more coercive. These internal structural relations may be affected by external pressures: generally, the greater the external pressures, the greater the rigidity and closure of the centre.

The classical must be distinguished from another type of revolution. The distinction is related to that between two types of traditional society: the imperial-feudal and the patrimonial. Patrimonial societies are characterised by the following features: lack of structural distinction between centre and periphery; high degree of status segregation; little political articulation of strata; little linkage between movements of protest, rebellion and central political struggle; little autonomy of secondary élites; and weak linkages among élites and between them and centres. These societies underwent far-reaching changes consequent upon incorporation into the emerging international systems. New economic, social and political structures arose; broad strata of the population were mobilised; élites were continually replaced and restructured. However, changes in different spheres were weakly connected, so that coalitions associated with modernising changes did not form to exert pressure on the centre.

The majority of these neo-patrimonial societies displayed certain preconditions of revolution, but none experienced a classical revolution. Only in colonial societies in the crucial phase of the struggle for independence did effective linkages between different protest movements develop. In other situations, isolated revolutionary groups did appear, but they were rarely able to create effective links with broader strata or to restructure central political processes. The existence of these groups has often been supported by international forces. Such forces may even help to produce revolutions similar to the classical: Mexico, Bolivia, Cuba and Portugal are examples.

Eisenstadt distinguishes the institutional from the symbolic components of revolution. The classical revolution was produced by a combination of capitalist economy, nation-state and radical Protestant ideology. It occurred because certain European societies were expanding in ways incompatible with traditional political institutions and ideologies. Their expansion – political and economic – carried their revolutionary ideologies to societies with very different sets of institutions. Thus, revolutionary movements grew up outside the European modernising 'core' with classical revolutionary ideologies, but without the institutional preconditions for a classical revolution. The symbolism of these movements has concealed – from both ideologists of various kinds and social scientists – the fact that they differ fundamentally from the classical model.

Eisenstadt's thesis that the classical revolution was unique is bold. Unfortunately, it wobbles. He states that, apart from the 'original' European revolutions, only the Russian and Chinese, and 'to some extent' the Turkish, Vietnamese, Yugoslav, and Mexican revolutions exhibited the features of classical revolutions. He also writes that 'our analysis of the similarities between the earlier and later revolutions indicated that once the breakthrough was achieved [i.e. the initial western push to modernity], its expansion could evoke in some societies responses similar to actual revolutionary ones'. But, since he calls the later events 'revolutions', it is clear that these responses to modernisation were not 'similar to', but were 'actual revolutionary ones'. What he means, but does not say, is that the responses were similar to early classical ones. But of the later revolutions, the Russian and Chinese unqualifiedly, and the Turkish, Vietnamese, Yugoslav and Mexican 'to some extent', exhibited the features of classical revolutions. Thus, the crucial distinction between the early classical and the later non-classical revolutions is blurred.

But even the list of later 'quasi-classical' revolutions excludes such events as that generally known as the Cuban Revolution. In discussing the impact of the modern international system on patrimonial societies, Eisenstadt says that many developed strong predilections to revolutionary symbolism under the influence of international revolutionary movements and the power politics of revolutionary states. But only in the cases of Mexico, Bolivia and Cuba did revolutionary efforts 'approach the pure revolutionary pattern'. This suggests that these revolutions, too, should be regarded as 'quasi-classical'. Having at first approached the pure revolutionary pattern, the Cuban events are later downgraded to 'semi-revolutionary processes'.

Eisenstadt is not self-conscious about method. It is hard to say how, if at all, he believes his theses should be tested. He does put forward propositions about cause and effect relationships: for example, that certain features of early modern Europe were necessary conditions for certain features of the revolutionary transformation to modernity. Perhaps these propositions might be formulated as testable generalisations, but it is not Eisenstadt's concern to do this systematically or with precision.

There is also a certain amount of *adhocery* in his explanations. For example, when the Cuban Revolution threatens to look like a classical revolution, despite having the wrong preconditions, international power politics is brought in to explain this development. This is indeed a plausible explanation, but it is not derived from a systematic theory; and because Eisenstadt does not reveal his underlying epistemology, we cannot tell what the status of these external explanatory factors is. This leaves a considerable degree of incoherence and indeterminacy in the theory.

If Eisenstadt's analysis suffers from imprecise definitions and unclear hypotheses, it has the merit of placing revolutions in an historical perspective. He offers an explanation-sketch of what is perhaps the most important single fact of modern revolutions: that their symbolism is indebted to European ideologies developed between the seventeenth and the nineteenth centuries, but is produced in societies which are structurally quite dissimilar. Also, because he analyses revolutions in terms of both social-structural and cultural preconditions, he can at least suggest explanations of various revolutionary outcomes. Despite a lack of system and rigour, therefore, he offers a much fuller understanding of modern revolutions than the apparently more rigorous system of abstractions offered by the method of Eckstein and Gurr.

Eisenstadt offers a framework for understanding modern revolutions which lacks rigorous proof of cause-and-effect relationships. One recent attempt to fill this gap is Theda Skocpol's *States and Social Revolutions*.[8] Like Eisenstadt, Skocpol is concerned with revolutionary social transformations in modern world history. Harking back to Brinton, her method is that of comparative history. Like Brinton and unlike Eisenstadt, she confines herself to a small number of revolutions: the French, the Russian and the Chinese. Her object is to explain the causes and outcomes of these three revolutions. Thus, she sharply departs from the approach of Eckstein and Gurr. Outcomes are to be explained as well as the occurrence of revolutions, and the strategy for doing so is the comparison in detail of a small number of revolutions within an explicit theoretical framework.

Social revolutions, says Skocpol, have been rare but momentous. They have transformed state organisations, class structures and dominant ideologies. Thus, in contrast to Eckstein and Gurr, and more in accord with Brinton and Eisenstadt, she identifies certain Great Revolutions as worthy of special attention. Skocpol defines social revolutions as rapid, basic transformations of a society's state and class structures, accompanied and in part carried through by class-based revolts from below. She rejects the assumption of many theories that revolutions are purposive. Revolutions and their outcomes are not to be understood primarily with reference to ideologies but to internal socio-economic and international conditions. Any valid explanation of revolution depends upon the analyst's rising above the viewpoints of participants to find important regularities across given historical instances. One must focus simultaneously upon the institutionally-determined situations and relations of groups within society, and upon the inter-relationships of societies within world-historically developing international structures.

The analysis of social revolutions must, then, be structural. In contrast to many earlier theories of revolution (including Marxism), Skocpol's analysis emphasises the importance of crises of the state. The political crises that have launched social revolutions have been direct expressions of contradictions in the structures of old regime states. Revolutionary leaders have used state structures to effect social transformations. And social revolutions have changed state structures as much as, or more than, they have changed class relations, societal values or social institutions. States exist in societies structured by class relations, but they are significantly autonomous institutions. States may be rivals with dominant classes in the allocation of societal resources. Even if the state normally has an interest in promoting the interests of the dominant classes, it has interests in its relations both with subordinate classes and with other states which do not necessarily harmonise with the interests of the dominant classes. The state is therefore situated between the class system in its own society and the international system of states. Pressures on the state may come from either direction or both. Whether the state can take the strain depends not only on its legitimacy but on the effectiveness of its coercive apparatus.

Skocpol employs a comparative approach, based on J. S. Mill's methods of agreement and difference. She seeks similarities of cause and effect in her three revolutions. A claim that cause and effect have indeed been discovered is strengthened by analysing cases where, in otherwise similar circumstances, absence of cause was followed by absence of effect. The method is acknowledged to have weaknesses. First, it is hard to implement the logic of comparison: the appropriate case may not exist. Where it does, perfect controls for all potentially relevant variables cannot be achieved. Consequently, 'strategic guesses' have to be made about what causes are likely to be at work. Secondly, comparison presupposes theory. Theory defines the subject, provides the criteria for the selection of appropriate cases, supplies concepts and hypotheses. These must come from 'the macro-sociological imagination', informed by contemporary theoretical debates and historical evidence. Comparative history is, however, an important check on theoretical speculation. It encourages us to make explicit the causal arguments suggested by grand theoretical perspectives. The ultimate objective, for Skocpol, is 'the actual illumination of causal regularities across sets of historical cases'.

It is useful to compare Skocpol's method with the weaknesses she acknowledges to inhere in it, with MacIntyre's account of comparative political science and the limitations to which he held it necessarily subject. Both believe that, in comparing what are apparently two cases of the same thing, the 'contexts' of the two cases present logical difficulties. But whereas, for Skocpol, the difficulty lies in the possibility of overlooking causally relevant variables, for MacIntyre a different context raises the question as to whether we really have a case of the same thing.

Yet it should be carefully noted that these two writers agree on what can and should be done in comparative politics. Skocpol seeks 'causal regularities' through her comparative method. MacIntyre advocates comparative history resulting in *de facto* generalisations. The similarity of their prescription is concealed by their different uses of the term 'theory'. For MacIntyre, 'theories' are high-level generalisations which explain lower-level, law-like generalisations.

For Skocpol, 'theory', though a source of causal hypotheses, is not necessarily a higher level of a pyramid of explanatory laws. Its function is more humbly heuristic.

Both Skocpol and Eisenstadt use a comparative historical method, though the scope of Skocpol's study is much narrower. Both use the Meiji Restoration in Japan as a case of non-revolutionary social transformation which can illuminate the revolutionary, but their explanations for non-revolution in Japan are characteristically different. Eisenstadt points to the absence of the requisite revolutionary cultural traditions (represented by Protestantism in Europe); Skocpol to the greater relative strength of the Japanese state *vis à vis* dominant social classes. In her conclusion, Skocpol addresses herself to the question of whether her analysis can be generalised to other revolutions, especially to recent revolutions in colonial societies. On this score, Eisenstadt's analysis of patrimonial societies goes well beyond anything Skocpol attempts. Both agree, however, that revolution and non-revolution in contemporary, economically backward societies are strongly shaped by their relation to the major political and economic powers, whose societies were themselves shaped by earlier revolutions.

Is a comparative science of revolution possible? MacIntyre's arguments imply that it is not. There are three main planks to his platform: (i) political science entails cross-cultural, law-like, causal generalisations which may be explained by theories; (ii) such generalisations cannot be established because political phenomena change their nature when they cross cultures: the notion of cross-cultural testing consequently becomes extremely dubious; (iii) the capacity of political agents for autonomous reflection makes it impossible for the would-be political scientist to state the sufficient conditions of such an *explanandum* as revolution. MacIntyre conceded that the comparative study of politics was possible, and that this could lead to generalisations, but not to the type of generalisations that constituted a genuine science.

In our survey of social-scientific approaches to revolution, we have seen various attempts to formulate generalisations. Brinton looked for *de facto*, empirical uniformities in a small number of somewhat homogeneous revolutions. He ordered these uniformities in terms of a common conceptual framework (very loosely applied), but made no attempt to show that they were causal or explanatory.

Eckstein and Gurr conceived the aim of their science in terms much closer to those of MacIntyre, but their results confirmed rather than refuted his scepticism: Gurr, who developed a much more elaborate theory than Eckstein, fell back on correlations rather than causal laws and retreated from the task of explaining revolutions or rebellions to the less interesting one of seeking the co-variants of levels and forms of political violence. Eisenstadt also sought ambitious generalisation, but in a quite different way: not quantified relations between variables but qualitative (and quite vague) comparative generalisations about the revolutionary potentialities of different types of civilisation. He did, briefly, claim to state the *sufficient* conditions of revolution, in opposition to MacIntyre's view that this could not be done, but the statement of the conditions is so vague that it does no serious threat to the sceptical position. Finally, Skocpol has returned to the Brintonian project of comparing a few revolutions in detail, but with the aim of establishing causal explanations. It might seem that she presents the strongest challenge to MacIntyre's scepticism, for she is able to establish certain limited cross-cultural causal relations, though they are extremely limited in scope and fall well short of MacIntyre's very exacting definition of science. However, we should remember that MacIntyre himself had conceded the possibility and advocated the desirability of such comparative generalisations.

Eckstein was, of course, right to say that 'revolution' was one of the classic themes of political theory. Not only has the term 'revolution' seemed to refer to a set of similar historical events but these events have seemed to raise certain important general questions. Barrington Moore, for example, has expressed the problems posed by revolutions as follows.

The contradiction between politics and morality, never far below the surface in so-called normal times, re-asserts itself with particular vehemence in times of revolutionary change. Why is it that revolutionaries sooner or later adopt, and sometimes intensify, the cruelties of the regimes against which they fight? Why is it that revolutionaries begin with camaraderie and end with fratricide? Why do revolutions start by proclaiming the brotherhood of man, the end of lies, deceit, and secrecy, and culminate in tyranny whose victims are overwhelmingly the little people for whom the revolution was proclaimed as the advent of a happier life? To raise these question is not to deny that revolutions have been among the most significant ways in which modern men – and in many crucial situations modern women – have managed to sweep aside some of the institutional causes of human suffering. But an impartial outlook and the plain facts of revolutionary change compel the raising of these questions as well.[9]

The point about these questions is not that they are particularly well posed, but that they are the sort of questions that seem proper to political theory and that they are *general*. If they are proper general questions, is it not proper to seek systematically (though not necessarily 'scientifically') for general answers?

Eckstein emphasised the importance of 'problemation' as a pre-theoretical operation: the formulation of significant and answerable questions. Eisenstadt and Skocpol, in formulating theories of the causes and outcomes of world-historical revolutions have succeeded in addressing themselves to such questions in a way that has proved impossible for those who, like Gurr, have followed Eckstein's insistence on quantitative theory.

The theories of Eisenstadt and Skocpol have quite severe weaknesses and limitations: the fomer in vagueness and inconsistency, the latter in extremely narrow scope. Neither meets MacIntyre's requirements for political science: but what of that?, we may well say. They both teach that any future revolution will not be like any past one, but it will not be utterly unlike, either. A causal theory of revolution along the lines they have pioneered may not lead to science, but it may lead to a greater political prudence. There may be no laws of revolution. But, if there are necessary conditions of certain effects and constant conjunctions of cause and effect, we would do well to know what they are. Science or not, the sociology of revolution has a future.

NOTES

1. Alasdair MacIntyre, 'Is a Science of Comparative Politics Possible?' in *Against the Self-Images of the Age* (London, Duckworth, 1971), pp. 260–79. See also Alasdair MacIntyre, 'Ideology, Social Science and Revolution', *Comparative Politics*, v, no. 3 (April 1973), pp. 321–42.
2. Crane Brinton, *The Anatomy of Revolution* (New York, Random House, 1965).

3. Harry Eckstein (ed.), *Internal War: Problems and Approaches* (London, Collier–Macmillan, 1964).
4. Harry Eckstein, 'On the Etiology of Internal Wars', *History and Theory*, IV (1965), pp. 133–4.
5. Eckstein, *Internal War*, pp. 23–4.
6. The Robert Gurr, *Why Men Rebel* (Princeton, Princeton University Press, 1970).
7. S. N. Eisenstadt, *Revolution and the Transformation of Societies* (New York, The Free Press, 1978).
8. Theda Skocpol, *States and Social Revolutions* (Cambridge, Cambridge University Press, 1979).
9. Barrington Moore, Jr, *Reflections on the Causes of Human Misery* (London, Allen Lane, 1972), p. 38.

II

LIBERAL AND DEMOCRATIC REVOLUTIONS

3 The American Revolution

H. G. NICHOLAS

Was there an American Revolution? Did the 'revolutionaries' think there had been? Under 'Revolution' the Chicago Dictionary of Americanisms gives as the initial meaning 'short for Revolutionary War'; 'Revolutionary War' itself it defines as 'the war for independence carried on by the American colonists against Great Britain'. 'Revolution' here thus appears so yoked to 'war' as to suggest that from the beginning it was virtually a synonym for the War of Independence i.e. that the revolutionary act lay in the waging of war against king and motherland. But was that all? John Adams thought not, in no uncertain terms:

> But what do we mean by the American Revolution? Do we mean the American war? The Revolution was effected before the war commenced. The Revolution was in the minds and hearts of the people; a change in their religious sentiments, of their duties and obligations. . . This radical change in the principles, opinions, sentiments and affections of the people was the real American Revolution. (Letter to Hezekiah Niles, 1818.)

Was the Revolution then something separate from and preceding the struggle for independence? This was certainly not the view of another patriot leader and close associate, Benjamin Rush, who in 1787 insisted

> The American war is over, but this is far from being the case with the American Revolution. On the contrary, nothing but the first act of the great drama is closed. It remains yet to establish and perfect our new forms of government and to prepare the principles, morals and manners of our citizens for these forms of government after they are established and brought to perfection.

In other words, independence is assured, the revolution is still to come.

The problem thus presented comes into being, for founding fathers and historians alike, because though the main grounds of colonial grievance are to be found in local abuses, these could not be relieved except by overthrowing an overseas yoke—in other words the *immediate* issue is separation. This is reflected in the classic statement of the colonists' case; it is a Declaration of *Independence* which they promulgate. But does this claim to independence constitute an assertion of self-determination? The Declaration is full of ambiguous wording. It refers to 'the population of these states', 'our people', 'our fellow citizens', even 'one people', but it stops short of claiming that the inhabitants of 'these United Colonies' constitute a distinct American nation; indeed it continues to refer to the 'ties of our common kindred', common, that is, with 'our British brethern'. Yet, while falling short of a claim to be bringing forth a new nation, the Declaration is at the same time universalist in its pretensions. It cites 'a decent respect to the opinions of mankind'; it submits its 'facts' to 'a candid world'. It is thus less than fully nationalistic, yet it claims the right of the inhabitants of North America to realise their own destiny within a framework of principles common to all human kind. But as to whether the need for independence springs from a developing sense of distinctiveness, a national self which seeks a separate voice, or whether it is the inevitable product of intolerable abuses—on this the Declaration speaks with no clear voice.

It is wise so to do. The fact is that the states in 1776 did not constitute a nation: they did not even constitute one by 1781. The nation was slowly and reluctantly created by a few far-sighted men whose success in this endeavour was correlative on the one hand to the external pressures which made for unity, and the internal particularities which worked against it, on the other. The Union was only *partly* a product of national self-consciousness; it was just as much a parent of it. And the tardy growth of its child was well evidenced by the fact that when the leading spokesman of Independence, Thomas Jefferson, had occasion to use the phrase 'my country', what he almost always meant was Virginia.

The fundamental difficulty in assessing the precise significance of Independence lies in the fact that the colonists' grievances were in actual fact good deal less than intolerable. At least 60,000 loyalists found them otherwise. Edmund Randolph, who declined to sign the draft Constitution of the United States because he thought it insufficiently republican, assessed the American Revolution as one which occurred 'without an immediate oppression, without a cause, depending so much on hasty feeling as on theoretic reasoning'. The conditions of life in British North America in 1776, however one may assess them, were very different from those in pre-1789 France, or pre-1917 Russia. The Declaration itself has to work hard to produce its inflated catalogue of 'repeated injuries and usurpations', 'of every act which may define a tyrant'.

Yet explosion there was, powerful enough to blow the 'tyrant' back across the Atlantic. The grievances *seemed* intolerable for two reasons which make eighteenth-century America quite different from most pre-revolutionary societies. 'The advent of parliamentary taxation', as Edmund S. Morgan describes it, 'inaugurated a quarter-century of political discussion in American that has never since been matched in intensity' (Edmund S. Morgan, *The Revolution as an Intellectual Movement*, in *Paths of American Thought*, ed. A. M. Schlesinger Jr and Morton White, p. 23). Whatever else George III and his Parliament did, they did not, to any effect, interfere with the torrent of pamphleteering and press argument which poured forth in every colony during the decade or so that preceded the Declaration. America certainly met one pre-revolutionary requirement: it was politically a highly activist society, eager to question all the accepted principles of the political order.

If this was the first, and efficient cause of the revolutionary explosion, the second was no less important. The society that found the pretensions and mild oppressions of king and parliament so intolerable was one which was already republican and self-determining in all but name. Not only had several of the colonies been founded by seventeenth-century puritans who, had they remained in England, would almost certainly have been anti-royalist in the Civil War and in the Glorious Revolution; more than this, the conditions of life throughout North America were such as in Europe were still the unrealised goals of revolutionary theorists. The colonists, long before the Stamp Act, were taking for granted a diffusion of property, a degree of social and economic equality, a pattern of religious diversity and independence which ran well ahead of anything enjoyed in Georgian Britain.

In the sense in which the term applies in Europe, there was in America no ruling class, certainly none that enjoyed hereditary privileges by law or legally sanctified custom. The feudalism which persisted in France into the century of Enlightenment had had no lodgement in America even in the seventeenth century when the colonies were constructed on a bedrock of faith. There were, of course, prominent and powerful families, but membership of a family did not of itself confer a privileged position in the conduct of public affairs – nor, for that matter, did wealth or education. Primogeniture and entail did indeed exist, as they did in the law of England; by the outbreak of the Revolution only two states, Pennsylvania and Maryland, had abolished primogeniture, and only South Carolina had abolished entail. But of course the potency of these legal relics of feudalism was vastly diminished in a country where the supply of available land was almost inexhaustible. When, in the wake of the Revolution, both insitutions were abolished the practical consequences were minimal. 'Apparently few estates had ever been entailed. Men had consolidated and broken up great estates before 1776 and would do so afterwards', (Jackson Turner Main, *The Sovereign States, 1775–1783*, p. 346).

Another characteristic feature of the *ancien régime*, that of a standing army, and, with it, the privileges and pretensions of a military class, was almost entirely lacking in the colonies. Such forces as did exist were either local and very part-time militia or British units – and indeed to that extent were an offensive symbol and instrument of royal power. But significantly they were an imported, not a local, imposition. The demand for their removal derived from the colonists' drive for independence rather than from their desire for revolutionary change *per se*.

Far more indigenous were the established Churches, an obvious appendage of an unreformed regime, and indeed a frequent source of discontent in colony after colony. Protestant sects and Catholics alike resented being forced to pay for the upkeep of whatever religion happened to be established by law in the colony in which they lived if they happened to be in the dissenting minority there at the time. Yet *de facto* disestablishment was already far advanced by 1776. The basic requirement of open public worship had been won by all the main dissenting groups almost everywhere. Moreover, education was already largely secularised. No religious tests were imposed on applicants to colleges and universities as in Britain and elsewhere then and long afterwards. And certainly, though fear of the imposition of an anglican bishop exercising spiritual lordship over North America was potent in the mounting revolutionary hysteria of the 1770s, the existing clerical establishments were not, in themselves, felt to be especially irksome. Indeed, the patriot movement was nowhere more vigorously endorsed than amongst the 'black clergy' of Calvinistic new England and the Anglican clergy of Virginia. And, of course, in certain states it was not until long after the Revolution that disestablishment was effected – in Connecticut in 1818, in New Hampshire in 1819, and in Massachusetts not finally until 1833.

In fact it was not the weight of a European-inherited *ancien régime* that impelled the colonists to rebel. It was the very absence of constraints, the peculiar freedom and mobility of American life, that made the colonists hyper-sensitive to measures and even proposals of imperial control which anywhere else in the then civilised world would have been regarded as exceptional in their mildness, as indeed a *sine qua non* of orderly government. While claiming only the rights and liberties of Englishmen, the colonists were in fact enjoying, for practical purposes, more of each than their brethren across the Atlantic.

It is this advanced degree of political development which is the basic reason why the Revolution, when it comes, brings internally no revolutionary change. Property, the symbol and substance of established order, undergoes a minimum of confiscation and depredation. Jackson Turner Main estimates that 'less than 4% of the nation's real and personal estates changed hands', and that of this 'at least three-fourths if not more' went to enrich 'the well-to-do traders, professional and speculators who alone commanded the capital or credit to buy it' (pp. 330–1). This is not to deny that a vast acreage became public domain, territory which previously had been the proprietary holdings of great families such as the Penns or the Fairfaxes. This went as freehold to previous tenants or new settlers, but the transfer was confined to a limited number of acres. More important, though representing no real transfer of wealth, was the opening up of the back country to settlement, where huge tracts, such as the entire Ohio region previously held by the British government, passed into the possession of the states. They in turn disposed of them in small lots to settlers who poured westward in large numbers, an estimated 200,000 in the half dozen years after the war. Opinions may differ as to the appropriate description for this disposition of western lands, a disposition which was to have such enormous significance for subsequent American development. Did it represent a movement from centralised control to local diversity? From collectivism to *laissez faire*? From bureaucracy to individualism? All have been associated, at one time or another, with revolutionary movements; none has been an essential common factor in them.

To one form of property the American Revolution brought little significant change at all: property in persons. Broadly speaking, the movement towards the abolition of slavery proceeded in inverse proportion to the numbers of blacks likely to be affected, i.e. tolerably broadly in New England, sluggishly in the Middle States (save in Pennsylvania, where Quaker influence and example had promoted emancipation well before 1776), and hardly at all in the South. The eloquent passage in Jefferson's penultimate draft of the Declaration, charging the King with keeping 'open a market where MEN should be bought and sold, . . . this execrable commerce', disappeard without trace from the Declaration as revised. It was too much to except that at a time when the slave-trade was still legal in Britain, the American South would cut its economic throat by emancipating the 450,000 slaves in its possession. Significantly, even the French Revolution was slow to move towards this; the initial resolution of the Assembly on this topic in 1790 specifically excluded the colonies from the operation of the new Constitution which was to forbid slavery in metropolitan France. It was 1794 before the Convention adopted the decree abolishing slavery throughout the colonies.

R. R. Palmer, in his *Age of the Democratic Revolution*, vol. I, (pp. 188ff), advances two criteria for assessing the impact of the Revolution: 'how many refugees were there from the Revolution, and how much property did they lose?' Applying the first test, he points out that the figure of 60,000 (a low estimate, many put it as high as 100,000) loyalists who emigrated to Canada or the United Kingdom represents 24 per 1000 head of population. He contrasts this with the figure of 5 per 1000 for the emigrés who fled the French Revolution a decade or so later. At first sight the contrast is impressive, but it is possible to read too much into the mere figures. Any realistic calculation should add to the total of French emigrés the 20,000 or so of those less fortunate who fell victim to the Terror and to whom no North American counterpart exists. How are they to be fitted into the equation? But over and beyond this it should always be borne in mind that to leave one colony for another, for example from Massachusetts for Quebec, or to return from colonial residence to one's mother country, constitutes a much less severe social, economic and psychological dislocation than to leave France for exile.

The second of Palmer's criteria is the economic: how much property did loyalists and emigrés lose? Palmer's calculations rest here on far shakier foundations – the indemnities paid respectively by the British government and the Bourbon restoration. His conclusion that revolutionary France, ten times as large as revolutionary America, confiscated only twelve times as much, still leaves the French losses larger. But in fact the basis of the calculation is too uncertain to make comparison reliable. Certainly the loyalists lost a great deal, in most cases almost everything, and their compensation, as always, was inadequate. But one might turn the comparison inside out: the very fact that so many were willing to leave and to lose what they did is a reflection of the contrast between the two societies. Unlike the deep-rooted landed aristocracy of the emigrés, the loyalists belonged to a mobile–indeed restless–culture to which change of locality and of status were already in some degree regular features of life. Of course flight or expulsion was painful and costly, but it was, even so, only a familiar experience in a painfully heightened degree. By contrast, every French emigré was pulling up roots centuries old, abandoning not merely home, but status, culture, almost everything that made life dear.

Compared with the incommensurables of such a felicific calculus, the historian can speak with more confidence of the impact of the Revolution on institutions and on the distribution of political power. Here one must distinguish between those changes which were an unavoidable consequence of the break with Britain and those which in themselves point in the direction of revolutionary reform. Thus the widespread employment of constitutional conventions to settle the forms of government, while having a hallowed history in seventeenth-century Britain, and a hallowed future in France and elsewhere as an agency of revolutionary change, was, if not a virtual necessity, certainly not a conspicuously revolutionary procedure once the given structure of royal government had broken down. The device could be employed for radical or conservative ends alike, according to the way the conventions were manned and the powers they were given or assumed. In only five states, Massachusetts, New Hampshire, Maryland, Pennsylvania and North Carolina, were the new constitutions submitted to popular ratification. The constitutions varied in their character, from the highly Whiggish product of the South Carolina planters, to the drastically democratic constitution of Pennsylvania which build on an already relatively democratic colonial government. Where state independence was such a generally cherished ideal, it is difficult to make comprehensive generalisations about the character of the constitutions thrown up in the still imperfectly united states. But in general they were conspicuous for their uniformity rather than their diversity and for their close adherence to the practices of colonial days.

A governor by that or another title provided an executive head. He might – as in Massachusetts, Vermont and New Hampshire – be elected by popular vote; but where this was not done he was chosen by the legislature. He had a fixed term, usually of one year. If these provisions had a markedly democratic flavour – perhaps more than any other features of the typical constitution – this was hardly surprising. The royal governor had represented the point at which the British shoe had pinched during the decades before Independence. Through him came the royal veto and the dissolution of legislatures. It was he who instructed the customs officials and tax collectors who so infringed the 'liberties' of the colonists. Surely his position, above all, must be made dependent on the sovereign people's will, directly or indirectly, if independence were to mean something more than a mere change of masters? An executive council (generally chosen by the legislature) acted, as in pre-revolutionary days, as the governor's advisers. But in any event, the separation of powers, a principle enshrined in the constitutional ethics of the period, but hardly revolutionary in intent or effect, curtailed the governor's powers in every state. Above all, however, the legislature which, significantly, the governor could neither adjourn nor prorogue, acquired a position of superiority, endowed now with many of the previous prerogative powers of the executive, notably over appointments and patronage. It was, all the same, normally bicameral (Pennsylvania, Georgia and Vermont being the only exceptions). It was rare for the Upper House, the Senate, to rest upon restrictive qualifications of property or seniority for membership, yet to a significant degree state senators did in fact approximate to the ideal of being leading establishment figures, whose political *gravitas* reposed on a solid property base. Without doubt, the new Lower Houses reflected a democratising trend – in lower or non-existent property qualifications for membership, in a re-apportionment of seats according to population, in annual elections, and in enhanced powers which gave the assemblies the upper hand over the Senates. Of course, at no point in the system was suffrage universal. The body politic still consisted of those who had a 'stake' in society; nor were religious qualifications for office-holding unknown. But these were societies in which property was very widely diffused, and atheism minimally professed. Combined with the Bills of Rights which were a feature of eight state constitutions, the structure of government was one which guaranteed expression of the popular will, respect for the individual, and institutions whose powers were limited by law as well as by consensus.

Just as the structure of government was never majoritarian so, of course, the structure of society was never egalitarian. The categories of colonial society were always of course much more fluid than those of eighteenth-century Britain. Yet aristocratic families there certainly were, even in post-revolutionary America, based on land and money, like the Byrds the Livingstons or the Saltonstalls; or on commerce and banking, like the Faneuils, the Jays, the Whartons and the Rutledges. John Adams did less than justice to the inherent mobility of American society when he affirmed that 'The poor are destined to labour and the rich, by the advantages of education, independence, and leisure, are qualified for superior status.' After all, John Harvard had been a butcher's boy. Nevertheless, the Adams view would have been echoed by almost all settlers before 1776, and by the great majority afterwards. 'Take none but gentlemen' was George Washington's advice on the selection of officers. And certainly the well-connected families, his own amongst them, who embraced the Revolution, did not think they were making America unsafe for aristocracy.

John Adams, in his *Thoughts on Government*, which was initially circulated in manuscript in 1776, expressed the philosophy which related this society to its post-Independence institutions. The aim, he insisted was

A plan [of government] as nearly resembling the governments under which we were born and have lived as the circumstances of the country will admit. Kings we never had among us, nobles we never had. Nothing hereditary ever existed in the country: nor will the country require or admit of any such thing. But governors and councils we have always had, as well as representatives. A legislature in three branches [i.e. governor, council and assembly–equivalent to king lords and commons] ought to be preserved, and independent judges. Where and how will you get your governors and councils? By elections. How, who shall elect? The representatives of the people in convention will be best qualified to contrive a mode. (*Diary and Autobiography*, III, p. 356)

That such an approach still left open the possibility of a radical, quasi-revolutionary set of institutions cannot be denied. That its main thrust was in the direction of as much conservatism as was compatible with the break with Britain is equally indisputable. No wonder that its author decried 'the plan of government' in Tom Paine's *Common Sense* as 'so democratical, without any restraint or even an attempt at any equilibrium or counterpoise, that it·must produce confusion and every evil work'.

In 1776, however, it had looked for a moment as if the Paine model would sweep the board. No infant revolution has ever had a foster-parent both so impatient and initially so successful in launching his child on the road to triumph.. The timing was perfect. Composed in that curious phase of hesitancy and debate that followed on Bunker Hill, *Common Sense* appeared in January 1776, just when it was needed to impel the last falterer towards Independence. As John C. Miller put it in his *Origins of the American Revolution* (p. 468), 'Tom Paine broke the ice that was slowly congealing the revolutionary movement.' With over 120,000 copies sold within three months, the pamphlet had a sensational impact on colonial opinion.

Yet it is no reflection on this masterpiece of radical pamphleteering to remind ourselves that as a key to the fundamental nature of the American Revolution it has its limitations. A good deal of its *réclame* was due to the fact that it was a rallying-cry issued by an émigré from tyrant George's kingdom, a volunteer who had thrown in his lot with the American cause. But this also meant that the Paine analysis and the Paine recipe were alike imported from another and an alien context. His was the voice of a British workingman whose emigration had been occasioned as much by the oppression of a class system that most Americans did not know as by the particular mis-government that they were actually resisting. And of course Paine's pen is being pushed for a purpose. His pamphlet seeks to sharpen the contrast and the conflict, to highlight the promise of the revolution and to appeal from the untidy complexities of the here and and now to the splendours and clarities of the world as it will be. In this, as in much else, Paine is in the true revolutionary tradition.

It is no accident that the moment of Paine's greatest impact is the moment of his first appearance. This is as much because of what *Common Sense* leaves out as because of what it asserts. The Calvinist preachers who read from their pulpits what appeared to be Paine's recognition of original sin – 'Government, like dress, is the badge of lost innocence' – lived to be shocked by the Paine who, in *The Age of Reason*, attacked the Bible as a forgery, and compared Christianity unfavourably with Mohammedanism and paganism. And even those whose private sentiments had strayed far from their Calvinistic upbringings, like Thomas Jefferson, learnt the wisdom of moderating the public expressions of their Deism. By the time Jefferson's draft of the Declaration had passed through the hands of Congress's Committee of Five (Jefferson, Adams, Franklin, Sherman and Robert R. Livingston), a significant omission had been made good; in the peroration had been inserted the words 'with a firm reliance on the protection of divine providence'. The Age of Reason had not yet fully taken over from the rule of the godly. In fact, as subsequent events demonstrated, the revolutionary American love affair with the Enlightenment was short-lived.

It is in the light of this awareness that we should read Tom Paine's trumpetings of universalism and millenarianism. 'The cause of America is in great measure the cause of all mankind.' 'We have it in our power to begin the world over again. A situation similar to the present has not happened since the days of Noah until now. The birthday of a new world is at hand, and a race of men, perhaps as numerous as all Europe contains, are to receive their portion of freedom from the events of a few months.' And later in the *Rights of Man*: 'The independence of America, considered as a separation from England, would have been a matter but of little importance, had it not been accompanied by a revolution in the principles and practice of government.'

But, in fact, these expectations of a *novus ordo seculorum* foundered on the sands of American pragmatism. For one thing, even as they embraced the overthrow of royal power, the Calvinistic clergy and their flocks had no intention of making independence, still less revolution, a substitute religion for the faith they knew and practised. There was never, in any part of the colonies, any disposition to let the ordinary culture of life, still less the culture of the Church, be taken over by revolutionary visionaries or fanatics. There was no Revolutionary Calender, no *Culte de l'Être Suprême*. Where the French had installed secular priests, the Americans resorted to lawyers. In place of the invocation of revolutionary ideology, there was appeal to an existing body of law, with the minimum of general principles to eke it our where necessary. Indeed a great deal of the effort expended on the Declaration of Independence and on similar related apologias was directed to proving the contention that what the colonists were attempting was not rebellion at all, but only a legitimate defence of their legal rights. Hence the long catalogue of 'facts', the list of 'repeated injuries and usurpations' of the tyrant king which takes up so much space in the body of the Declaration. It is not the existing form of government as such that is being attacked, but the way in which it has been practised.

Of course behind the 'facts', the 'grievances' and the protests there was a philosophy, but it was a philosophy – what Jefferson significantly called 'the common sense of the subject' – which was taken for granted by all who had grown up in the world of contract theory, who had read their Locke (and perhaps, but by no means necessarily, their Rousseau), who viewed the laws of Nature and of Nature's God, and the Natural Rights which went with them, as reasonable, universal and self-evident. It was a philosophy which could be fitted into a religious setting or not, as one preferred, but it could not be divorced from law, and it gave no easy licence to *any* ruler, including revolutionary ones. In America, where there was no real centralisation of power either before, during or after the Revolution, it could not be used to set up a tyranny of revolutionary principle. In fact, in a country where habits of pragmatism were already well developed the temper of the people guaranteed that it would find its lasting expression in a Constitution which, for all the generalities of its Bill of Rights, set up a government against government, and entrusted the oversight of it all not to a majority of the sovereign people but to a majority of a supreme court.

And yet, when one has demonstrated its uniqueness, its American-ness, its moderation and its legalism, that is not quite all. Somewhere here there is a resonance, a sense of a new page opened in the history not just of thirteen American, English-speaking colonies, or even of their consequential Union. As soon as Lafayette 'took a house in 1783', we are told in his *Memoirs*, 'he placed in it the Declaration of Independence with a vacant place, "waiting" [as he said], "the declaration of rights of France" '. When Ian Smith seized power in Rhodesia in 1965 he drew, however shadily, on the ringing phrases of Thomas Jefferson's prose. It may be true that the American case was unique rather than universal, that if offers little or nothing in the way of a usable blueprint. The fact remains that it broke the eighteenth-century code of custom at a stroke. Something – a lot – must be allowed to the exceptional literary powers of the spokesmen, not only of Jefferson in his Declaration, but also of Paine and Madison and others who contrived to chisel classic expressions of what men in all sorts of subsequently diverse conditions have wanted to say about liberty and equality, justice and government. Only our own century with its puny powers of self-expression would commit the elementary blunder of underestimating the role of words in the transmission of beliefs. But beyond this remains the fact that what happened in America, whether a revolution or not, was an indisputable success. The War of Independence was won, and at a price which was less than many feared. The colonists composed their internal differences – even if at the price of sending many a loyalist packing. The framework of society and government which they established was erected with a remarkable freedom from dissension and bloodshed. The Union which was born of Independence lived and thrived. The future was shown to work. If it was not a *novus ordo seculorum* it promised, none the less, a fitting home for all sorts and conditions of men provided they were each willing to become a member of Crèvecoeur's new breed, *homo Americanus*, 'this new man'.

4 The French Revolution

NORMAN HAMPSON

During the first half of the twentieth century there emerged in
France a way of looking at the Revolution of 1789 that Professor
Soboul, its latest exponent at the Sorbonne, likes to describe as
'classical'. By 1945 this had hardened into orthodoxy. Its own
merits, the remarkable erudition of its advocates, and the hier-
archical structure of French universities, meant that it was difficult
for young scholars to see that complicated and important period
from any other perspective, and leanings towards heterodoxy were
somewhat vigorously discouraged.

In a general sort of way, this interpretation rested on what was
assumed to be a Marxist basis. Pre-revolutionary French society
was described, rather loosely, as 'feudal', with a landed nobility as
its ruling class and its political institutions centred on an absolute
monarchy that still showed many traces of its medieval origins.
Within this society there had developed an alien bourgeoisie whose
economic interests and consequent mental attitudes were at variance
with prevailing ideas and practices. This emergent middle class had
evolved its own ideology – the Enlightenment – which reflected its
rationalist and utilitarian values and posed a theoretical challenge
to the existing order. The latter increasingly inhibited the economic
development and frustrated the social ambitions of those who were
in the process of becoming the dominant sector of society. By the
1780s the scene was therefore set for the overthrow of the *ancien
régime* and its replacement by a new bourgeois society. The occasion
for this social revolution was provided by the bankruptcy of the
monarchy, which found itself unable to govern. The initial assault
came, not from the bourgeois, but from the nobility, the only
section of society with the corporate institutions (*parlements*, pro-
vincial assemblies, the assembly of the clergy) that enabled it to
challenge the royal government. When the nobility forced Louis xvi
to convene the Estates General in 1789, this provided the bourgeoisie with the political machinery that allowed it to emerge as an

autonomous force, defeat both the initial protagonists, and seize power in its own right. Convinced that it represented not the interests of a single class, but those of the nation – indeed, of humanity itself – the bourgeoisie was able to enlist the support of a minority of the nobility and of the mass of the urban and peasant population.

This initial success led to the transformation of French society, but provoked growing resistance from the representatives of an old order that had been defeated but not destroyed. A period of unstable compromise was ended by the outbreak of war. The war soon became an ideological crusade, with the old order in Europe intent on crushing the new forces in France that threatened its survival. Within France itself, the war ended the attempt at compromise between the *ancien régime* and the Revolution and led to the insurrection of 10 August 1792 and the overthrow of the monarchy. Faced with a desperate struggle to defeat the armies of the counter-revolution, the French bourgeoisie was driven to make a new compromise, this time with the *sans culottes*, the urban working class. This split the middle-class politicians, with the Girondins clinging to bourgeois principles, and the Montagnards ready to make such temporary concessions as were required to enlist popular support. In this way, they were able to dispose of their Girondin rivals, but their alliance with the *sans culottes* was a marriage of convenience that lasted only as long as the military crisis. Victory in the field led quickly to the overthrow of Robespierre, the dismantling of the Terror, and the final emergence of a fully-fledged bourgeois society.

This relatively straightforward interpretation was complicated by influences from two different quarters. The first of these was a form of nationalism that derived from Michelet, who had seen the Revolution as a new gospel of salvation for all the nations. The *French* Revolution thereby acquired a more universal significance than those of England and her American colonies. If the peoples of the world had two *patries*, their own and France, all good revolutionaries had two revolutions, and non-French versions owed this inspiration to the 'révolution notre mère' that was the mother of them all. Projecting this backwards, the preservation of the Revolution in France, in the 1790s, had rightly taken precedence over the interests of the sister-republics that were created along the French frontier – a kind of anticipation of 'socialism in one country'. In the second place, from Mathiez onwards, French historians had tended to see Robespierre as the incarnation of the Revolution, and to equate its fortune with his own career, which had given rise to some ingenious mental acrobatics.

This is not, I think, an unfair description of a certain school of French historiography, but it is a much oversimplified one, that takes no account of the differences between Mathiez, Lefebvre and Soboul, its main exponents. Such differences, however, were matters of emphasis rather than of principle.

The 'classical' explanation had a certain hypnotic quality. All its parts cohered and, to those inclined towards an economic interpretation of history, there was a kind of inherent probability about it. It was supported by an intimidating body of evidence, and it did explain why contemporaries as different as Blake, Fox, Kant and Goethe should have regarded the Revolution as something of enormous importance to the world at large. If one could bring oneself to ask, however, whether the emperor really had any clothes on, there was no need of exhaustive research in order to pose some awkward questions. *Could* the middle class have been the dominant economic force in eighteenth-century France when it was far from being anything of the kind in England (despite the fact that England's 'bourgeois revolution' was a hundred years old)? *Were* men like Montesquieu, Voltaire and Rousseau really the spokesmen of the bourgeoisie, and if they were, why did they disagree so much? When the bourgeoisie 'intervened' in 1789, why were most of their leaders nobles? Why did a commercial and industrial middle class, in whose interest the Revolution was being made, prove so coy about leading it? and why did it allow war and inflation to play such havoc with the economy? Was Napoleon really the kind of ruler that the bourgeoisie wanted? If they had seized power in 1789, why did they have to do it all over again in 1830? and why did bourgeois and revolutionary France prove so backward in the nineteenth century when compared with conservative and aristocratic England? There were answers to these questions, but not necessarily convincing ones. In retrospect, one is inclined to wonder at the willing suspension of disbelief that allowed the 'classical' explanation to survive for so long as almost 'all ye know on earth and all ye need to know'. This is not to deny, of course, that it inspired some very fine research and in many areas uncovered evidence that would not otherwise have been sought or understood.

Since 1945 the interpretation has been progressively undermined, at first in England and America and latterly in France itself. Guérin in *La lutte des classes sous la première république* (1946) attempted a specifically Trotskyite interpretation of the Revolution. This made the *sans culottes* the heroes at the expense of Robespierre, but otherwise confronted the orthodoxy with no more than minor heresies. In the 1950s, Palmer and Godechot posited the existence of an international 'Atlantic' revolutionary movement. As Palmer himself has insisted, this is a rather separate issue, in the sense that the Atlantic hypothesis neither confirms nor invalidates the central arguments of the 'classical' theory. It has nevertheless been vigorously rejected by Soboul as a product of the 'cold war'. This reflects both his concern to see France as the forerunner of Russia rather than the culmination of liberal (and 'Anglo-Saxon') revolutionary movements and also, one suspects, some reluctance to see a uniquely French event deprived of its exclusively national character. Soboul's alignment of the French with the Russian Revolution had been suggested, from a very different point of view, by Talmon, whose *Origins of Totalitarian Democracy* (1952) presented Robespierre and Saint-Just as the heirs of a Rousseauist collectivism that was finally to triumph under Stalin.

The first direct challenge to the 'classical' theory came from Cobban in his inaugural lecture, *The Myth of the French Revolution*, whose argument was elaborated in the Wiles Lectures, and subsequently published as *The Social Interpretation of the French Revolution* (1964). Cobban seems to have seen himself as challenging the Marxists, but much of his own argument consisted of showing not that Marx was mistaken, but that his followers had drawn the wrong conclusions from their misinterpretations of the evidence. When Cobban wrote, 'It was a revolution not for, but against capitalism', he was claiming by implication to be a more accurate Marxist than Soboul. Just as one suspects that behind Soboul's interpretation lies an unconscious pride in the *French* Revolution, Cobban seemed to have an equally pronounced leaning in the opposite direction. 'There is nothing surprising in the fact that, the economic development of English society being so far in advance of that of France, its political evolution should also have shown much greater maturity.' Patriotism apart, there was more than a hint of economic determinism here! Like all pioneers, Cobban had to cut his way through, without being able to see precisely where he was going. His book has rightly been acclaimed for its effect in encouraging everyone to look at the evidence with new eyes. Its main contribution was, however, negative. The society of the *ancien régime* was *not* feudal; the commercial bourgeoisie did *not* play an active part in the Revolution; the insurgent peasantry was *not* the natural ally of a revolutionary middle class, and so on. The result was to knock large holes in the 'classical' theory, without putting anything else in its place. It also cut the Revolution down to size so drastically that one was left wondering why Wordsworth found it 'bliss in that dawn to be alive'; and why Goethe, in the Prussian camp after Valmy, thought he was present at the beginning of a new age in the history of the world. The 'classical' theory had provided an admirable answer to that and, even if it was an erroneous one, the fact still needed explaining.

More recent work has fragmented the picture that the 'Marxist' historians had presented in sharp, if illusory focus. In two brilliant articles ('Types of Capitalism in Eighteenth-century France', in the *English Historical Review* (1964), and 'Non-capitalist Wealth and the Origins of the French Revolution', in the *American Historical Review* (1967)), G. V. Taylor demonstrated that there was no sharp distinction between the economic interests of the nobility and those of the middle class under the *ancien régime*, both being primarily interested in what he described as 'proprietory capitalism'. Betty Behrens, in a sensitive study (*The Ancien Régime* (1967)), showed that the 'privileged orders' were to some extent an invention of revolutionary propaganda. Anyone of any importance in eighteenth-century France enjoyed privileges of one kind or another, and successful businessmen had learned to exploit the peculiar anomalies of the *ancien régime*, which they might be in no hurry to dismantle. Doyle disputed the existence of a 'feudal reaction' in the exploitation of seigneurial rights ('Was there an aristocratic reaction in pre-revolutionary France?', *Past and Present* (1972)). Forster, in his examination of the French nobility (*The Nobility of Toulouse in the Eighteenth century* (1960); 'The Noble Wine-producers in the Bordelais in the Eighteenth Century', *Economic History Review* (1961)), showed that the nobility were often thrustful entrepreneurs. This was demonstrated, in more general terms, by Chaussinand–Nogaret (*La Noblesse au XVIII c Siècle* (1976)). Also in France, Furet went back to de Tocqueville, stressing the extent to which the Revolution represented continuity rather than a fresh start in French history. For him, its unique contribution was ideological rather than social. Recent studies have emphasised the autonomous role of politics during the Revolution, the existence of political machines and the tactical reasons for the adoption of particular political options. A number of excellent regional studies have drawn attention to the diversity of the revolutionary experience. The combined effect of all this effort has been to make things very much more complicated. Whether or not it will eventually lead to some new synthesis that will command as much support as the old one, it is impossible to predict. On the whole it seems unlikely.

The present situation is therefore unsatisfactory – especially for the harassed student – in the sense that no one is abreast of recent research can write a unified history of the Revolution that will keep all the balls in the air at the same time. Doyle's recent masterly study of the controversies about its causes (*Origins of the French Revolution* (1981)) offers no simple synthesis with the compelling power of Lefebvre's *1789*. However disappointing this may be, it is probably healthy. At least it is some sort of safeguard against the Procrustean processes that were used in the past to make the evidence fit. It does, however, reflect a climate of professional agnosticism that may not last, and it makes it very difficult for specialists to present the Revolution in terms that will prove interesting, or even comprehensible to the informed public or to practitioners of other disciplines. Within the context of the present volume, the most important aspect of the French Revolution is perhaps its ideology, and the remainder of this chapter will therefore consist, not of any up-to-date consensus about the Revolution as a whole – which scarcely exists any more – but of a brief personal view of the ideas professed by the revolutionaries themselves and the ways in which these were influenced by the pressure of events.

If one reads what the future leaders of the Revolution were writing in the years before 1789, it becomes immediately obvious that they derived their inspiration from Montesquieu and Rousseau and from virtually no one else. Marat, for example, wrote in the summer of 1789, 'If Montesquieu and Rousseau were still with us, the best thing the nation could to would be to beg them on its knees to give us a constitution.' The message of *De l'Ésprit des lois* was diverse and contradictory. Conservative *parlementaires* were particularly attracted by the earlier part, in which Montesquieu stressed the role of an hereditary nobility in checking the tendency of monarchies to degenerate into despotisms. Revolutionaries preferred to concentrate on the later part. Here Montesquieu judged political societies by the extent to which they ensured liberty, by which he meant individual liberty and what we now understand by civil rights. He believed men's opinions to be determined by many factors – historical, geographical, social and religious – whose combined effect produced an *esprit général*. This was an amalgamation of innumerable divergent wills and interests, since each citizen was the point of intersection of a unique combination of allegiances to the state, his religion, his family, etc. The *esprit général* determined not merely what was possible, but what the members of a community would regard as desirable. Legislation that frustrated or defied it, from whatever motive, would prove in its application to be tyrannous. When he reached this stage of his book, Montesquieu had discarded his earlier admiration for the classical city-state, whose inhabitants were assumed to have been united by a *vertu* so all-embracing that they lost their individual identity within it. Looking at the world about him, he concluded that power corrupted and '*vertu* itself needs limits'. He therefore advocated a political system in which 'power checks power', and he believed this to be ideally manifested in the political institutions of Great Britain.

So far as the revolutionaries were concerned, Montesquieu was the man who knew about constitutions. His followers emphasised the primacy of individual freedom; they tended to look across the Channel for an example; they welcomed private initiative as conducive to national prosperity; they thought in terms of continuous gradual amelioration; and they wanted political power to be fragmented. As Mercier wrote in the conclusion to his *Notions claires sur les gouvernements* (1787),

Where is sovereignty in such a state? I don't know. . . . There are scattered sovereignties; I see forces in balance and that is what is needed . . . the more that states are simplified, the more dangerous they are, because then they become military. Governments must be complicated; human liberty finds its ramparts amidst these oppositions.

The question of Rousseau's influence has been unnecessarily confused by arguments about the extent to which people were familiar with *Du contrat social*. Much of the essence of that enigmatic book had already appeared in Rousseau's article, 'Economie politique', in the *Encyclopedia*, and was therefore easily available. In any case, his influence had little to do with the tantalising ambiguities of the *volonté générale*. Rousseau served his generation as a kind of deist Wesley, recalling those who had gone astray in the arid wastes of rationalism, to belief in the heart, the natural goodness of man and the benevolence of a responsive god. Brissot, Mme. Roland, Mercier and, by implication, Robespierre, all testified to a kind of spiritual rebirth under his influence. This was effected by his work as a whole, by the *Nouvelle Héloïse* and *Emile*, rather more than by his specifically political writings.

In the first place, Rousseau *converted* people to the belief that men were naturally good and were made evil only by vicious social and political institutions. The essential aim of political activity was, therefore, to reverse the process and regenerate both individuals and society. The specific form this regeneration must take was dictated to him by his obsession with the idealised values that he attributed to the classical city-states (or at least to Sparta and republican Rome, for he never had much use for Athens). This may have originated with Montesquieu. To recover the lost glories would require the most literal imitation of the ancient institutions. He therefore advised the Corsicans to aim at the self-sufficiency of each family unit, and to dispense with trade altogether, even on a basis of barter. He recommended the Poles to base their military tactics on those of the Parthians and the Spartans. His ideal society was based on subsistence agriculture, approximate economic equality, and a Spartan life in more ways than one, in which the state would provide by public festivals and manifestations of collective enthusiasm whatever might be lacking in the satisfaction of the material or spiritual needs of the individual. He was the first to agree that such arduous delights would prove beyond the grasp of his effeminate contemporaries, apart from favoured exceptions such as the Corsicans and the Poles, but he did admit of one exception: 'In the duration of states there are sometimes violent epochs, when revolutions act upon men like the crises in illness and horror of the past takes the place of loss of money, and the state, blazing with civil war, is reborn from its ashes.' If regeneration was to be achieved at all, its consolidation would depend on the implanting of *vertu* by means of republican institutions, which could only be devised by a 'legislator' of the calibre of Solon or Lycurgus. Such a legislator would create a society in which each would find the satisfaction of his personal needs in the fulfilment of a collective purpose. There should, therefore, be no intermediate bodies to provide distracting foci of allegiance between the individual and the institutions of society as a whole. Individual rights acquired their meaning only within the context of the interests of the community; unanimity was the goal and divergence from the collective will was a sign of ignorance or perversity.

None of the revolutionaries swallowed Rousseau whole – even if Marat in 1793 did propose mobilising the entire adult population and equipping everyone with Roman swords. His influence was nevertheless deep and pervasive. His devotees saw politics essentially as a moral crusade for national regeneration. They were inclined to equate opposition with whatever was the deist equivalent of anti-christ. They thought in terms of an agrarian society and distrusted commerce. They tended to ascribe *vertu* to the poor who were, however, in need of enlightenment and guidance from their social superiors. Like Rousseau himself, they were ambivalent on the question of property, but saw it as a social institution, in the sense that the subsistence of the poor had priority over the economic freedom of the rich – they assumed, unlike Montesquieu, that the enrichment of some automatically implied the impoverishment of others. Whatever their knowledge and understanding of the *volonté générale*, as Rousseau struggled to define it in *Du contrat social*, they believed that what was understood to be in the interest of the community as a whole was, in some sense, sovereign, independent of and superior to the wishes of individuals, or even of the majority. As Prieur de la Marne, one of the members of the Committee of Public Safety, put in in 1793, 'If it were true that only a minority [in Savoy] had accepted the constitution, one would have to conclude that, in this respect as in many others, the people had been deceived.' Robespierre too thought that '*Vertu* is always in a minority in this world.'

In fact, the conclusions of Montesquieu and Rousseau were antithetical. The former started with men as they were and looked for political institutions that would allow them to remain what they wanted to be. Rousseau aimed to transform them into what they ought to have wanted to become. 'Good social institutions are those which most effectually denature man, replacing his absolute existence with a relative one and transporting his "I" within a common unity.' It was nevertheless possible, after a fashion and up to a point, to combine elements of both in a rather hazy synthesis, at least if one was writing pamphlets before 1789 and not actually implementing policies. There was some talk of a coming 'revolution', by which men seem to have meant something much less dramatic than what actually occurred. Rousseau's ends, at least in the vague sense of a moral reformation, were to be achieved by Montesquieu's means, a constitutional monarchy that would guard against usurpations of power. If people actually wanted what was good for them – which was not too difficult to predicate in the golden future – the *esprit général* and the *volonté générale* would amount to the same thing. Rousseau had intended to liberate people, not to enslave them, and perhaps everything would work out for the best. The fact that some such heady mixture was common to so many thinking people before 1789 was of considerable importance. It meant that the French Revolution, unlike those in England and America, had its ideology worked out in advance. When a political crisis broke, with the convocation of the Estates General, not many people were thinking of a return to the past. The occasion was widely hailed as one for the drafting of a new social contract that would establish the French monarchy on entirely different foundations.

The Revolution began with a widespread conviction that the millennium had already arrived: Marat's *Offrande à la patrie*, published in March 1793, was perhaps the only optimistic thing that he ever wrote. The events of that unforgettable year were some of the most dramatic in France's long history – the fall of Bastille, in particular, caught the imagination of the whole of Europe – and they were relatively bloodless. On the night of 4 August 1789, representatives of the nobility and the clergy offered to sacrifice many of their privileges. It was this that committed the Assembly, not merely to give France a Constitution, but to remodel the organisation of the Church (which involved education, poor relief and hospitals), the legal system and local government. This was won not merely by consent, but as a voluntary sacrifice by the previous beneficiaries. In this mood, *esprit général* and *volonté générale* did indeed seem to amount to much the same thing, and it looked as though a universal commitment to regeneration meant that there would be no need to sacrifice the liberalism of Montesquieu to the sterner principles of Rousseau.

For the next year or two Robespierre concentrated on trying to keep the Constituent Assembly true to the principles it had professed in the glorious summer of 1789. When he launched a newspaper in the spring of 1792, he called it *Le défenseur de la constitution*. Saint-Just, in two works that he wrote in 1791–2, criticised Rousseau from a point of view that came close to anarchism. If men were really good by nature, all coercive legislation was illegitimate. He considered it unpardonable of Rousseau to have accepted the death penalty, since 'laws that depend on the executioner perish in blood and infamy'. He accused Rousseau of smothering liberty with its own hands, and rejected the absolute sovereignty of the general will, which 'must also be just and reasonable. It is not less criminal for the sovereign to be tyrannised by itself than by someone else.'

It was all too good to be true, and certainly too good to last. The consensus to which the revolutionaries aspired was rejected by the King and a substantial part of the clergy and nobility, not to mention the more conservative members of the Third Estate. The Legislative Assembly resorted to what it intended to be a limited war in the hope of breaking the ensuing deadlock. France was faced with impending Prussian invasion, and on 10 August 1792 the Tuileries were stormed and the monarchy overthrown. This transformed both the course of the Revolution and the way in which its leaders conceived of it. When France became a republic in September 1792, this meant much more than the abolition of the monarchy. For Robespierre at least, the magic word implied a commitment to the ideal of the classical city-states. 'Thus has begun the finest revolution that has ever honoured humanity, indeed the only one with an object worthy of man: to found political societies at last on the immortal principles of equality, justice and reason. Frenchmen, remember that the destinies of the universe are in your hands.'

More prosaically, the national consensus had broken down. When a new Convention was elected, there could be no question of admitting monarchists to it, and no means of knowing how numerous they were. When the Girondins were purged in June 1793, most Frenchmen were by now probably out of sympathy with their alleged representatives. There could be no turning back and it was impossible to relax the control of the central government when invasion threatened the survival of the Revolution itself. Force of circumstances drove the revolutionaries to act in a way that corresponded to Rousseau's theories: in the name of the national interest, to assert the legitimacy of policies that the majority of the population might not want but could not be given an opportunity to reject. When Robespierre joined Saint-Just on the Committee of Public Safety in July 1793, and the Committee gradually took on the appearance of a war cabinet, the two men found themselves sharing in the responsibilities of government. They could not help being aware of a divergence between the general will, as they claimed to embody it, and what people actually wanted. Robespierre, in a speech that he made on Christmas Day 1793, wrestled with the ghost of Montesquieu in an attempt to persuade the Assembly and himself that acceptance of the Terror did not mean basing the state on *crainte*, the emblem of despotism. His distinction between periods of constitutional government, when the rights of the individual took precedence over those of government, and revolutionary periods when the roles were reversed, was sensible enough, but it did not provide a theoretical justification for long-term measures designed to make people want what was good for them. Saint-Just had fewer inhibitions: 'A revolution has occurred within the government, but it has not penetrated civil society. The government rests on liberty, civil society on aristocracy.' In the previous year he had already paraphrased Rousseau to the effect that it was for the legislator to make men what he wanted them to be.

None of the practical measures proposed by the two men had much effect, but they do show how the pressure of events had driven them in the direction of extreme Rousseauist attitudes. Robespierre championed an Education Bill that provided for several years of compulsory training for girls and boys, in comprehensive boarding schools, where they would be brought up like little Spartans. No social levelling underlay this commando course in *vertu*: at the age of ten or eleven the children were to be restored to their families to receive the kind of training appropriate to their future positions in society. The Convention approved the Bill, but did nothing to implement it. In the spring of 1794 Robespierre persuaded it to endorse a new state religion that was copied from the penultimate chapter of *Du contrat social*. He was overthrown before it could have much effect and few of his colleagues had much sympathy with it.

Saint-Just, in the spring of 1794, put forward a plan for the confiscation of the property of 'suspects' for the benefit of the poor. This was not intended as a primarily egalitarian measure, since he declared the property of *patriotes* to be sacred, and his main concern was to deprive suspected counter-revolutionaries of the political influence that money could buy. As tensions became unbearable in the summer of 1794, Saint-Just argued desperately that Salvation could come only through the transformation of social attitudes by the adoption of republican institutions. A rough draft of some of the things he had in mind was found in his pocket when he was arrested. It was a bizarre mixture of agrarian primitivism ('every citizen ought to derive his livelihood from his land and use industry merely to supplement his wealth'), healthy life crankiness (no meat for those under sixteen and thereafter only on seven days in every ten; he perhaps did not realise what an increase in consumption this would have implied for the majority of the population), and general busy-bodying (white scarves for those who completed sixty years of virtuous life, black for murderers, death for women who entered military camps, etc.)The whole thing was inconceivable as the basis for any kind of actual society, but it was strikingly similar to Rousseau's advice to the Poles and the Corsicans. Since his plans for Corsican society were not published until the nineteenth century, this makes the correspondence between his views and those of Saint-Just all the more striking.

Both Robespierre and Saint-Just had reservations about the attitudes they had been driven to adopt. Robespierre turned on an over-enthusiastic Jacobin who wanted to deport a colleague for atheism, with the remark that there were some truths better left in the pages of Rousseau. To the end, Saint-Just insisted that government was only necessary for the wicked and that the virtuous must be left free to go their ways independently. In practice, this cannot have been of much comfort to anyone but Saint-Just himself, since he also said that anyone who criticised the government as dictatorial thereby exposed himself as an enemy of the Revolution. Robespierre and Saint-Just, in fact, had reached the *reductio ad absurdum* of Rousseauist logic, where the general will was equated not with the majority of the population, the Convention, the Montagnards or even the Committee of Public Safety, but with themselves and one or two of their associates.

Their overthrow coincided with the winding up of the Terror and for long enough after that, Rousseau was to be associated with the bloody measures that had been justified in his name. Montesquieu fared little better. The Thermidoreans believed that political power should reflect social realities, in the sense that its exercise should be restricted to those with wealth and education. 'A country ruled by property-owners is within the social order; one in which men without property govern is in a state of nature.' This was to make the state the instrument of one section of society, whereas Montesquieu had insisted that it should hold the balance between them all. In any case, France was too bitterly divided between warring factions with scores to settle and atrocities to avenge for there to be any hope of identifying an *esprit général* that might serve as the basis for a new consensus. Mercier, one of the survivors from the wreck of so many hopes, may serve as the disenchanted spokesmen for those who were left: 'They wanted to make entirely new men of us and all they did was to make us practically savages.' It would be ridiculous to pretend that this was all Rousseau's fault, but a good deal of it had been justified in the name of his principles.

III

TOTAL
REVOLUTION

5 Nazism and Revolution

JEREMY NOAKES

'We are not improvers, but revolutionary reformers', wrote Hitler on 17 July 1922, and a few days later he told a Munich audience: 'Let there be no doubt. We Nazis are not a second Gironde.'[1] A number of similar quotations could be used to illustrate the point that, from an early date, Hitler claimed that he and his movement were bent on a revolution. Moreover, after 1933, Hitler and other leading Nazis continued to refer to the 'National Socialist revolution', though sometimes as something which had taken place in 1933 and sometimes as something that was still in progress – with each reference depending on the political context in which it was used.[2]

But if the Nazis themselves repeatedly declared that they had either carried out or were engaged upon a revolution, this claim has by no means met with unanimous acceptance by subsequent historians, nor is there agreement about what exactly the intended or purported revolution consisted of. The situation is not helped by the fact that to use the term 'revolution' is to enter a semantic minefield. It has become ideologically loaded to a high degree, carrying with it a whole set of connotations of either a positive or a negative kind depending on the standpoint of the person using it. Moreover, so much depends on what each author considers to be the essential or determining features of a social order that it is difficult to use it in its dictionary sense as simply a neutral measure of the degree of political, economic, and social change which has occurred or is intended to occur in a particular case.

Two of the more interesting studies of Nazism have made it clear where they stand in their titles: Hermann Rauschning's *The Revolution of Destruction* and, more recently, David Schoenbaum's *Hitler's Social Revolution*, although they do not agree as to what kind of revolution was involved.[3] Other students of Nazism believe that while Nazism was revolutionary in intention – aiming at nothing less than 'a revolution against the modern world' – it nevertheless failed to carry out either an economic or a social revolution.[4]

The most categorical denial of Nazism's status as a revolutionary movement comes from Marxist historians for whom it was neither revolutionary in intention nor in effect.[5] These historians regard Nazism as a particular form of Fascism which emerged in response to a severe crisis in late capitalism and, in particular, to the failure of the bourgeois political order of Weimar democracy to guarantee the reproduction of the conditions necessary for the production and realisation of surplus value. This failure, it is argued, compelled the bourgeoisie to accept a Fascist regime which sometimes imposed measures which were unpalatable – at any rate for some – but which they were obliged to tolerate, since Fascism offered the only chance of preserving the capitalist system. Indeed, the crucial point for most Marxist historians is their claim that whatever the revolutionary and anti-capitalist rhetoric of Nazism, and whatever measures may have been taken against individual capitalists, overall when judged in terms of concrete results, the Nazi regime worked to the advantage of monopoly capitalism. This point has been well put by Ernest Mandel:

> Whether Krupp or Thyssen looked upon this or that point of Hitler's rule with enthusiasm, reservation, or antipathy is not essential. But it is essential to determine whether Hitler's dictatorship tended to maintain or destroy, consolidated or undermined the social institutions of private property in the means of production and the subordination of workers who are forced to sell their labour power under the domination of capital. In this respect the historical balance seems to us clear.[6]

On the positive side of this 'historical balance' are some undeniable facts: first, the destruction of the independent political and economic organisations of the working class, and the introduction of legislation which strengthened the position of the employer *vis à vis* his employers; secondly, the increase in profits as a proportion of national income; thirdly, an acceleration of the trend towards concentration in industry; and, finally, the extent to which large-scale private industry and, in particular, the chemical industry (IG Farben) was involved in running the German economy after 1938 – particularly during the war years under the Speer system of 'industrial self-government' – and the extent to which it benefited from Nazi imperialist policies, for example through business acquisitions and the reorganisation of markets in the occupied territories.

Nevertheless, the fact that big business benefited from Nazism in the decade 1933–43, though significant, cannot in itself prove that the Nazi regime was the servant of big capital, or that the phenomenon of Nazism can be reduced to a function of capitalism. Indeed, in the light of the historical evidence, a number of Marxist historians and theorists have been unable to accept that Nazism was merely the 'agent' of monopoly capitalism. They have argued that the political regime had a measure of 'autonomy' from the economic 'base'.[7] This autonomy is seen as deriving from a crisis within the system as a result of intensified contradictions between the classes and, in particular, the failure of any one class or class fraction to impose its hegemony. This 'equilibrium' between the bourgeoisie and the proletariat (Thalheimer-Gramsci), or between the class factions within the ruling 'power bloc' (Poulantzas) created a kind of free space in which the Fascist regime could operate autonomously. The extent and significance of this autonomy is, however, highly contentions. Some historians see its function as being to preserve the capitalist system and, in particular, to establish the hegemony of big monopoly capital. Similarly, 'the continuing tendency of the highly centralized state apparatus to become independent' has been seen as originating in the efforts of the big bourgeoisie to change the balance of power on the world market. 'The all-or-nothing politics of Fascism are carried over from the social-political sphere into the financial sphere; it encourages permanent inflation and finally allows no alternative but foreign military adventure.'[8] Other Marxist historians, however, see it as a more extreme form of autonomy in which the political sphere has so far emancipated itself from the economic base as to acquire 'primacy' and has become, in effect, dysfunctional, indeed destructive.[9]

But if Marxist historians dispute the revolutionary intentions and effects of Nazism, as we saw, Hitler and most of his leading supporters claimed and indeed almost certainly believed, that Nazism was a revolutionary movement. The Nazi leaders did not envisage their revolution in the form of a sudden major social upheaval leading to a drastic redistribution of political, economic and social power between the existing social classes such as had characterised the Russian and – to a lesser extent – the French Revolutions. On the other hand, they did not intend to restrict themselves to a mere change of political regime. Their initial aim was certainly the overthrow of the existing political system, replacing the parliamentary democracy which had been introduced under the Weimar Constitution of 1919 by a one-party dictatorship under their leader, Adolf Hitler. But this *political* revolution was intended merely as the preliminary to a much more far-reaching transformation of Germany.

Hitler's goals are well-known.[10] Briefly, he aimed first, to restore Germany's military strength and free her from the restrictions of the Versailles peace settlement; secondly, to acquire *Lebensraum* in the East; and thirdly, to solve the so-called 'Jewish problem'. The new living space would not only provide the territory and resources with which to achieve an unassailable economic and strategic position for Germany in its struggle with its international rivals and, in particular, with 'world Jewry', but would also enable the government to reverse the hitherto inexorable trend towards industrialisation and urbanisation which, in Hitler's view, posed such a threat to the racial health of the German people, by settling large numbers of Germans in rural settlements in the East.

In terms of their influence on developments in the Third Reich, however, as significant as the goals themselves were the ways in which Hitler believed they could best be achieved. They were based on an approach which he had developed during his earliest years in politics. Considering Germany's position in the post-war world, defeated and bound by the Versailles settlement, he was convinced that the nation's future lay in its own hands. In his view morale was the key to Germany's revival, and morale in turn depended upon the indoctrination of the German people with a new ideology (*Weltanschauung*) with which to replace the debilitating liberal-democratic values which, in his view, had sapped the energy and will power of the German people. The main components of this ideology were anti-semitism and a racist form of Social Darwinism or, as Hitler himself preferred to put it, an acceptance of the 'laws of nature'. While Hitler sometimes referred to the actual takeover of power in 1933 as 'the National Socialist revolution', he seems, in fact, to have regarded the revolution as a long-term process of indoctrination. As he put it in 1934:

The victory of a party is a change of government, the victory of a *Weltanschauung* is a revolution which transforms the conditions of a nation profoundly and in its essence. One does not become a National Socialist in one year, in fact many years are necessary and generations will no doubt pass before we shall have buried the victory sign of our Reich in the hearts of everybody. And only then will the National Socialist revolution have succeeded and the German people have been finally saved.[11]

Such a fundamental reorientation of the German people's mentality required, on the one hand, a massive programme of re-education and indoctrination and, on the other hand, the suppression of those individuals and organisations which put forward views which were regarded as liable to undermine national morale – by encouraging class conflict, by stressing the rights of the individual as against those of the community (as interpreted by the new regime), or by encouraging a pacifist view of international relations. The measures undertaken by the Nazis after 1933 to a large extent reflected these priorities.

Hitler's Social Darwinist ideas and his priority in internal politics of achieving an ideological revolution clearly had important implications for his attitude and behaviour towards the existing economic and social order. Thus, as far as he was concerned, Nazi economic theory was 'not a theory at all but an understanding of nature, an understanding of the primitive laws of life, of its preconditions, an acknowledgement of the experiences derived from life and nothing else.'[12] He professed himself impatient with questions concerning the organisation of the economy: 'There is so much talk of a private enterprise economy and a communal economy, of a socialised economy and of a private property economy. Believe me the decisive thing here too is not the theory but the performance of the economy'.[13] His view of the superior performance of a capitalist economy compared with a socialist economy was determined by his belief that the individual entrepreneur, in competition with other individuals, would prove more effective than an economy run by civil servants whose advancement was determined by seniority rather than by survival and success in the market-place. Hitler was clearly unaware of, or chose to ignore, the significance of the monopolistic tendencies of a mature capitalist economy which were increasingly eroding the market. As far as he was concerned, performance was the major criterion and he was happy to work with and reward the big fish who gobbled up the smaller fry so long as they delivered the goods required by the political leadership of the state. Hitler's view of the relationship between politics and economics was a crude one. Politics was for him of prior importance. It was the responsibility of the politicians to create favourable conditions for the economy by securing sufficient land and raw materials in a struggle with other races for survival. The economy must, in turn, see its main function as supplying the politicians with the means – in the shape of armaments – with which to secure land and raw materials.

Hitler's attitude to the existing social order was complex and ambiguous and this was true of Nazi ideology in general.[14] One of the main themes of Nazi ideology was the idea of a society in which social position would no longer be determined solely by birth and by the possession of wealth and educational qualifications and the advantages accruing to them. Instead, it would combine a fundamental equality with stratification based on personal achievement (*Leistung*) assessed in terms of service to the community. Thus, all citizens would be members of the national community (*Volksgemeinschaft*) and, as such, equal in their subordination to it – they were all *Volksgenossen*. At the same time, however, these *Volksgenossen* would be stratified in terms of income and capital according to their performance within the occupational market-place, but an occupational market-place which must in future be geared to the needs of the community. It seems plausible to suggest that this ambivalence on the questions of social stratification and equality reflects the outlook of those who felt that their upward movement was being frustrated by traditional barriers of one kind and another, a group which was strongly represented within the Nazi leadership and of whom Hitler himself appears a good example. Thus, for all his emphasis in propaganda speeches on the need for social solidarity in a 'national community', he was a strong élitist. His attitude to the German upper and middle classes, however, was ambivalent in the extreme. On the one hand, his Social Darwinist outlook tended to persuade him that success was a proof of quality. Those who were at the top had the right to be there – they had shown themselves to have 'personality'. Their achievement gave them the right to wield authority over the less successful. This was particularly true of the economic élites for whom he believed the market performed a kind of Darwinian process of selection. As he put it in a speech in 1944: 'there is nothing apparently so cruel, but also nothing so sensible as the economic life struggle'.[15] This attitude was reinforced by an element of petty bourgeois deference towards social superiors which lingered even after 1933. On the other hand, he often professed to regard the aristocracy and bourgeoisie with contempt. He echoed the Pan-German criticism of the performance of the pre-war German establishment, while its abject capitulation in the revolution of November 1918 had confirmed his view that the German aristocracy was decadent, corrupted among other things by marriages to Jewish heiresses. 'This paper aristocracy', he told a meeting of party officials in the summer of 1933, 'these degenerate shoots of ancient noble families have still one thing left, to die in beauty.'[16] Similarly, he insisted that he would

not be deceived by these captains of industry either! Captains indeed. I should like to know what ships they navigate! They are stupid fools who cannot see beyond the waves they paddle! The better one gets to know them the less one respects them. . . . today's bourgeoisie is rotten to the core! It has no ideals any more; all it wants to do is earn money.[17]

In theory, Hitler envisaged the emergence of a new racial élite to supplant the existing decadent ruling groups. As he remarked in 1941: 'I do not doubt for a moment, despite certain people's scepticism, that within a hundred years or so from now all the German élite will be a product of the SS – for only the SS practises racial selection.'[18] But this was a long-term goal. In practice, Hitler was pragmatic about such questions. Unlike some other Nazi leaders, notably Himmler, he appears to have had no hard-and-fast rules based on pseudo-scientific criteria about what constituted racial quality: Jews were in a uniquely pernicious category of their own; coloured people were beyond the pale, (though a tactical exception could be made for the Japanese); his contempt for the Slavs derived from the cultural arrogance of his Austro-German background. But, important tactical considerations apart, his own physical appearance must have precluded too narrow a definition of the Aryan type. Indeed, within Germany his definition of racial quality tended to be synonymous with support for his own movement and the holding of Nazi views. 'No, my party comrades', he told a group of his officials in the summer of 1932, 'we shall not discuss the growth of a new upper class. We shall create it, and there is only one way of creating it: battle. The selection of the new Führer class is my struggle for power. Whoever proclaims his allegiance to *me* is, by this very proclamation and by the *manner* in which it is made, one of the chosen.'[19] In other words, in his view, the Nazi movement before 1933 was acting as a kind of racial magnet attracting those individuals who were racially fittest. For, since he believed that Nazism alone embodied an outlook which reflected the laws of nature, those who were attracted to it, and at a time when to do so was to court ridicule if nothing worse, must represent the least decadent section of the nation. This was, of course, a very convenient definition of race for a movement bent on securing power. After

1933, when Nazism became the official movement of the state and, therefore, attracted large numbers of opportunists, the process of racial selection became more difficult. Essentially, however, as far as Hitler was concerned, it remained a matter of commitment to a particular set of values and was measured by the ruthlessness with which the individual was prepared to discard moral scruples in the service of the German people in its struggle for hegemony.

In 1933, however, Hitler's own ideas and future goals were only one factor in a complex political equation. First and foremost, he needed to retain and consolidate his power. Indeed, one of the keys to understanding what happened in Germany after 1933 lies in the contradiction between Hitler's long-term goals, and the immediate steps needed both to consolidate his position and to secure a basis for achieving these goals. He had come to power, on the one hand, through an alliance with the existing élites and, on the other hand, with the support of a million or so members in his party organisation and with less than half the electorate voting for him in the last relatively free election in March 1933. To ensure himself a strong position *vis à vis* the élites he needed both the support of public opinion and to entrench his own party organisations within the new power structure. On the other hand, he could not dispense with the support of the élites if he wished to improve the economic situation which was essential if he was to retain – let alone increase – his public support; and secondly, if he was to achieve his initial major objective of a revival of German power. A key question, then, was the relationship between the Nazi movement – in particular its leadership – and the existing élites.

In January 1933 the Nazi movement was still, in terms of its social basis, predominantly lower middle-class.[20] The national and regional leadership was of a slightly higher social status than the party membership as a whole and, in general, appears to have been upwardly mobile. The years 1930–3, and particularly the year 1932, however, saw a considerable influx from the upper middle class, with the result that by 1933 their proportion within the party was somewhat higher than in the population as a whole; though of course they still formed only a small minority within the party. This influx of members of the upper and upper middle classes into the party reflects the changing attitude of the German élites towards the NSDAP during the years 1930–3. Whereas between 1925–9 the élites had regarded the Nazis as a marginal group of radical anti-semites who were beneath their notice, from the autumn of 1929 onwards they began to take them increasingly seriously. This growing rapprochement between the NSDAP and the German élites followed the breakdown of the Republican consensus, which had existed between 1924 and 1928, under the strain of economic crisis.

The influx of members of the upper classes, which had begun after the September 1930 election and had gathered pace during 1932, became a veritable flood during 1933. Before 1933, the Nazis had already succeeded in infiltrating and, in some cases in taking over many middle-class professional and interest organisations (e.g. the main agricultural organisation, the *Landbund*), so that the process of 'coordination' (*Gleichschaltung*) of these organisations after the Nazi takeover of power was greatly facilitated. As far as the economic élites were concerned, the Nazis benefited from the fact that the relationship between agriculture and industry and between the various sectors of industry had broken down by 1933 so that the political leadership had considerable freedom of manoeuvre in working out its policies *vis à vis* the various economic sectors. And initially, at any rate, the economic élites could unite in support of the measures against the parliamentary system in general, and the trade unions and political parties of the Left in particular. The civil service, already demoralised by salary cuts introduced by the Brüning government in 1931, was happy to co-operate with the new regime which had come to power by legal means and, with its hostility to parliamentary government, appeared to offer civil servants the opportunity of regaining the dominant position within the political process which they had enjoyed before October-November 1918. Finally, in the course of the 1920s, the army had become more professional in its approach and – after the experience of total war during 1914–18 – more conscious of the need for an effective mobilisation of the nation's resources and of the importance of morale. The army leadership, therefore, looked to the Nazis to provide not only the material resources for an accelerated programme of rearmament, which had been denied them under the democratic system of Weimar, but also for the encouragement of a climate of opinion within the country at large more favourable to mobilisation. They were reassured by the strong nationalist commitment of the Nazis and by their hostility to all pacifist tendencies. They were relieved that the new regime offered them the opportunity to concentrate on military matters and leave politics in the reliable hands of others. Co-operation from the élites was also ensured – particularly during 1933–4 – by the indirect threat represented by the massed ranks of the SA and the Factory Cell Organisation (NSBO) and also by the more radical members of the party leadership both at national (*Feder*) and at regional level (certain *Gauleiter*). Hitler was able to pose as a statesmanlike figure who would be prepared to restrain his more militant comrades and the rank-and-file, provided he met with full co-operation from the existing authorities.

Thus the influx of upper middle-class sympathisers – many with professional qualifications and managerial experience – into the ranks of the NSDAP, together with the increasingly sympathetic response from the various élites to the Nazi movement, removed the need to carry out a revolutionary purge – apart that is from the overtly political posts in regional and local government. Hitler was fully aware that if he was to achieve his major initial goal of the mobilisation of the German people for war he needed the skills and expertise of the existing élites. The result was that change in this sphere tended to be – in David Schoenbaum's phrase – 'more a matter of subversion than of radical reorganisation'.[21] During the first phase of the regime, there was a purge of the civil service under the Law for the Re-establishment of the Professional Civil Service of 7 April 1933.[22] The law provided for the purging of Jews (Art.3) and known political opponents of the regime (Art.4), and also for the suspension or transfer of officials for technical reasons; a course of action which had previously been prevented by civil service regulations. The effects of this law, however, were comparatively small, though marginally greater in Prussia than elsewhere. In the army, although a few high-ranking officers known to be unsympathetic to the new regime were soon retired or transferred, this was carried out by the army leadership itself, and did not go beyond the bounds of normality. In effect, the army retained, for the time being, its operational independence, in return for its abdication from the political sphere and for gestures of ideological conformity. Moreover, while there was a considerable reduction in the proportion of aristocrats within the officer corps, during the course of the Third Reich, this was inevitable given the enormous expansion of the armed services.[23]

The most important factor governing recruitment into the officer corps, the higher ranks of the civil service and the professions continued to be the requirement that candidates had to be in possession of the school-leaving certificate (the *Abitur*) and, in the case of the civil service and the professions, of a university degree as well. In the civil service – particularly in the new ministries such as Propaganda – exceptions were made on political grounds, but they remained exceptions. Since both secondary and university education continued to be fee-paying, they remained an overwhelmingly middle-class preserve. Similarly, industry, big business, and the banks continued to recruit their executives from the same social strata as before 1933.

The main change introduced by the new regime into the existing structure of the élites was of course the new party organisations. These organisations varied somewhat in their social composition. The regional party bosses or *Gauleiter* certainly came, on average, from a lower level of society than was traditional for a German élite group, and were also younger than average.[24] The same was true of the lower-level functionaries within the political cadre of the party – the local branch and district leaders. In some cases the party was able to integrate itself into the local establishment by recruiting a local notable, in others there was a degree of tension between the local party leadership, on the one hand, and the traditional local social élite, on the other, with both sides coexisting in a kind of uneasy stalemate. The political cadre, however, was by no means the most important of the party organisations.[25] Indeed, until the last three years of the war, it was comparatively unimportant. Its most successful achievement had been to capture a large measure of control over local government appointments. Otherwise, except in the case of a few particularly tough and aggressive *Gauleiter*, its influence was mainly sporadic rather than consistent and disruptive rather than decisive. The most important Nazi organisation – the SS – on the other hand, concentrated on trying to recruit members of the existing élites, forming various bodies for this particular purpose, e.g. riding associations to attract the aristocracy, and Himmler's 'circle of friends', consisting of important businessmen – although this form of membership was largely nominal.[26] The SS was particularly successful at recruiting young graduates in law and in political science who tended to join the SD. Indeed, the extent of student sympathy for Nazism during the last phase of the Weimar Republic– by 1931 the German student unions had already been captured by the Nazi student organisation – ensured that there were large numbers of young, educated, middle-class recruits who could fill posts in various spheres of the regime.

Thus there was no single coherent élite. Instead, the traditional élites continued to exist (with some of their members having become Nazis) side by side with new party organisations which contained members from various social backgrounds, and who tended to have in common only a relatively low age. Only in the SS were there the beginnings of a fusion of the old and the new élites. Attempts by the party to establish special schools or colleges to train a new Nazi élite proved largely ineffective.[27] One set of schools, the so-called 'Napolas', became virtually identical with the previous military-style boarding schools, (the *Kadettenanstalten*), whose alumni preferred to go in for conventional élite careers in the army or business. The other Nazi schools – the Adolf Hitler Schools and the Nazi colleges (*Ordensburgen*) – suffered from having curricula which were more appropriate to educating physical training instructors than a modern political-administrative élite capable of coping with the demands of a complex industrial society. The graduates of the *Ordensburgen* were notorious for the way in which they combined a breathtaking arrogance with remarkable incompetence. The problem was that with the existing élites still functioning on the Nazi party had no pressing need for a new élite, and no clear idea of the criteria for one other than vague concepts of 'leadership', defined largely in terms of a ruthless and aggressive personality, to be inculcated mainly by physical training and crude ideological indoctrination.

To sum up, since Hitler believed that the most vital reforms needed in Germany were ideological and psychological in character – a restoration of morale and the inculcation of racist and Social Darwinist views – since even before 1933 the party had succeeded in co-opting members of the existing élites and infiltrating their professional organisations, and finally, since the Nazis' initial objectives of the destruction of the Left and a major rearmament drive were enthusiastically endorsed by the traditional élites, there was no need to carry out a major transformation of the economic and social order. At the same time, however, the Nazis were committed to the idea of an open élite. The career open to the talents had been an article of faith since the very earliest days – indeed, it was a plank in the party's 1920 programme. Moreover, this commitment had behind it a powerful wave of lower middle-class resentment at the traditional barriers to upward mobility posed by birth, property and education, and also at the extent to which their own interests had been ignored and their own values flouted by the dominant élites.

This populist resentment, which was also directed above all at what was seen as the failure of the governing classes to unite the nation and mobilise its energies effectively in the national cause, had its origins in the Pan-German movement of the pre-war period, but had acquired added impetus from the experience of the first world war and of the post-war era.[28] It had now found expression in the Nazi movement.

This raises the question of how far the Nazi regime introduced increased possibilities of upward mobility.[29] In view of the shortage of relevant data, the answer is not easy to determine, but the increase in upward mobility does not in fact appear to have been very significant. Politics certainly provided an avenue of upward movement continuing – indeed accelerating – a trend which had already become established in the Weimar Republic. But the effects of this should not be exaggerated. Thus, although the proliferation of the Nazi party bureaucracy enabled large numbers of people to become functionaries of one kind and another (probably getting on for 2 million or so), most of these were part-time and unpaid, contributing to an enhancement of their sense of status rather than a change in their real economic position. As we have seen, secondary and university education continued to be fee-paying and in a society where educational qualifications were still the key to social advancement in most spheres, this remained the biggest single obstacle to upward mobility, which was not compensated for by the few Nazi schools.

The impact of the Nazi regime on the élites, however, was not confined to the challenge of new men, but also involved the effects of new values, and of a new mentality. Even before 1914 these 'new men' of the radical Right had not shared the values of the traditional élites. Moreover, the experience of the war – and of the latent civil war of the early 1920s – had radicalised these views still further producing a mentality which regarded the remnants of the Christian ethic and of the humanitarian impulses of the Enlightenment, which found expression in traditional conservative and liberal ideologies, with contempt as 'bourgeois' or 'philistine' (*spiessig*).[30] They preached instead a new barbarism which gloried in its contempt for ordinary, everyday life. They made a cult of instinct as against reason, of physical strength and brutality, of youth and violence. They were happy to sacrifice the individual before the altar of abstractions such as the *Volksgemeinschaft* and rationalised their amorality in terms of an alleged natural law and of the struggle for the survival of the fittest. There was nothing new about these ideas, which derived from the debased forms of idealism and rationalism current at the end of the nineteenth century. What was new was that they had now become the official ideology.

The combination of this threat of new men and new official values provoked a degree of tension between what one might call the ideologically committed Nazis on the one hand – many though by no means all of whom had joined the party before 1930 – and, on the other hand, elements within the traditional élites. This tension came to the surface in the summer of 1934 at the time of the Röhm purge, again in 1938 on the occasion of the Blomberg/Fritsch crisis, and culminated in the attempts to assassinate Hitler during the war years. But the mixture of social pride, religious principle, moral scruples and professional interest which produced this opposition was by no means characteristic of the élites in general. Their traditional values had already been eroded by the pressures of a changing world. For many, the temptations of power, status and profit offered by the new order at a time of crisis when their economic and social position seemed to be jeopardised by a serious threat from below; the hope of retaining their position by compromising with it; the beguiling similarity of some of its major objectives with their own – all proved too much. And, once one compromise had been made, it was all too easy to make the next until one was totally compromised. Thus the Nazis could rely on a long-term process of subversion, whereby the ideological and social cohesion of the various élites would be progressively sapped. Cynicism, opportunism, the priority of self-advancement at all costs seen became the ruling ethos of the Third Reich.

Nazi ideology and practice was a complex amalgam of contradictory features, simultaneously modern and anti-modern and, in consequence, has continued to baffle historians trying to define its character.[31] These contradictions owe something to the nature of the party's social base and, in particular, to the differences of interest and mentality which existed between the so-called new *Mittelstand* of white-collar workers and officials and the old *Mittelstand* of peasants, artisans and retailers who together formed the bulk of the party's rank-and-file.[32] Thus, while on the one hand, the new *Mittelstand* of medium-and low-ranking civil servants such as primary school teachers, salesmen and clerks were behind the modernizing concept of the career open to the talents and an open mobile society, the old *Mittelstand* tended to advocate measures which would slow down – if not reverse – the impact of social and economic developments and provide them with a haven of stability.

The 'Janus-faced' (*Bracher*) nature of Nazism derived above all, however, from the contradiction between the anti-modernist ideology and the means necessary to achieve its goals. Thus, although the Nazis began by trying to satisfy the needs of their social and economic clientele in agriculture and the old *Mittelstand*, and although they allowed themselves initially to be influenced to some extent by ideological principles in the economic sphere (e.g. the Entailed Farm Law of September 1933), it soon became clear that the programme of mobilisation for war was producing results which directly contradicted Hitler's often expressed long-term goal of a shift in emphasis from industrialisation towards rural settlement. Since rearmament inevitably encouraged existing trends towards industrial growth and urbanisation. In other words, the means necessary to achieve the goal, namely the conquest of *Lebensraum*, and the creation of a society governed by the ideology of blood and soil contradicted the goal itself.

In consequence, the economy and society of Nazi Germany up to the outbreak of war presented a picture combining elements of both continuity and change, but with the elements of continuity predominating.[33] The regime did not engineer a fundamental change in the composition of the élites, nor a marked increase in upward social mobility, nor a radical shift in the distribution of wealth between the classes. Moreover, it neither engineered a counter-revolution against the dominant trends of the modern world, nor did it preside over a major impetus towards the modernisation of the economy and society. Instead, there occurred a continuation or, at the most, a slight acceleration of existing economic and social trends, the most marked of which was of the increased role of the state in the economy. At the same time, however, there were some changes which contradicted existing developments, notably in agricultural and *Mittelstand* policies, changes reflecting both ideological and political priorities. The war-time period saw rather more drastic changes, particularly after 1941 in the wake of the shift to a total war economy. There was, for example, a more thorough attempt to rationalise the retail trade and small artisanal sectors. But even then, the kind of revolution which would have been necessary to

mobilise and concentrate Germany's resources was rendered largely
unnecessary by the large quantities of raw materials and in particular,
the large numbers of foreign workers who were imported to service
the German war machine. Arguably, it was the effects of the defeat
itself and, in particular, the loss of the *junker* estates of East Elbia
and the massive migration of refugees from East to West which
proved the single most revolutionary socio-economic development
of the years 1933–45.

But if the actual changes in the German economy and society
were as limited as has been suggested, why does the Nazi regime
appear to have been such a drastic innovation? and in what ways can
it be distinguished from its predecessors? In his study of class and
status in Nazi Germany, David Schoenbaum has drawn attention to
the crucial distinction btween objective social reality and its interpretation by the individual. He accepts that objective reality was the
opposite of what Hitler had promised, and of what most of his
followers had expected. As he puts it:

In 1939 the cities were larger not smaller; the concentration of capital
greater than before; the rural population reduced not increased; women not
at the fireside but in the office and the factory; the inequality of income and
property distribution more not less conspicuous; industry's share of the
gross national product up and agriculture's down; while industrial labour
had it relatively good and small business increasingly bad. The East Elbian
estates continued to be run by the gentry, the civil service by the doctors,
and the Army by generals whose names began with 'von'.[34]

At the same time, however, Schoenbaum suggests that interpreted
social reality 'reflected a society united like no other in recent
German history, a society of opportunities for young and old,
classes and masses, a society that was New Deal and good old days
at the same time'. Moreover, he suggests that this interpreted social
reality in turn had its own objective reality or, as he puts it, 'Being
[Sein] influences consciousness (*Bewusstsein*) as Marx maintained.
But under National Socialism the reverse was also true.'

Few would wish to deny that mentality influences social behaviour,
or that it need not correspond with social reality. The question is,
however, to what extent Nazism actually succeeded in changing the
mentalities of the various social groups so that their behaviour was
significantly modified as a result. As we have seen, this was indeed
the main objective of Hitler's so-called 'internal reforms'.

Schoenbaum is not alone in suggesting that the Nazis had a good deal of success in their endeavours. Ralf Dahrendorf has argued that in order to secure their political position Hitler and the Nazis were obliged to seek total power, and in order to achieve total power they were in turn compelled to remove the autonomy of all spheres of social life and incorporate them within their totalitarian system.[35] In the process of this totalitarian coordination of social life, they were forced to destroy the traditional loyalties of the German people – loyalties to their region, religion, family, class, and so on. These traditional loyalties, Dahrendorf argues, had hitherto acted as barriers to the development of responsible citizenship in Germany with people actively participating in their own self-government; indeed, these traditions had provided the basis for authoritarian political structures and for a deep hostility to liberal values. During the Third Reich, Dahrendorf suggests, organic relationships were destroyed and replaced by mechanical ones. The Nazi organisations – the Hitler Youth, the Labour Front, the Labour Service and later the army – served to iron out differences of ethnicity, class, religion, education, and so on. In place of a multiplicity of social roles was substituted the single role of '*Volksgenosse*' (a compatriot). The individual was forced out of his traditional role of being simply a passive subject of an authoritarian regime for whom private life and private virtues were the main preoccupation, and was compelled to become an active participant in public life. In short, he was politically mobilised even if his participation only took the form of gestures which were manipulated and controlled from above. Thus Dahrendorf sees the Third Reich as a form of social revolution which brought about the modernisation of German society by destroying traditional loyalties, norms and values which had hitherto prevented the Germans from coming to terms with the modern world. Paradoxically, because of its need for total control, a movement which had set out to create a *Volksgemeinschaft* had ended up by creating a *Gesellschaft*.

It is certainly a suggestive line of thought, but the question is: how much truth is there in it? It also leads one to consider the question of how far the Nazis succeeded in imposing their ideology on the German people. How successful was Hitler in carrying out the revolution which he conceived as essential – a revolution of mentality? Research into mentalities is at the best of times fraught with difficulties of one kind and another. In a dictatorship which controls the expression of opinion through the machinery of terror, and distorts it through the machinery of propaganda, it appears almost impossible. As far as Nazi Germany is concerned, the most fruitful avenue of research has proved to be the records of those agencies whose responsibility it was to monitor public opinion, of which there were a number whose records have survived in varying degrees of completeness.[36]

One obvious test of the impact of Nazism on the German mentality is to what extent the regime succeeded in imposing its racist and Social Darwinist ideas on the German people. This, after all, was the core element of Nazi ideology. Here, according to recent research into attitudes in Nazi Germany, it appears the Nazis had little success. While Nazi propaganda had probably strengthened somewhat the latent anti-semitism which had already been wide-spread before 1933, it had failed to mobilise an active, racist anti-semitism.[37] Similarly, despite extensive propaganda, including a film designed to extol the benefits of a euthanasia programme, the public response to the mass-murder of thousands of handicapped people launched in the autumn of 1939 was such that the government was obliged to end the programme officially, though it continued unofficially on a reduced scale: clearly, the public had not yet been successfully indoctrinated.[38]

Another test of the extent to which the Nazis succeeded in their objective of an ideological revolution is the attitude of the working class. One of Hitler's main aims had been to extirpate 'Marxism' and to inculcate a fanatical nationalism in the German working class. He believed that Germany owed its defeat in 1918 to the collapse of morale among the masses, and he was determined to ensure that the defeat of November 1918 did not repeat itself under his regime. Here, the interpretation of the evidence is even more difficult and controversial, although evidence from Gestapo and SD reports, and from reports to the Social Democratic Party in exile, suggest that while Hitler himself had succeeded in winning a measure of support among the working class, most other Nazi leaders and the party itself were unpopular.[39] On the other hand, the attitude among some sections of the working class – at any rate at certain periods–appears to have been more positive than a mere sullen acquiescence which, in turn, suggests that some aspects of the regime had some appeal, but was very long way from the whole-hearted commitment Hitler sought. This is a field in which more research is necessary, and even then it may be impossible to reach firm conclusions.

The peasantry and *Mittelstand* were disappointed in the great hopes they had invested in the regime which on the contrary had followed policies which had enabled big business to increase its wealth and power at the expense of the small man, and had favoured industry and labour at the expense of agriculture. Although there is evidence that this had produced a degree of disillusionment by the outbreak of war, there was no real sign of hostility to the regime itself. In part, this was no doubt because the government had fulfilled some of their demands – more, at any rate, than any Weimar governments had done.[40] Moreover, the rhetoric and symbolism of the regime had gone out of its way to flatter the self-image of the *Mittelstand* and publicly to adopt its values – praised as *gesundes Volksempfinden* (healthy common sense) – as the essence of National Socialist morality.[41]

Thus while there were limits to the impact of Nazi indoctrination, Schoenbaum's suggestion that a gap had developed between social reality and the way in which it was perceived and, in particular, that the impression of a more egalitarian society had been created, may well be true for some sections of the population, particularly among the *Mittelstand*. It was possible to be quite critical about certain aspects of the regime – particularly of material issues – while at the same time retaining a generally positive view of it overall. In this connection, Hitler's role as a focus of loyalty was of crucial importance as a legitimising force as Ian Kershaw has shown.[42] But to describe this gap between social reality and interpreted social reality and this subjective impression of egalitarianism as a 'social revolution', as Schoenbaum appears to, surely goes too far. And Dahrendorf's argument that the regime carried out a revolution of modernisation through its totalitarian practices is largely unconvincing. Rather, the evidence suggests that the image of German society under the Third Reich as a mass of atomised individuals whose traditional ties and loyalties had been destroyed is a distorted one. For example, while there is some evidence of a slight decline in religious practice and of church membership during the years 1933–9, it was not very substantial. In 1939, 94.5 per cent of the German population still belonged to a Christian church, while only 3.5 per cent described themselves as 'believers in God' (*gottgläubig*—the Nazi phrase for having left the Church but still retaining a belief in

God), and only 1.5 per cent were without faith.[43] Similarly, despite the fact that in some cases the Hitler Youth exacerbated tension between parents and children, there is no evidence that the family as an institution had collapsed under totalitarian pressures. Also, class solidarity undoubtedly remained a powerful force, particularly among the older generation. Finally, although people were politically mobilised to an unprecedented extent, there is little evidence that this turned people into active citizens after 1945. If anything, the experience of politics in the Third Reich contributed to the '*ohne mich*' mood of the early post-war era. As suggested earlier, it is probable that the experience associated with defeat and reconstruction in the years 1944–7 did more to modernise the mentality of the German people – in Dahrendorf's sense – than did the first eleven years of the Third Reich, although even then the elements of continuity remained strong.

Any discussion of the revolutionary character of Nazism must of course take account of the fact that Nazism was defeated in war before it had a chance to implement its full programme and, therefore, it can never be finally determined how revolutionary the movement and regime really were. It has been argued that for the Nazis the peace-time years were 'only a preparatory phase, a staging ground so to speak, for a far-reaching transformation of German society to be effected in the wake of a Nazi military triumph'.[44] Certainly, during the pre-war years, the Nazis were limited in their actions by a number of factors – the need to accommodate the existing élites, limited economic resources, public opinion at home and foreign opinion abroad, among others – some of which would have been removed or considerably reduced in significance had the Nazis been victorious. The war itself removed some of these obstacles, producing a significant radicalisation of Nazi goals which had not been feasible during the pre-war years (a notorious example is the euthanasia programme for the handicapped). Moreover, during the phase of the war in which the Nazis appeared to have a good chance of success – the years 1941–2 – plans were not only mooted but, as Alan Milward has shown, in some cases had already begun to be put into operation which indicate that some, at any rate, of Hitler's more far-reaching plans should not simply be regarded as fantasies.[45] Support for this view is provided by the long-term planning, and indeed the actual implementation of the initial stages of the grandiose architectural projects intended by Hitler to provide symbolic representation of Germany's world hegemony.[46] Finally, the regime's population policy, which began as early as July 1933 with the Sterilisation Law, and continued with measures to prevent marriages between those with hereditary defects, and a whole range of other actions, indicates how seriously the regime took its objective of improving the 'racial health' of the German people.

On the other hand, it has been argued that schemes such as the settlement of large numbers of German soldier-peasants in eastern Europe were so contrary to the trends of the time – in general, a drift away from the land into industry and the cities and, in particular, a continuing population shift from East to West – that they can only be described as utopian.[47] This may well be true. On the other hand, the massive resettlement programme carried out in Stalin's Russia during the 1940s provides an ominous example of the power of modern dictatorships. The Nazis themselves had succeeded in resettling some 950,000 ethnic Germans by 1944. Similarly, the extermination of the Jews would almost certainly have been described as utopian after 1945 had it not actually been carried out.

Despite the undeniable benefits which accrued to German employers, to capital in general, and to the largest companies in particular between 1933 and 1943, the case for Nazism – either as movement or as regime – primarily serving the interests of monopoly capitalism, remains unconvincing. The fact that the more sophisticated Marxist historians have developed theories admitting varying degrees of autonomy for the political sphere suggests an awareness of the limitations of such a reductive approach. Indeed, in a recent article by a Marxist, who is among the best-informed historians of the Nazi state, Nazism is seen as part of the crisis of capitalism rather than its resolution – an extreme and ultimately self-destructive form of the autonomisation of politics.[48]

An emphasis on the political sphere provides the best insight into the nature of Nazism, and here the case for its revolutionary character is arguably strongest. It lies precisely in its nature as a movement. Before 1933, the Nazi party had developed as an organisation bent above all on political mobilisation, and had acquired a leadership cadre which repudiated not simply parliamentary democracy but the traditions and practices of the German state itself as they had developed over the previous century or more. After 1933, the impact of the dynamic unleashed by the Nazi movement – the progressive penetration of the effects of the charismatic style of authority and the forms of organisation developed within the Nazi party before 1933 into the existing framework of the German state – contributed to its progressive demoralisation and disintegration into the atavistic quasi-feudal structure of authority which became more and more characteristic of the Third Reich.[49] In the words of a civil servant who had begun as an admirer of the Nazis, but who by 1937 had become thoroughly disillusioned:

'The clear objective task of the civil service and of the individual official is more and more lost to sight since the formerly unified state power has been split into a number of separate authorities: party and professional organisations working in the same areas overlap with no clear divisions of responsibility, while the whole is not always given priority over the particular aim, nor the cause over the individual. The civil service, as well as the individual official lacks both clear directives from the state as well as objective backing when acting according to its laws. The civil servant too often stands alone and unprotected.[50]

In short, the civil service from being the representative of the authority of the state had been degraded to the level of one among the number of competing bureaucracies, and this reflected the fact that the state itself was no longer regarded, in the traditional German fasion, as the embodiment of the best interests of the community – that role having been taken over by Hitler acting as charismatic leader of the German people.

More important even than the atomisation of the state and the downgrading of the civil service, however, was the fact that the political system of the Third Reich represented the destruction of the *Rechtsstaat*, which had formed the basis of German government since the mid-nineteenth century, indeed the destruction of law itself. In practice, this meant that while the state appeared to continue much as before – laws and legal regulations still remained on the statute books; new ones were still issued according to formal processes; civil servants still administered them; the Code of Civil Law (BBG) still remained in operation and was enforced by the judiciary; and so on – this façade of normality was, in fact, progressively being undermined by organisations, activities and measures which derived their authority directly from the Führer – the exception became increasingly the rule. This development was reflected in the emergence of separate legal systems for the party and for the SS/police. Nor was it confined to the conventional political sphere. The whole legal system was in effect politicised through its subjection to the arbitrary will of the Führer, and the precepts of an irrational ideology. Thus, according to a decision of the highest court, the *Reichsgericht*, of January 1943:

The basic ideology of National Socialism, grounded in the racist [*völkisch*] laws of life and customs, has general validity for the interpretation and assessment of existing laws and agreements, and it defines the content of the concepts of 'good faith' [ss. 157, 242 of the BBG] and of 'good morals' [ss. 138 of the BBG].[51]

Ultimately the will of the Führer represented the supreme law.

This erosion of a relatively rational, bureaucratic and legal order was – even in Marxist terms – arguably undermining the 'super-structure' essential to the successful reproduction of the conditions of a capitalist system. The process gathered pace during the war years, which in effect acted as a forcing-house for Nazism. And it found expression, above all, in the growing power, or 'autonom-isation', of the party cadre, on the one hand, and of the SS on the other – both organisations representing Hitler's exceptional author-ity as Führer, which fought for control of the virgin political soil of the occupied territories, particularly in the East.

In this view, then, it was, above all the nature of the Nazi movement itself and, in particular, the charismatic basis of its authority which, when transferred to the German state after 1933, acted as a solvent of the existing order which had already been gravely weakened by the strains imposed by the preceding years of crisis. The essence of charismatic leadership is that it is the form of authority appropriate to crisis. The leader derives his authority from his apparent vocation to lead his followers in a crisis. Nazism was rooted in crisis, and its whole system of politics was geared, in effect, to the maintenance of crisis as a permanent state. In its practice rules, regulations, administrative routine, the concept of law itself other than as the fiat of the leader; in short, all the mechanisms for ensuring a measure of rationality, predictability and hence of relative stability, were anathema. In its ideology, Nazism glorified conflict as the essence of nature. Moreover, to the existing revanchist ambitions shared by the majority of the élites, Hitler added a view of the role of his regime in terms of a much more fundamental crisis than that which appeared to face the German people. It was a crisis of cosmic significance – the threat of Jewish world domination, and of the destruction of the Aryan race. Hitler's major aim was the defeat of this Jewish 'threat', and the acquisition at the very least of an impregnable and ideally hegemonic position for Germany in a world governed by a racial war for survival. Furthermore, he saw the key to success in overcoming the conflicts which divided the German people by mobilising them behind the ideology of integral nationalism which would overcome class conflict. These were essentially irrational goals and, because they were irrational, were bound to be destructive. Thus, both the nature of the system itself and the ideology of its leadership created mutually reinforcing pressures leading to the supreme crisis of war. Arguably, therefore, the Nazi revolution was war – not simply because war accelerated political, economic and social change to a degree which had not occurred in peace-time, but more profoundly because in war Nazism was in its element. In this sense Nazism was truly 'a revolution of destruction' – of itself and of others on an unparalleled scale.

NOTES

1. Cf. E. Jäeckel, *Hitler, Sämtliche Aufzeichnungen 1905–1924* (Stuttgart, 1980), pp. 652, 670.
2. See Hitler's speeches, especially during 1933–4, in M. Domarus, *Hitler, Reden und Proklamationen 1932 bis 1945* Bd. I (Wiesbaden, 1973).
3. Hermann Rauschning, *The Revolution of Destruction. Warning to the West* (New York, 1939); David Schoenbaum, *Hitler's Social Revolution. Class and Status in Nazi Germany* (New York, 1966). For Rauschning, Nazism was 'action pure and simple, dynamics *in vacuo*, revolution at a variable tempo, ready to be changed at any moment. One thing it is not – doctrine or philosophy', *op. cit.*, p. 23. For Schoenbuam, the Third Reich was 'a double revolution', 'a revolution of means and ends. The revolution of ends was ideological – war against bourgeois and industrial society. The revolution of means was its reciprocal. It was bourgeois and industrial since, in an industrial age, even a war against industrial society must be fought with industrial means and bourgeois and necessary to fight the bourgeoisie', *op. cit.*, p. xxii.
4. Cf. K. Hildebrand, *Das Dritte Reich* (München-Wein, 1979), p. 138.
5. There is a substantial Marxist literature on Nazism, see W. Abendroth (ed.), *Faschismus und Kapitalismus. Theorien über die sozialen Ursprünge und die Funktion des Faschismus* (Frankfurt, 1968), *Das Argument*

issues of 1965–6; L. Trotsky, *The Struggle against Fascism in Germany* (London, 1975); N. Poulantzas, *Fascism and Dictatorship* (London, 1974); for a representative selection of recent work by East German authors see D. Eichholtz and K. Gossweiler (eds.), *Faschismus-forschung. Positionen-Probleme-Polemik* (East Berlin/Cologne, 1980).

6. E. Mandel, Introduction to Trotsky, *op. cit.*, p. xiii.
7. See, in particular, A. Thalheimer, 'Uber den Faschismus', in Abendroth, *op. cit.*, pp. 19–38; and A. Gramsci, *Prison Notebooks*, (London, 1971), pp. 291ff.
8. Mandel, *op. cit.*, p. xxii.
9. Cf. T. W. Mason, 'The Primacy of Politics – Politics and Economics in National Socialist Germany', in S. J. Woolf (ed.), *The Nature of Fascism* (London, 1968), pp. 165–95.
10. For Hitler's goals, see A. Hitler, *Mein Kampf* (London, 1974); *Hitler's Secret Book* ed. G. Weinberg (New York, 1961); *Hitler's Secret Conversations* 1941–1944 (New York, 1953); E. Jäeckel, *Hitler's Weltanschauung* (Middletown, Conn., 1972).
11. Cf. Domarus, *op. cit.*, p. 371.
12. Cf. 'Hitler vor Bauarbeitern in Berchtesgaden über die Wirtschafts-politik am 20.5.1937', in H. von Kotze und H. Krausnick (eds.), *'Es spricht der Führer' 7 exemplarische Hitler–Reden* (Gütersloh, 1966), pp. 200ff. On Hitler's economic views, see also H. A. Turner, 'Hitler's Einstellung zu Wirtschaft und Gesellschaft vor 1933', in *Geschichte und Gesellschaft* (1976) pp. 89–117.
13. ibid.
14. Cf. W. Struve, *Elites against Democracy. Leadership ideals in bourgeois political thought in Germany 1890–1933* (Princeton, 1973), pp. 415–63.
15. von Kotze and Krausnick *op. cit.*, p. 341.
16. H. Rauschning, *Hitler Speaks* (London, 1939), p. 49. On Hitler and the aristocracy, see G. H. Kleine, 'Adelsgenossenschaft und National-sozialismus' in *Vierte jahrshefte für Zeitgeschichte*, 26 (1978), pp. 100–43.
17. H. Rauschning, *op. cit.*, p. 30.
18. *Hitler's Secret Conversations*, *op. cit.*, p. 125.
19. Rauschning, *op. cit.*, p. 49.
20. Cf. M. Kater, 'Sozialer Wandel in der NSDAP im Zuge der national-sozialistischen Machtergreifung', in W. Schieder (ed.), *Faschismus als sozialer Bewegung* (Hamburg, 1976) pp. 25–68. On the relationship between the Nazis and the élites in 1933–4, see H. Mommsen, 'Zur Verschränkung traditioneller und faschistischer Führungsgruppen in Deutschland bei Ubergang von der Bewegungs – zur Systemphase', in Schieder, *op. cit.*, pp. 157–82. On the impact of the élites on the Third Reich, see also W. Zapf, *Wandlungen der deutschen Elite. Ein*

Zirkulationsmodell deutscher Führungsgruppen 1919–1961 (Munich, 1966).

21. Schoenbaum, *op. cit.*, p. 247.

22. Cf. H. Mommsen, *Beamtentum im Dritten Reich* (Stuttgart, 1966) pp. 39–61; and J. Canlan, 'The Civil Servant in the Third Reich', D. Phil thesis (Oxford, 1973), pp. 140ff.

23. Cf. D. Bald, *Vom Kaiserheer zur Bundeswehr. Sozialstruktur des Militärs: Politik der Rekrutierung von Offizieren und Unteroffizieren* (Frankfurt, 1981), pp. 26–7, 38. Bald terms the change from 31.5 per cent of aristocratic officers in 1931 to only 7% in 1943 'revolutionary', though later (p. 80) denies assertions that 'Nazism intended a social revolution in the officer corps'.

24. Cf. R. Rogowski, 'The Gauleiter and the Social Origins of Fascism', in *Comparative Studies in Society and History*, 19 (1977), pp. 399–430; and W. Jannen, 'National Socialism and Social Mobility', in *Journal of Social History*, 9.3 (1976), pp. 339–66.

25. On the political cadre, see D. Orlow, *The History of the Nazi Party. Vol. 2 1933–1945* (Newton Abbot, 1973); and J. Noakes, 'The Nazi Party and the Third Reich: the Myth and Reality of the One Party State', in J. Noakes (ed.), *Government, Party and People in Nazi Germany* (Exeter, 1981), pp. 1–33.

26. On this aspect of the SS, see H. Höhne, *The Order of the Death's Head* (London, 1969), pp. 121–47; and G. C. Boehnert, 'The Jurists in the SS-Führerkorps 1925–1939', in G. Hirschefeld and L. Kettenacker (eds.), '*Der Führerstaat'. Mythos und Realität. Studien zur Struktur and Politik des Dritten Reiches* (Stuttgart, 1980), pp. 381–92.

27. Cf. D. Orlow, 'Die Adolf Hitler Schulen', in *Vierteljahrschefte für Zeitgeschichte* pp. 272–84; H. Überhorst (ed.), *Elite für die Diktatur. Die Nationalpolitisch Erziehungsanstalten 1933–1945. Ein Dokumentarbericht. (Düsseldorf, 1969); H. Scholtz, Nationalsozialistische Ausleseschulen. Internatsschulen als Herrschafts Mittel Führerstaates* (Göttingen, 1973).

28. On the background from which the Nazi movement emerged, see G. Eley, *The Reshaping of the German Right* (New Haven, 1981); D. Stegmann, 'Zwishen Repression und Manipulation: Konservative Machteliten und Arbeiter-und Angestelltenbewegung 1910–1918. Ein Beitrag zur Vorgeschichte der NSDAP', in *Archiv für Sozialgeschichte*, 12 (1972), pp. 351–432; U. Lohalm, *Völkischer Radikalismus. Die Geschichte des Deutsch-völkischer Schutz-und Trutzbund* (Hamburg, 1970).

29. Schoenbaum argues that there was a significant measure of upward mobility, in *op. cit.*, pp. 99, 240ff. This has been disputed by Tim Mason, in T. Mason, *Soziaolitik im Dritten Reich. Arbeiterklasse und Volksgemeinschaft* (Opladen, 1977), p. 274.

30. See the literatue in note 28; and also K. Sontheimer, *Antidemokratisches Danken in der Weimarer Republik* (Munich, 1962).
31. Cf. H. A. Turner, 'Fascism and Modernization', in *World Politics* (24 April 1972), pp. 547–60.
32. On the concept of the *Mittelstand* see T. Geiger, *Die soziale Schichtung des deutschen Volkes* (Suttgart, 1932), pp. 108ff.
33. For the following see Mason, *op. cit.*, and W. Zorn, 'Sozialgeschichte 1918–1970', in H. Aubin, and W. Zorn (eds.), *Handbuch der Deutschen Wirtschafts-und Sozialgeschichte* Bd. 2 (Stuttgart, 1976), pp. 876–933.
34. Schoenbaum *op. cit.*, pp. 285–86.
35. R. Dahrendorf, *Society and Democracy in Germany* (London, 1968), pp. 268ff.
36. Of these reports selections from the SD reports for the war years have been published in H. Boberach (ed.), *Meldungen aus dem Reich* (Neuwied/Berlin, 1965). A selection of police and other reports from Bavaria have been published in M. Broszat *et. al.* (eds.), *Bayern in der NS-Zeit. Soziale Lage und politisches Verhalten der Bevölkerung im Spiegel vertraulicher Berichte* (Munich-Vienna, 1977). See also the reports of SPD contact men in Germany to the headquarters in exile, in *Deutschland Berichte der Sozialdemokratischen partei Deutschlands (Sopade) 1934–1940* (Salzhausen-Frankfurt, 1980), 7 vols.
37. Cf. I. Kershaw, 'The persecution of the Jews and German Popular Opinion in the Third Reich', in *Leo Baeck Institute Year Book XXVI* (1981), pp. 261–90; and 'Anti-semitismus and Volksmeinung. Reaktion auf die Judenverfolgung', in M. Broszat and E. Fröhlich (eds.), *Bayern in der NS- Zeit. Herrschaft und Gesellschaft im Konflikt* (Stuttgart 1979) pp. 281–348.
38. Cf. K. Dörner, 'Nationalsozialismus und Lebensvernichtung', in *Vierteljahrshefte für Zeitgeschichte*, 15 (1967), pp. 121–52; and L. Gruchmann, 'Euthanasie und Justiz im Dritten Reich', in *Vierteljahrshefte für Zeitgeschichte*, 20 (1972), pp. 235–79.
39. Cf. I. Kershaw, 'Popular Opinion in the Third Reich', in Noakes (ed.), *op. cit.*, pp. 57–75; and S. Salter, 'Class Harmony or Class Conflict. The Industrial Working Class and the National Socialist Regime 1933–1945', *ibid.*, pp. 76–97.
40. On the peasantry, see J. Farquarson, *The Plough and the Swastika. The NSDAP and Agriculture in Germany 1928–1945* (London/Beverley Hills, 1976), pp. 262–4. On the *Mittelstand*, see A. von Saldern, *Der Mittelstand im Dritten Reich* (Frankfurt, 1979); and H. Winkler, 'Der entbehrliche Stand. Zur Mittelstandspolitik im "Ditten Reich" ' in *Archiv für Sozialgeschicthe*, XVII (1977), pp. 1–40.
41. Cf. L. Kettenacker, 'Sozialpsychologische Aspekte der Führerherrschaft', in Hirschfeld and Kettenacker (eds.), *op. cit.*, pp. 98–131.

42. Cf. I. Kershaw, *Der Hitler-Mythos. Volksmeinung und Propaganda im Dritten Reich* (Stuttgart, 1980).
43. Cf. Zorn, *op. cit.*, p. 915.
44. Turner, 'Fascism and Modernization', *op. cit.*
45. Cf. A. Milward, *The Fascist Economy in Norway* (Oxford, 1972).
46. Cf. J. Thies, *Architekt der Weltherrschaft. Die 'Endziele' Hitlers* (Düsseldorf, 1976).
47. Cf. Farquarson, *op. cit.*, pp. 262–4.
48. Cf. J. Caplan, 'Theories of Fascism: Nicos Poulantzas as Historian', in *History Workshop* (1977), pp. 94–6.
49. On the quasi-feudal aspects of Nazism, see R. Koehl, 'Feudal Aspects of National Socialism', in *American Political Science Review*, LIV (1960), pp. 921–33. On this process of disintegration see M. Broszat, *Hitler's State* (London, 1981), pp. 294–327.
50. J. Noakes and G. Pridham (eds.), *Documents on Nazism 1919–1945* (London, 1974; New York, 1975), pp. 258–9.
51. Quoted in B. Rüthers, *Die unbegrenzte Auslegung. Zum Wandel der Privatrechtsordnung im Nationalsozialismus* (Frankfurt, 1973), p. 219.

6 Russia in 1917: Revolution or Counter-Revolution?

TERRY McNEILL

Revolutions, as Trotsky observed, are especially prolix affairs: an observation no less true of the one in which he himself was so conspicuous and to whose prolixity he greatly added. The literature on the Russian Revolution is indeed immense and varied; it is also, particularly on the Soviet side, highly partisan and political. In the latter case it ranges from the intellectual pyrotechnics of Trotsky's own efforts, to the febrile palimpsest of the Stalin years, on to the leaden expurgations of today's official productions. Non-soviet writing on the Revolution is similarly vast, though, with a number of notable exceptions, less overtly political in its intent. Given the contention that attends any revolution, and given the enormous and still unfolding consequences of this revolution in particular, it is not surprising to find that the voluminous literature that it has sparked contains much that is controversial. Not all the controversy, however, falls within the province of genuine scholarly disputation, for although many aspects of the Russian Revolution are undoubtedly problematical and subject to legitimate disagreement, much of what purports to be reasoned debate is little more than ideological axe-grinding.

Take, for instance, the issue of characterisation of the Revolution. There are few who would deny that it was a revolution, in the sense that it was about making a fundamental change in the social and political system and not merely about changing rulers. But was it one revolution or two? and if the latter how should they be distinguished? Soviet historians insist that there were two distinct revolutions, the first primarily bourgeois in character, and the latter unambiguously proletarian. Many non-soviet historians, while they would agree that there were two distinct revolutions, would prefer to call the February one *popular* rather than bourgeois, and the October one they would dub a party-based *coup*, rather than a revolution as such – revolution being a term reserved to describe what the Bolsheviks actually did when in power, but not the means by which they came to power. This, which is probably the most hotly contested issue arising out of the Russian Revolution, and one on which a great deal of intensive research has been carried out, turns out on closer inspection not to be a proper question for historians at all, for it is not something that can be settled on grounds of evidence. What is in fact being argued about is possession of legitimacy. According to Soviet historians, the Bolshevik seizure of power was legitimate, not only because the Bolsheviks were the true custodians of the people's interests, but because the masses had become disenchanted with the Provisional Government and had deserted them for the Bolsheviks. Liberally-inclined historians, on the other hand, tend to the view that the Bolsheviks usurped power from a government that stood for the kind of policies the people really wanted, and that the basis of their victory was not popular support, but a conspiratorial organisation aided and abetted by subverted military. Neither assertion, unfortunately, can properly be put to the test, for neither the Provisional Government (perforce) nor the Bolsheviks (by choice) subjected their rule to electoral sanction; both simply assumed power in the name of the Revolution. Therefore, the question of which was the legitimate government cannot be resolved by empirical reference, and to pursue the matter on any other grounds invites speculation about what was the *true* nature of the Revolution and what was the *real* will of the people, – speculations that properly belong to the realms of metaphysics and ideology.

Rather than launch into such thickets, the present analysis will confine itself to areas of inquiry that are more amenable to evidential explanation. To be precise, consideration will be focused upon three issues: why did the Revolution occur? Why did it take the course it did? What has been its significance? The terms February Revolution and October Revolution will be used throughout, as this accords with accepted usage, but they will be viewed not as separate revolutions to be distinguished by ideologically-determined criteria, but as discrete stages in an increasingly radical convulsion that gripped Russia throughout 1917.

Systemic Contradictions

Although the immediate precipitants of the upheaval of 1917 may be located in the effects of a grinding war, threatened starvation and the breakdown in authority, a more profound cause may be discerned in the unresolved contradictions between the social and politial structures of tsarist Russia.

By the turn of the century, the tsarist system was coming under increasing pressure from a combination of new and traditional social forces. With industrial development there emerged, on one side, an urban middle class which began to press for constitutional reform and a say in national affairs, and on the other, a proletariat, which likewise began to agitate for redress in the spheres of life that most concerned it. Besides these, there were the peasants with their age-old land hunger, and their ingrained sense of grievance about excessive taxation, burdensome military service, and oppressive land redemption payments. Industrialisation, it is true, eased the peasants' plight to some extent by opening up new employment prospects, and by syphoning off some surplus rural population, but it did so at the expense of heightening other social problems. In particular, the acceleration of urban growth that accompanied industrial development outpaced the provision of services and housing, giving rise to appalling privation and squalor. Increasingly, the government was called upon to act, but was draggingly slow in its response. Provoked by this inaction, the workers resorted with growing frequency to the strike weapon, the better-educated classes became susceptible to revolutionary agitation, while the peasants vented their rage in bouts of savage destruction. Tensions were thus rising anyway, and in 1905 were brought dramatically to a head when, with an unexpected military humiliation at the hands of the Japanese, it became evident that the regime was as incompetent as it was indifferent. The people took to the streets, radicals put themselves at the head of the insurrectionary upsurge and the future of the regime hung in the balance.

Faced with being toppled, the Tsar was forced to make concessions directed at defusing the key sources of discontent. The middle classes were given a parliament (*Duma*) and pledges of civil rights; the intellectuals were given university self-government; the workers were permitted to unionise, and strikes were made legal; the peasants, with the passage of the Stolypin measures, were given the opportunity of acquiring more land and creating self-contained smallholdings. In other words, steps were taken in the direction of accountable government and a freer society. Had the Tsar been better advised (which implies, among other things, that he should have married someone else) he might have viewed the concessions wrung from him *in extremis* as a means of constructing firmer social foundations for his regime. The middle class, for example, who may be seen as his best potential allies, had been poisoned by the violence of the upheaval they had just experienced, and were ready to support the restoration of public order, provided there was something in it for them. But the sovereign was unwilling to countenance the legitimacy of their aspirations. His aim was to re-establish the integrity of autocratic rule, and there was no place in this for junior partners. So, as soon as it was propitious, he set about clawing back the concessions forced from him. Thus the *Duma*, which might have become the institutional setting for nurturing the growth of a pro-monarchist moderate centre, was denied any meaningful political influence. As a consequence, a moderate centre failed to materialise in any sizeable way, and the goal of a parliamentary democracy remained as inherently revolutionary as the more explicitly revolutionary ambitions of the radical Left.

The parties of the middle class, for their part, were powerless to resist the reassertion of autocracy. The reason for this lies in the weakness of the social stratum from which they drew their support. Not only was the Russian middle class numerically small (perhaps no more than 5–6 million, including children, out of a population of 160 million), but it was far from homogeneous, and had developed little capacity for united action or coordinated political pressure. The explanation for its extraordinary weakness lies in the peculiarities of Russia's industrial development. For her, industrialisation was not only slow by comparison with western Europe; unlike the latter it was not in the main the product of spontaneous domestic economic forces, but instead, came about by state action and foreign financing. Implied in this is the fact that indigenous entrepreneurs played only a marginal role in Russia's industrialisation, and as a consequence failed to acquire to any significant degree the kind of economic strength that could be eventually converted into political muscle. It was their realisation of this, to quote Lenin, 'amazing, almost unbelievable powerlessness' that convinced both Trotsky and him that the Russian bourgeoisie would be incapable of independently establishing its political authority, and that the revolution, when it came, was unlikely to stabilise under their hegemony, but would be shaped by the stronger proletarian and peasant forces.

Industrialisation, although it may have failed to give birth to a strong middle class, did however generate its other corollary – an industrial proletariat. It was also a proletariat which, while not numerous, was highly concentrated, and this concentration gave it a cohesion and a capacity for action that greatly compensated for its lack of numbers. The virtual absence of effective legislative regulation meant that factory conditions were generally bad; wages were also low. At the same time peaceful improvements were made difficult as the concession of independent trade unions granted in 1905 was soon withdrawn, and strikes once again forcibly suppressed. These repressive measures ensured that labour remained an alienated force, and that industrial unrest retained an inherently political character amenable to revolutionary persuasion.

But of all the forces of unrest, it was not the middle class or the proletariat that, in the eyes of the regime, constituted the greatest threat, but the sullen masses of the Russian peasantry. Making up some 80 per cent of the population, these 'dark people', as they were nicknamed, driven by want and privation, expressed their bitterness in periodic acts of outrage and atrocity. Characteristically, their hostility was not directed against the Tsar personally, whom many revered as a father-figure, but against the gentry, the police and the tax officials – those who could be identified immediately as their oppressors. Because their sense of grievances was thus personal and circumstantial, their sense of class solidarity and their capacity for collective action were accordingly weak. This meant that as long as the military – the peasants in uniform – remained loyal, and as long as peasant disturbances did not take place in the context of a more general social upheaval, the regime found the peasant problem containable.

The intelligentsia presented a different sort of problem. This social grouping was the most consistently alienated element in tsarist Russia, and what it lacked in numerical force it made up for in intellectual weight and in unwavering hostility to the established order. In an accounting of the forces that helped bring about and shape the Russian Revolution, it would be difficult to overstate their importance. Berdyaev, probably their most acute critic, has likened them to a monastic sect whose distinctive characteristic was an obsessive interest in metaphysical issues. They produced many creeds, typically utopian in character, and usually derived from western ideas. These ideas, however, in the process of transference lost whatever they had of openness, scepticism and inquiry, and became instead dogmatised, absolutised and unconditional.

Positivism, Marxism, economic materialism, neo-Kantianism, empirico-criticism in turn suffered this deformation: each creed becoming the object of devotion, of 'idolatory', to its particular neophytes. Philosophy was seen by them not as a pursuit in its own right, but as a justification for politics, 'an instrument of social revolution'. Each sectarian splinter-group preached a different brand of salvation. For the liberal intelligentsia, the abstract verities of liberty and constitutionalism were the foundation of all happiness; the populists idealised the peasantry, and saw them as the harbingers of a truly communal society; the Marxists found their god among the proletariat; the nihilists preached the total destruction of everything so that a brave new world could rise like the phoenix from the ashes.

Parallels have been drawn between the part played by Russia's revolutionary intelligentsia and that played by intellectuals in the political process of developing nations generally. In the latter cases it has been young, western-educated elements that have taken the lead in the drive for national independence and for social and economic transformation, often in the teeth of the opposition from entrenched élites. But to depict the Russian intelligentsia simply as modernisers of this type would be inadequate. Modernisation, as it is presently understood, was not their prime objective. Rather, as Berdyaev has observed, what motivated them was a quasi-religious pursuit of redemption and salvation through the creation of a new order, based on an 'equalising justice' and regenerated man. In the nature of things, revolution for many of them became an end in itself, not just a means.

Beset by enemies on all sides, the Tsar could not even look to that traditional ally of the monarchy, the landed aristocracy, for support. Unlike most of its western counterparts, the Russian aristocracy, because of peculiarities in its historical formation, did not develop into a strong, independent social class. Instead, it survived as a parasitic appendage of the court, debt-ridden, and at the mercy of imperial handouts. It could neither offer the regime significant support, nor could it pose an effective challenge to it. Hence while slavishly committed to the perpetuation of the system for the sake of its sinecures and privileges, it was able to do little to sustain it. On top of this, the aristocracy was riven by internal feuds' many of which had their origin in court intrigues and machinations within the royal family, which the weak and indecisive Nicholas was unable to contain. Then, to cap all the other problems, came the war.

THE WAR

War is probably the supreme test for any system. It tests the competence of its government, the readiness of its military, the loyalty of its people, and the strength of its economy. The Great War was the first in history that called for total and sustained mobilisation of the nation's resources: of all the powers entering the fray, Russia was the probably least prepared. Crises developed everywhere. The transport system proved incapable of supplying the fronts and simultaneously provisioning the towns. There were soon not enough guns or ammunition. Casualities were high, the commanders incompetent, and the conscripts badly trained and poorly armed. At the top, the government fumbled with various improvisations for paying for the fighting. A tax on excess profits was levied which, according to one estimate, covered the costs of about twenty minutes' fighting. A graduated income tax was imposed that fell heaviest on the poor. The printing presses were then speeded up to meet the bills. The result was galloping inflation, the degeneration of trade into barter, and the increasing refusal of the peasants to supply food in return for worthless paper.

As if he had not troubles enough, the Tsar added to them by personally assuming the post of Commander-in-Chief, thus tying the fate of the dynasty directly to the fortunes of war. Even more imprudently, in his absence he left the running of the country to his wife. Within a short space of time, she had managed to get rid of the few competent ministers, replacing them at the behest of her guru, Rasputin, with a succession of nincompoops. All told, in the first two years of war there were no fewer than four Prime Ministers, three Foreign Secretaries, three Ministers of War and five Ministers of the Interior. This dizzying dance of the portfolios not only strengthened the impression that the government had simply no idea what it was doing but, in the minds of some, fanned the suspicion that a German faction at court headed by their German Empress was out to sabotage the Russian war effort.

By 1916 exhaustion had set in: the summer saw a wave of strikes; there were riots in the autumn. Morale at the front was beginning to weaken, and reports began to speak of troops fraternising with the enemy. At home, the real value of wages steadily plummeted, essential goods ran short, and signs of rural unrest multiplied. The secret police who in general knew more about that was going on than most now repeatedly warned of the imminence of an uprising.

THE FEBRUARY REVOLUTION

A bad war generally spells trouble for any government. In England it led to the overthrow of Asquith by Lloyd George, in France to the assumption of power by Clemenceau. In Russia, there is a tradition that a bad war means revolution. The Napoleonic invasion was followed by the Decembrist Revolt; the failures of Crimea were followed by the 'revolution from above' of the 1860s; defeat by Japan sparked the insurrections of 1905. Strictly speaking, in 1916 Russia was not yet defeated, her armies though badly mauled were still more or less intact, and no great area of the country had yet been ceded. (In fact, militarily, Russia was more badly battered and had lost far more territory in the initial stages of the second world war than she had by the end of 1916.) Yet defeated she was, none the less: defeated in the same sense that the Kaiser's Germany was two years later, when the imperial forces surrendered, despite the fact that not a foot of national soil had been taken. Defeats such as these are systemic rather than military. By the beginning of 1917, the tsarist system was simply falling apart; the authorities were losing control the economy was stalling; war weariness had set in; the dynasty was discredited. The emergence of a military dictator might have saved the situation, but no one came forward. In any case the Tsar was adamantly against any diminution of his autocratic prerogative, the birthright of his sickly son. Some affrighted liberals in the *Duma* – those associated with the Progressive bloc – toyed with the idea of imposing a new government on the Emperor, and even went so far as to draw up a portfolio of ministers and a set of policy outlines. But in the end they did nothing. Lack of self-confidence and fear of creating a situation that might encourage mob violence paralysed them.

When the crisis finally broke, there was little unexpected about it: just about everyone from the German Chancellor and the British Ambassador, to the lowliest typist in the Ministry of the Interior had been proclaiming its inevitability: only Lenin seems to have been taken unawares. What was unexpected, however, was the ease with which it all happened. Rioting women in a bread queue, strikes in the Vyborg district of the capital, refusal by the Cossacks – and eventually by the police – to obey orders, and within a few days the foundations of the *ancien régime* had been swept away. The moderates in the *Duma* panicked at the sight of the mob, and tried to induce some other members of the royal family to assume power, but their efforts failed and, with great reluctance, they were forced to constitute themselves as a government. And so the Provisional Government came into being.

From the outset, however, it was confronted with a potential rival in the form of the Petrograd Soviet. And the latter's reach steadily increased as the message of the revolution spread out into the provinces, and local soviets began to spring up metastatically across the country. For a time, the conflict inherent in this odd institutional dualism remained muted, partly because an overlapping membership helped to smooth out frictions, but principally because the revolutionary hardliners had not yet returned to the capital.

Indeed, the most striking feature of the February Revolution was the absence of the professional revolutionaries from the centre of events. This was very much a revolution that happened, rather than was made. The top Bolshevik leaders were either in Siberia or abroad when the uprising broke out, and their rank-and-file strength in the capital was meagre. For instance, they had only about 150 members out of the 20,000 workers in the vitally important Putilov Works, and out of the 1500-odd members who made up the Petrograd Soviet, they could muster only about forty. The main peasant party, the Socialist-Revolutionaries, was much larger than the Bolsheviks but, since it was largely made up of politically unsophisticated masses now drawn to the action, it tended to respond to events rather than to shape them. The third revolutionary party of note, the Mensheviks, endorsed what had taken place, but, as their creed reconciled them to the legitimacy of a successful 'bourgeois revolution', they saw little role either for themselves or the proletariat in the immediate situation.

To different people the revolution meant different things. To the moderate political *literati*, it was the fulfilment of a dream: Russia was to become a parliamentary democracy in the best European tradition, and could now join the ranks of civilised states. To the workers, it meant free trade unions, the eight-hour day, industrial arbitration, and better wages and conditions; only an insignificant minority at this stage were agitating for workers' control. To the peasants, the meaning of the revolution was just one thing – the land would be theirs. To the ethnic minorities, the revolution meant recognition and respect for national rights. To the townspeople, it meant that there would now be enough food and fuel, and the spectre of famine would be averted. In general, it was thought to mean the end of the war though, strangely, there was no immediate pressure for this; the war seemed to recede into the background.

Altogether, therefore, a great deal was expected of the new revolutionary administration, and it was expected very quickly. Problems came, not because the new regime failed to respond, but because it took as its priority matters that were peripheral to the main concerns. Thus, while it instituted trial by jury, freedom of press, conscience and association, the separation of Church and state, the abolition of capital punishment, political amnesty, civil rights for soldiers and such like, it failed to press ahead with land redistribution, to arrest the plunge towards economic disaster, or to meet the nationalities' hopes of self-determination. Their inaction, while it may be put down to inexperience and internal feuding, also owes something to a sense of constitutional propriety. As a provisional government, the new administration viewed itself in a caretaker capacity, lacking the proper mandate that only a democratically convened national convention could confer. The trouble was that such a body was not scheduled to meet until almost a year hence; meanwhile, problems had to be tackled which could not wait. An added difficulty was the government's dependence on the Petrograd Soviet. The Soviet commanded the streets, and, more important, it commanded the Petrograd garrison. The Provisional Government, on the other hand, had no real force at its disposal. The government therefore needed the backing of the Soviet. The latter was loath to give it, for the idea of propping up a bourgeois regime was repugnant to those who had been lifelong revolutionary socialists. Even without Lenin to stir things up, it could be seen that the uneasy coexistence between the two institutions was heading for trouble.

And when trouble came, the peasants were in the forefront. They had not anticipated that the distribution of the land would not be a simple handover. So, when the authorities started talking about land surveys, statistical reports and the need for committees and investigations, they naturally smelt treachery, and reacted accordingly. The increasing ferment in the villages in turn affected food supplies to the towns. Despite government requisitioning, which in itself further exacerbated rural feelings, the daily bread ration was steadily cut back. Shortages of essentials became acute; the supply of flour to the troops was reduced to little more than a quarter of what was needed. This and subversion began to sap morale and, after the failure of the June offensive, soldiers began to vote with their feet for an end to the war. The government temporised, highmindedly proclaiming that such a move would be a betrayal of the alliance, which they now held to be a democratic crusade against dictatorship. More practically, they feared that it would also jeopardise the prospects of obtaining badly needed French and British investment.

The decision to continue the war had fateful consequences. Not only was it an enormous drain on resources, but it also meant that a solution to the land question had to be postponed lest it trigger mass desertion from the Front, with peasant conscripts flocking back for their cut of the handout. Secondly, effective prosecution of the war meant that the economy had to be restored. In the eyes of the regime this implied the priority of a stable currency. Inflation was tackled by resort to wage control. The effect of this was to antagonise the workers, but without achieving its objective. And in the end, like Weimar Germany, the authorities were issuing treasury bills for currency in uncut wads. The situation was bad. The war made everything worse, and the people could not see the point of further sacrifices. It was a situation ready-made for demogogic and simplistic solutions.

Lenin's recipe went right to the heart of the problem. Whereas the other revolutionary parties were fumbling for some way to stop the revolution from collapsing into anarchy, Lenin said simply, let it all collapse. To the soldiers he said: forget about the war and about peace treaties, just stop fighting and go home. To the peasants: ignore the government and its legal niceties, seize the land and distribute it among yourselves. To the workers: take control of the factories and throw the bosses out. To the soviets: forget about democratising the state, destroy it. Nothing of the old society should be saved, let it collapse, and out of the ruins something entirely new will be built. 'Land, peace and bread' summed it all up in unambiguous language that even the simplest could grasp.

Demagogic though Lenin's appeal was, it was in tune with the feelings of an increasingly widening section of the population fed up with the dithering of the government in the face of mounting chaos. The peasants were already beginning to act in accord with Lenin's exhortation. In March, disturbances were reported in thirty-four districts, in April the figure was 174, in May 236, in June 280. By late summer nearly every important agricultural region was in a state of uproar with peasants seizing the estates and putting their owners to flight, or worse. In the towns factory seizures, strikes and lock-outs were likewise increasing in frequency.

Momentarily, it looked as if the military would be able to turn the course of events when, in August, General Kornilov attempted to stage a *putsch*. But the man 'with the heart of a lion and the head of an ox' was no Napoleon. The *putsch* was poorly organised and was easily thwarted by worker defence squads, and the refusal of the railwaymen to let the conspirators through. The fact that armed detachments under Bolshevik control had played a key part in defending the government against the mutinous military underlined their claim to be the most resolute force, and made it extremely difficult for the authorities to take action against their subversive activities. Besides, against all the evidence, the liberal ministers refused to believe that there was any real threat from the Left. They persisted to the end in the myopic belief that the main danger lay in an attempted monarchist restoration. And the end was coming rapidly, as the country slid steadily into general anarchy. The Bolsheviks had only to catch the favouring wind and fill their sails.

The October Revolution

It is not surprising that the Bolshevik *coup*, when it took place in late October, met with such little resistance. The seizure of power had already been prepared for in the events that preceded it. Engels had once noted, in a letter to Vera Zasulich, that Russia was one of those exceptional cases where it would be possible for a handful of men to effect a revolution. Lenin, almost alone among his comrades, perceived this, and saw that the time was right. His personal contribution to the Bolshevik victory was enormous but, at the same time, he could not have succeeded without the Bolshevik organisation. The key factor here was the strength the party managed to acquire in the big industrial centres, in the main garrison towns, in the northern armies and, in particular, in the Baltic fleet. Also, by October, they had attained dominance in the crucial Moscow and Petrograd soviets.

In its essentials, the Bolshevik *coup* conforms to the model of modern urban revolution in that control of the radio, railway, telephone and telegraph were the first objectives. At the same time, key government buildings were occupied and the incumbents arrested. The numbers actually involved in the operations were small compared with the masses active in the February insurrections; in October the main moves were carried out by designated military units. The effortless manner in which they succeeded is a tribute not only to the skill with which the whole operation was handled, but to the degree to which the takeover had been prepared for in the propaganda victories and political successes already registered.

The takeover in the capital and then in Moscow was, of course, not the end of the story. It took a further three years of savage civil war before Bolshevik power was finally secured. Indeed, it might be argued that final victory was not assured until Stalin had broken the back of peasant resistance with the enforced collectivisation of the land in the late 1920s.

SIGNIFICANCE OF THE BOLSHEVIK VICTORY

With the coming to power of the Bolsheviks, the Russian Revolution ceased to be a purely national affair. This was partly fortuitous in that their *coup* was the signal for foreign intervention against them. But in a deeper sense, it ceased to be purely national because the Bolsheviks saw themselves not just as actors on a Russian stage, but as the catalyst of world revolution. The Soviet state was to be but the first unit in an international fraternity of socialist republics. Not unlike President Wilson, they saw themselves as the architects of a new world order based on principles that would persist, irrespective of the immediate fate of the Russian Revolution itself. Not until Stalin said otherwise did any of them imagine that the Russian Revolution could survive, let alone prosper, on its own.

The fact that the Russian Revolution failed to ignite similar conflagrations elsewhere did not seriously diminish Bolshevik expectations that this was but a temporary hiatus in the onward march of history towards socialism. Nor did it lead them to question their assumption that their own revolution was the archetype for those that were to follow. It was taken as incontrovertible that the Bolshevik achievement was a faithful realisation of Marx's prognoses pertaining to proletarian revolutions. This in turn made it entirely justifiable in their eyes that they should expect other communist parties to learn from Bolshevik experience and apply it in practice. It also made it necessary for Lenin and his followers to deny that their revolution was in any important respect unique or had essential features that were specific only to Russia. The truth is, however, that the Bolshevik revolution had many crucial features that were not allowed for in Marx's model. Comparing Marx's key criteria on one side with those characteristic of the Bolshevik revolution on the other, we find that (in the latter case) party substitutes for proletarian as the main agency, anarchism for political consciousness, economic backwardness for industrial development, socialist opponents for the bourgeois state, and a minority-based party-military *coup* for class action. The remarkable thing might seem that these substitutions were carried out without repudiating one iota of Marxism. But, upon reflection, it could not have been otherwise, for without a Marxist rationalisation, the Bolsheviks could not have justified their political existence, still less their seizure of power. Nor could they later have justified their claim to hegemony over all other communist parties.

Furthermore, just as the Bolsheviks needed Marx as their legitimation, so, in an odd way, Marx needed the Bolsheviks. For, had not the October Revolution taken place, it seems entirely possible that Marxism would have atrophied into an increasingly peripheral social critique. Its economics had already been found wanting and, as apostates like Bernstein had begun to point out, its predictions about the nature of social change were equally unsound. Also, as a political force, it was beginning to lose its drawing power, with the realisation that under democratic conditions there were alternatives to revolution as a means of redress. In fact, its most numerous adherent, the German Social Democrats, had in all but name already abandoned it. The Bolshevik victory in the name of Marxism, and with it the establishment of an avowedly communist state, gave what was becoming an increasingly moribund doctrine a new lease of life. And it did so, not by demonstrating the doctrine's correctness, but by showing its possibilities in areas of the world and under conditions not catered for in the original theory. Put another way, the October Revolution changed Marxism from a eurocentric creed directed at the transformation of advanced industrial society, into a recipe for accelerated modernisation in the Third World, carried out by self-selected élites using administrative methods. If this is a paradox, it is not the only one; there is another that is more profound and more tragic.

The October Revolution, its makers believed, marked a decisive break with the Russian past. It set out not to negate the aspirations of the February Revolution, but to fulfil them. The Bolsheviks promised not merely democracy, but social democracy; not just liberty, but also equality; not just representative government, but government by the people; not just concessions to ethnic minorities, but independence; not just redress against unfair employers, but workers' control of the means of production; not just a free Russia, but a Russia that would be the cornerstone of a free world. This was the promise. Yet within ten years Russia was becoming the nightmare world of Stalin's *gulags*, a tyranny darker than that of any of the tsars, an empire more tightly bound than ever before, its peasants effectively re-enserfed, workers conscripted into labour armies, and the whole population gagged and threatened by a draconian police state. Autocracy had become totalitarianism.

How did the promise degenerate into the nightmare? Clearly no one, not Lenin and probably not Stalin, willed it. In his last letters Lenin showed an awareness that the revolution was not turning out as expected, but he was uncertain as to what should be done. Trotsky, writing later, blamed the rot on a bureaucratic malaise, but was unable to say clearly how it came about. Others on the Left said it happened because the Revolution failed to triumph beyond Russia. Present-day Soviet explanation – in so far as there is one – pins 'mistakes of the past' on Stalin's personality. None of these explanations touches the heart of the problem. The supposition that the Revolution might have been 'saved' had it spread beyond Russia and produced other socialist states is particularly fatuous. The chronicle of Sino-Soviet or Sino-Vietnamese relations – to mention but the two most glaring cases – hardly provides much substance to the theory of natural socialist fraternity. A more convincing argument seems to be that the seeds of disaster were present from the outset; they were inherent in the nature of Bolshevism itself.

Bolshevism represents the fusion of two traditions: the tradition of the extremist, maximalist, dogmatic intelligentsia, and the tradition of tsarist statism. When the utopian vision of the Bolsheviks had to confront the recalcitrant reality of Russia, they had to choose between settling for less, or else forcibly changing reality. That they would resort to violence was fore-ordained. It was implicit from the outset in Lenin's attitude, in his belief that the Bolshevik party was the repository of a higher consciousness. It was implicit too in the assumption that this party had a binding, compelling historical obligation to realise the vision of communism, and it flowed from the fact that the majority of the people neither shared nor sympathised with that vision. Thus it was necessary from the start that the Soviet republic be a one-party state, and that it operate as a dictatorship. In the nature of things, the Bolshevik socialist transformation would have to be imposed from above, a transformation wrought by administrative means in the manner of that of the great tsar-revolutionaries of the past.

Resort to violence was made more likely too by the absence of moderate political traditions and civic culture. It was also made more probable because the Revolution had swept away the nascent Russian middle class who might have exercised some restraint upon the resurgent statism of the new soviet power élite and their return to the habitual violence of Russian government. With the benefit of hindsight, it can be seen that it was the aspirations of this middle class and hence the Revolution in February that marked the real break with the Russian past; what happened in October was in a sense a counter-revolution, in that it represented a reinstatement of the principle of state absolutism, albeit in a new ideological garb and for supposedly humanitarian purposes.

The Bolshevik revolution has dominated the politics of Left radicalism in this century in the way that the French Revolution did in the previous century. The odd thing is that it is a revolution that has won its pre-eminence more in spite of its failures than on account of its successes. For it is hardly deniable that the western democracies, based on older values that Bolshevism avowed to transcend, are today more prosperous and congenial societies than is the Soviet Union or any of its offspring. The appeal of the soviet model is largely confined to those areas of the world that have never experienced genuine democracy and where pressing social and economic problems are being encountered. In these conditions, the soviet way seems seductively attractive. It presents a simple, seemingly easy-to-operate, political mechanism and appears to signpost a faster and a cheaper route to development and enhanced national status than is possible to attain by leaving development to spontaneous domestic forces. It also appears to be able to promote growth without relapse into neo-colonial dependence.

On closer inspection, it can be seen that many of the supposed advantages of the soviet model are illusory. Copying soviet-style socialist transformation is invariably a bloody affair, and the alternative economic model does little more than trade neo-colonial dependence for a client state relationship with the USSR.

How much longer the sway of the Bolshevik revolution is likely to last cannot easily be foreseen. It is instructive to note, however, that in its homeland, and in the facsimile states that it has spawned, it is coming under increasing threat. Within the USSR long-suppressed pluralist tendencies are beginning to manifest themselves – dissidence, nationalisms, youth culture, political opposition. Ideological conviction is waning not just in society, but within the party itself: what sustains the system is a combination of police measures and promises of material betterment. Material betterment, however, is increasingly hard to come by. An enfeebled agriculture, an unwieldy and counter-productive planning system, and looming shortages of essential resources (in part the product of past prodigality) are beginning to impose excessive economic strains. Added to this is the heavy drain of a huge military budget and the other costs incurred in financing super-power status and globalist pretensions. On top of all this, Soviet paymasters are faced with the prospect of having to bail some of the crippled economies of their East European appendages. Clearly something will have to give. In the past, the Kremlin has responded to pressure points in its economic development with a sharp dose of austerity, secure in the knowledge that the terror apparatus could be relied upon to keep the people in line. But times have changed, terror, at least in a naked form, has not been invoked for some time, and today's Soviet population is more confident and sophisticated than their forebears. The imposition of an unwelcome austerity may not be greeted with the kind of docility which Stalin could automatically expect. There are already acute shortages of a number of staple foodstuffs. It is not inconceivable that any further reductions could bring down upon the Kremlin a crisis of Polish dimensions. And it is hard to imagine the outbreak of such a crisis without it triggering a spiral of unrest throughout eastern Europe, bringing with it the threatened unravelling of the whole bloc system. In considering what it should do, the Soviet leaders would do well to bear in mind that a regime ushered in as a result of a riot in a bread queue could go out the same way.

Economic failure and popular repudiation may lessen the appeal of the Soviet model in those regions of the world where it is presently found attractive, but they are hardly likely to dull the appetite for other panaceas. The search for the *genuine* revolution, unbetrayed and permanent, shows little sign of abating.

7 The Chinese Revolution and the Chinese Tradition of Political Thought*

JAMES COTTON

In the past one hundred years western revolutionary ideologies have undoubtedly comprised an influence upon Chinese political thinking and conduct. It is the purpose of the present essay to discuss the importance of the role these ideologies have played in recent Chinese history, by way of a consideration of their reception and application. Having reviewed the initial attempts of Chinese intellectuals to come to terms with notions of revolution, nationalism and socialism, the more contemporary impact of these ideas will be examined by way of some remarks on the thought of Mao Tse-tung and on the character of recent historiography in China.

The provenance of the modern Chinese term for revolution (*ko-ming*) is a particularly telling example of the relationship between the traditional and the external in modern Chinese ideology. The term itself is present in two of the earliest examples of the classical literature, and is used to refer to the salutary 'changing of the mandate' whereby one dynasty gives way to another, heaven taking the right to rule from the last and invariably corrupt representative of the old ruling house, and investing it in the virtuous founder of the new. But the term only began to take on the connotations of the western political meaning of 'revolution', and came to be used to translate that word from the European languages, in imitation of Japanese works on the West. In 1895, Sun Yat-sen, then a revolutionary though not yet greatly influenced by socialist ideas 'is said to have been the first to recognise his enterprise as *ko-ming* [revolutionary], when he read a report of his own activities in the Japanese

* I should like to thank the Research Grants Committee and the Faculty of Social Sciences of the University of Newcastle upon Tyne for their generous support which greatly facilitated the research for this essay.

press'.[1] Significantly, until that time, Chinese accounts of western revolutions used a term (*luan*) which carried with it suggestions of popular tumult and disorder. By the early 1900s it was possible, therefore, for the Chinese to engage in quite sophisticated debate concerning the relative merits of reform and revolution.

The modern idea of revolution can only have meaning if connected with notions of fundamental overthrow and renewal, and, as will be shown, nationalism and socialism came to comprise much of the context for the activity of Chinese revolutionists. The indigenous intellectual tradition, however, was not without its millenarian strains (often of a Taoist variety), and it is important to note that the ideologists of the Taiping movement of the mid-nineteenth century, as well as being directly influenced by (a wildly interpreted) Protestant Christianity, derived much inspiration also from their understanding of some passages of the classical Confucian literature. And of course their very name refers to that time of 'Great Peace' (*t'ai-p'ing*) when the virtuous shall rule and all men shall be brothers. More particularly, K'ang Yu-wei (1858–1927), a pivotal figure in the development of modern Chinese ideology, and an influence upon many early socialists (and the young Mao), affirmed a millenarian doctrine explicitly drawn from the 'new text' school of Confucianism, a school which had its origins in the Han period, and which had undergone a revival in the eighteenth and nineteenth centuries.[2] The 'new text' school rests its interpretation of the Confucian canon upon an esoteric reading of a number of the texts thereof, as well as upon the claim that it has recorded the essentials of an oral tradition which is a guide to the sage's true meaning. This school claims to find in the *Spring and Autumn Annals* (the chronological official records of Confucius's state of *Lu*) reference to three ages which are supposed to pertain to the history of the world, this insight being placed together with an apparent scheme of historical periodisation found in the *Book of Rites*, where mankind is described as having passed from an era of great harmony (ta-t'ung) characterised by universal regard for others, and an absence of private property to a lesser one of 'small tranquillity'.

There is a curious parallelism here with Rousseau and some other western thinkers, since the 'new text' school reverses this schema and applies it to the movement of world history. K'ang Yu-wei is writing explicitly within this tradition when he expresses the belief that history is bound to devolve ultimately into a period of 'Great

Harmony', when differences between nations shall disappear, and all men and women shall enjoy equality.

It is noteworthy that K'ang's 'Great Harmony' is also that of Mao, who affirms the view that this final epoch will come about when classes finally disappear. Other reformers employed both this notion of stages, and the idea of a harmonious and just end stage. Liang Ch'i-ch'ao, K'ang's star pupil, who wished to see the Chinese as 'a people made new', understood history to be divided into three periods: the first in which all men were devoid of rights, the second where some possessed rights, and the third where all had rights. Now this millenarian strain in Chinese thought has been noted in order to show that notions of renovation and renewal are not foreign to the indigenous tradition. It provides the context for the movement, on the part of K'ang Yu-wei, Liang Ch'i-ch'ao and others, from Chinese to western thinking of this type, a movement facilitated by their belief that both had a fundamentally similar character. Thus, in the late 1890s when the translator of Bellamy's *Looking Backward* referred to that author's socialist vision of the future as a 'Great Harmony', Tan Ssu-t'ung, a friend of K'ang's and an early martyr of the reform movement, could identify that vision with the position of 'new text' Confucianism.[3]

When we turn to consider the role of nationalism in modern Chinese ideology, we encounter a similar procedure whereby certain traditional ideas and practices have comprised the foundation for a partly foreign edifice. Joseph Levenson has made much of the fact that for China to be a nation amongst nations a profound re-evaluation of national identity was required. This is apparent from the fact that the customary appellations for the nation and its state, 'the middle county' (chung-kuo) or, 'all under heaven' (t'ien-hsia) seemed to exclude the notion that nations could be equal in the possession of nationhood.[4] Yet this is perhaps to take the Confucian tradition too much at face-value,, as welll as to misunderstand the phenomenon of modern nationalism. The history of Chinese dynasties has often been the history of external conquest, so much so that some interpretations of Chinese history find in the changing character of the Chinese frontier or periphery the crucial feature or determinant of that history. Although the Ch'ing period was characterised by a degree of xenophobia and the assertion of cultural superiority, China under previous dynasties had been open to and partially transformed by foreign ideas – perhaps the most notable example of which is the influence of Bhuddism in the T'ang period – and both the Ming and Ch'ing dynasties had maintained complex commercial and even diplomatic relations with China's neighbours, particularly the Persians, and later the Russians. Moreover, in the ideology of European nationalism, there has never been a firm division between national unity and self-rule on the one hand, and national self-assertion on the other. Thus Liang Ch'i-ch'ao, whose earlier view of nationalism saw it as consisting of internal popular rule, and the external recognition of the rights of other nations, had by 1901 come round to the view that nationalism now entailed 'national imperialism', a bloody competition between nations and the subordination of the population to the state. In this, as in other areas, works in Japanese, and Japanese translations of western writings, had introduced Chinese intellectuals at the turn of the century to the phenomenon of imperialism, evidence for the existence of which Chinese intellectuals found in abundance in their everyday experience. The other ideological component in the development of Chinese nationalism was an explicitly racial anti-Manchu sentiment which had a history going back to the seventeenth century, which had again come to prominence in the propaganda of the Taiping movement and which had fired the youthful Sun Yat-sen to his first revolutionary endeavours.[5] In 1906, anti-Manchuism was incorporated in the platform of Sun's *T'ung-meng-hui* (League of Common Alliance), it being argued there that the Manchus were racially inferior, oppressive and corrupt as a ruling élite, and bound to bring disaster to China with their belated and feeble attempts at reform.

In the light of subsequent developments in European nationalism it is perhaps significant that some Chinese in this period (for example, Ch'en T'ien-hua in Hunan) were able to see the struggle between nations as in essence a contest between races. It is noteworthy also that for the Chinese, if nationalism is about the nation (*kuo*) it is also about the people (*min*) such that the term used to denote nationalism (*min-tsu chu-i*, another Japanese neologism) was more obviously concerned with the latter rather than the former.

The form of government which the nationalist revolutionists were to inaugurate they variously described as republican or democratic and constitutional, though Liang Ch'i-ch'ao drawing partly on German theorists of 'state socialism' was to argue the case against the spokesmen of the *T'ung-meng hui* for a period of enlightened absolutism or tutelage before popular rule would be possible.[6] It is significant, however, that from its foundation the *T'ung-meng hui* understood part of its task to be the introduction of socialism into China by means of the policy of 'land nationalisation'. To the introduction of socialist ideas into China we now turn, though this requires us to back-track slightly in time.

Once again in the case of the acquisition of socialist ideas traditional ideas play a part, and the Japanese appear in the role of midwives to the Chinese intellect. National schemes for the equalisation of landholding have a long history in China. The *Mencius* and other Confucian works refer to the existence of a well-field (*ching-t'ien*) system of land ownership whereby the countryside is divided into plots each of nine fields, every eight families tilling a field on their own account, and tending the ninth for the community or state. Reformers at various times (including Wang Mang, and Wang An-Shih), up to and including the Taipings sought to restore or introduce this system: K'ang Yu-wei was to interpret Fourier as a theorist of the well-field, and in similar vein Liang Ch'i-ch'ao in 1899 was to refer to it as 'on the same plane as modern socialism',[7] both men thereby interpreting advanced western nations in terms of a traditional point of reference. In a masterful discussion, Joseph Levenson is able to show the waning of the importance of this point of reference as time elapsed, though he also concedes that this most unlikely piece of folklore has now become incorporated into the modern myth of the Chinese past as evidence of a universal primitive communal ownership which existed according to Engels before slave society.

The Chinese term for socialism (*she-hui chu-i*) is another Japanese neologism which first appeared in the 1870s, and Japanese materials seem to have been crucial in the acquisition of ideas of socialism by Chinese intellectuals, though a possible additional influence may have been *The Review of the Times*. This latter work, edited by missionaries Dr Young J. Allen and Dr Timothy Richard, first appeared in 1889, and carried, amongst many other items, articles (between 1894 and 1899) discussing the ideas of Henry George.[8] However, Japanese influence was much more significant not merely for cultural and linguistic reasons, but because by far the greatest concentration of Chinese students studying overseas were to be found in Japan, that country also being the obvious refuge for reformers and revolutionaries in the closing years of the Ch'ing dynasty. Drawing upon Japanese sources Liang Ch'i-ch'ao wrote a number of articles from 1899 which discussed the struggle between capitalist and proletariat, and in 1902 and 1903 he introduced Chinese readers to some of the leading figures of socialism (including Marx).

Liang also assisted in the founding of a publishing house in Shanghai which brought out, in 1903, translations of three Japanese works on socialism, the first books in Chinese on that subject; a year which also saw translations of Japanese works on anarchism and on the Russian revolutionary movement. At this time a number of Chinese journals favourable to socialism appeared, and it was only three years later in the *Min-pao* (The people) of the *T'ung-meng hui* that the first translation of Marx into Chinese appeared, the text in question being the ten-point programme from the *Communist Manifesto*.[9] At about the same time Chinese interest in anarchist theory emerged amongst students in France.

But if in this period socialism for the Chinese intellectual meant Marx and his theories, it also meant Henry George, and indeed there was much argument on the Left regarding the applicability of George's single tax proposals to China in the years immediately after 1905. Sun Yat-sen may first have discovered George in the reading-room of the British Museum in 1897; it is undoubtedly the case that he understood the policy of 'equalisation of land rights' affirmed by the *T'ung-meng hui* and some of its predecessors in a specifically Georgian sense, an irony in view of that western sage's low assessment of the Chinese.[10] It is noteworthy in this connection that even the westernised Sun, who had spent many years in Hong Kong, Hawaii and further afield, and who was not even properly literate in Chinese, at least according to his Chinese opponents, had been preoccupied from the first with the idea of the people's livelihood (*min-sheng*), a traditional term and one which occurs in his earliest reform proposals. What is more striking is that in later years Sun used 'people's livelihood-ism' (*min-sheng chu-i*) and the Japanese term for socialism (*she-hui chu-i*) interchangeably (of the European as well as of the Chinese ideology)[11] which may explain why Chinese socialists in the early years of the century devoted so much of their time to the highly traditional difficulties of the agrarian sector, a preoccupation which extends to the present time. In the years immediately after 1905, then, when the newspaper of Sun Yat-sen's movement (*Min-pao*) carried a profusion of articles on Marx and on socialism written by associates of Sun (including Hu

Han-min – later to be an influence on the young Mao – Wang Ching-wei, Chu Chih-hsin and Feng Tzu-yu), although all these figures were strongly influenced by socialist notions they also interpreted these notions through the same prism as did Sun. Feng Tzu-yu, for example, similarly identified 'people's livelihood-ism' with western socialism, believed that the putative well-field system of ancient China had affinities with later socialist arrangements, and though a proponent of land nationalisation and the single tax system of Henry George found the latter directly equivalent to the 'Single Whip' land taxation of the Ch'ing period.[12]

Before the collapse of the Manchu dynasty in 1911, then, it can be seen that Chinese intellectuals were quite familiar with that triad of twentieth-century ideology: revolution, nationalism and socialism. It is also apparent, however, that their discovery of these notions was assisted by Japanese cultural and linguistic intermediaries, and their awareness of these ideas incorporated significant traditional components and preoccupations.

Amongst the commonplaces of texts on Chinese history are the statements that K'ang Yu-wei was the last Confucian, and that western and modernising ideas and ideologies grew to the ascendant in China with the May Fourth movement of 1919, to be followed soon after by the foundation of the Communist Party in 1921, and the Soviet-inspired reorganisation of Sun's party (now the *Kuomintang*) in 1923. The slogans of the May Fourth movement of intellectual and cultural iconoclasm, which began with demonstrations against the humiliation of the country at the Versailles peace conference, included 'down with the old and up with the new', and the even more telling 'smash the Confucius shop'.[13] Now the movement prompted and inaugurated great changes in literature, education and philosophy, and it is customary to link the growth of interest in Marxism with the intellectual ferment of the time, in which there was much discussion of notions of progress, science and democracy. Whilst it is true that the intellectual founders of the communist movement in China, Li Ta-chao and Ch'en Tu-hsiu, were participants in this debate, we have seen that socialism originated in a different and earlier context. It needs to be determined, therefore, whether Mao, whose history is largely the history of socialism in modern China, was a legitimate child of this cultural renaissance, or whether significant features of his thought derive from other perhaps earlier origins.

The formation and lineaments of Mao's ideology is a complex topic which has yet to receive a definitive treatment, but it does appear clear that Mao carried about with him the most curious farrago of intellectual baggage. Although one of the earliest (1917–18) of Mao's writings is a commentary on a neo-Kantian work, Paulsen's *System of Ethics*[14] and we know that he read the translations made by Yen Fu and others of Mill, Spencer, Rousseau and Montesquieu, he also received his earliest education in the classics, and throughout his life quoted and drew on Chinese popular novels and stories, ancient military writings, and other non-Confucian literature. His intellectual relationship with the May Fourth movement finds a curious parallel in his personal position in Peking at that time. As a lowly assistant in the University Library he found it difficult to make contact with significant intellectual figures in the capital, and he was himself to record the most significant of his experiences of that memorable year as walking on the ice of the gulf of Pei Hai, walking around the walls of Hsuchou (of *Three Kingdom's* fame) climbing T'ai Shan, and visiting the grave of Confucius.[15] The most vivid impression of the effect on Mao's thinking of these disparate influences may be gained by reading the table-talk recorded in the Red Guard compilations of his sayings, where his rather sketchy knowledge of western history and ideas is supplemented by references to *The Dream of the Red Chamber*, or characters from folktales. And Soviet critics point out that there are more references in his writings to Chinese literature and philosophy than to the Marxist classics, a good selection of which were not available in translation before 1935.[16] Mao knew no western language, and before his trip to Russia in 1949 had never been beyond China's boundaries.

Throughout the period before Mao's rise to absolute pre-eminence in the Chinese Communist Party his opponents and critics were men of foreign learning and experience (notably Wang Ming and his 'Returned Student' clique) and there can be little doubt that he took great pleasure in being, for them, the final authority in such western esoterica as dialectical materialism. The periodic purges and persecutions of western-trained intellectuals in China since 1949 may be attributed, in part, to Mao's distrust of foreign influences, a distrust which was reflected in the extraordinary xenophobia of China in the later Maoist period. And even Mao's insistence after about 1958 that class struggle continues under socialism and perhaps never entirely disappears, which seems to derive from a revenge of the dialectic (if dialectics never cease, neither can their social reflection, class struggle) may also be inspired by a voluntarist style of politics which incorporates the most traditional notions of rule by the self-disciplined virtuous. The exaltation of 'Legalism' (the Confucian school's historical opponent) and the praise accorded to Ch'in Shih Huang, and the identification of Mao with the first emperor, are further evidence of Mao's indigenous roots and appeal. Finally, Mao's preoccupation with the peasantry, the original motor of his revolution and ever the recipient of his solicitations and utopian projections, has more to do with traditional Chinese orientations than classical Marxism. If parallels can be drawn between the practices of traditional Chinese governments, with their all encompassing bureaucracies, control of commerce and industry, attention to irrigation and land regulation, and those of the present regime, many traditional features may be discerned also in the still official ideology of the People's Republic.

For Joseph Levenson, however, these and other traditional features are only a shattered and unstructured remainder. In the final section of this paper, therefore, I shall discuss this the most elegant statement of the discontinuity thesis, particularly in connection with modern historiography in China which Levenson claims provides crucial evidence for his argument.

It is one of the arguments of Joseph Levenson's fascinating, complex, and learned work, *Confucian China and Its Modern Fate*, that from the middle of the nineteenth century onwards there has occurred a fundamental change in the character of Chinese civilisation and its political culture: essential traditional elements thereof have passed irreparably into history. For the Chinese mind, China now has a past like that of other nations. Though the Chinese past may be more subtle and rich than that of other civilisations, it is nevertheless a *past*, and as such can offer no real prescriptions for the present. Traditional features in thought and in politics may persist, but these are mere fragments. This passing of the traditional civilisation is no more evident, according to Levenson, than in the field of political ideas where, successively, Chinese intellectuals appropriated the key elements of contemporary western ideology in the form of notions of revolution, nationalism and socialism,[17] notions which were quite inconsistent with the traditional world-view. According to Levenson's argument, the notion of revolution cannot be appropriated to the Chinese tradition, as those erstwhile radicals K'ang Yu-wei and Liang Ch'i-chao both stated after 1911, since the chief emphasis of that tradition was upon continuity and prescription. Nationalism is quite inconsistent with that world-view, for to become a nation in a world of nations, the 'culturalism' of the civilisation, that is, its insistence that Chinese culture was the only real culture, must be rejected. And although traditional points of reference (such as the well-field) played an important role in the discovery and appropriation of socialist ideas by Chinese intellectuals, these points of reference were soon forgotten or ridiculed by younger socialists of the May Fourth generation.

In his endeavour to show that China now has a past like that of other nations, Levenson discusses in parts two and three of his third volume key evidence in historiographical material. The adoption of the Marxian scheme of historical periodisation in China signifies the rejection of the traditional and prescriptive approach to history, though the concomitant insistence that China had experienced *all* those stages of history which had transpired in other civilisations (and would have evolved to socialism if left to her own devices) raised her to an equality with other nations. The Confucian literature ceased to be the repository of timeless values and instead became the subject of Marxian scrutiny, with Confucius himself 'museumified' according to (sometimes conflicting) interpretations of Chinese classical history. And the whole civilisation and its culture began to be approached from the point of view of an external, or perhaps cosmopolitan standpoint, where, for example, Taoism became interesting because of its connection with chemistry or its anticipations of modern physics.

Levenson's thesis would seem to be supported by the efflorescence of innovative historical writing which has appeared since the death of Mao, some items of which take explicit issue with tenets of Maoist historiography in a scientific and critical fashion. Since 1976, for example, the allegedly 'progressive' character of the Taiping and Boxer movements has been queried, and some scholars have gone so far as to express open disagreement with Mao by questioning the positive role of peasant wars in Chinese history, arguing that by themselves peasant uprisings could do nothing to develop the productive forces, and may even cause them harm.[18] But there is still a significant body of material which would appear to adhere to quite a different conception of history. To determine whether this conception conforms to some of the characteristics of the traditional historiography (and is thus damaging to Levenson's thesis), these characteristics must be briefly delineated before some examples of this writing are examined.

According to Robert Hartwell, the traditional historiography evinces the characteristics of classicism, moral didacticism and historical analogism. For Etienne Balazs, the most notable features of this historiography are the official status of its writers (it is a history by officials, of officials, for officials), its incorporation of much material quoted directly from sources, and its form, which is generally dynastic, exhibiting 'the habit of cutting history up into dynastic slices'.[19] For present purposes I should like to synthesise these features to offer the following as essential characteristics. First, traditional history is most usually official history in the sense that it is not merely written by functionaries, for functionaries, but matters of interpretation are generally political in nature. Further, the selection of historical evidence does not conform to a critical method. Here Hartwell's 'classicism' and Balazs's penchant for quotation are combined. Now it would be foolhardy to affirm that an uncritical use of sources has always characterised Chinese historiography – Ssu-ma Kuang could be regarded as the inventor of the critical method in history writing, a method which is again to be found in some history writing under the Ch'ing – but it can be maintained that this has often been the case. Secondly, history is very often concerned with drawing analogies from the past with the intention of deriving some moral or political lessons for the present: its form is that of 'historical analogism' and 'moral didacticism' as Hartwell expresses it. Finally, history is normally about dynasties, and being about dynasties it is usually subordinated to a rather rigid understanding of the dynastic cycle, the dynasty being founded by a man of singular virtue and brought to ruin, after vigour and then decline, by a corrupt or vicious character enmeshed in the intrigues of eunuchs and concubines, and unwilling or unable to revivify the bureaucracy and reappropriate lost state revenues. How much are these four features in evidence in recent popular historiographical writing?

Is history official history? We certainly have evidence for this having been the case before the death of Mao. A number of articles attest to the manipulation of academic discussion for political purposes, the most singular of which is a piece by the editorial department of the history journal *Li-shi yen-chiu* published in December 1976.[20] It complains of direct interference by the 'Gang of Four' in the editorial policy of the journal, citing numerous examples. But *plus ça change* because it also refers, in now rather sadly dated language, to 'the great victories of the Proletarian Cultural Revolution', 'the Campaign to Criticise Lin-Piao and Confucius [which was] personally started by Chairman Mao', and 'the wide leadership of the Party Central Committee headed by Chairman Hua'. More recently there has been favourable reference to the (Maoist) slogan 'making the past serve the present', and it has been stated that the praise of legalism in Mao's declining years 'was a political plot to usurp Party and state power on the pretext of assessing historical figures'.[21] Further, virtue has been rediscovered in the notion of self-cultivation as proposed by Mencius, and this has been explicitly linked to Liu Shao-ch'i's recently recycled tracts which quote Mencius approvingly on this topic. And lest practitioners of social science were in doubt, Hu Ch'iao-mu, in an address to the Academy of Social Sciences Party Congress, made it clear that party members in the Academy should aim to combine 'real learning' with 'party spirit', the latter being attained only if such individuals 'consciously . . . march in step politically with the party'.[22] At certain levels, then, history still seems to retain its official character as a vehicle of state-inspired instruction. What of the other features?

Concerning the selection of historical evidences, traditional procedures are not entirely absent in much popular historiography. An article on Ch'in Shi Huang incorporates, as its only evidence, a series of quotations from SSu-ma Ch'ien's biography of him. A statement on some of the differing opinions concerning Confucious employs two pieces of evidence neither of which are reliable sources concerning his conduct or views, though they are both employed in traditional accounts of his thought.[23] Finally, the figure of patriotic general Yue Fei of the southern Sung reappears having being condemned as a 'capitulationist' by the Gang of Four. His good name, much revered in the old historiography, is rehabilitated, though many of the conventional details of his life and conduct may well be later invention.[24] Again there is, therefore, some evidence for the persistence of the traditional approach, though this persistence is even more marked when the third feature of that approach, the moral didacticism and historical analogism of Chinese historiography, is reviewed.

Here the evidence in popular history writing is in the form of discussions of some aspects of previous dynasties and periods, of feudalism, and of Confucius. Now it is apparent that none of this material is really intelligible unless it is understood to be written in order to draw parallels between past and present, and to derive instruction and example for contemporary practice. This is most transparently the case in articles on the emperor's personal servants, and on the despotic and irresponsible fashion in which eunuchs and the empress's relatives wielded power after having gained the emperor's confidence, or otherwise placing him under their control.[25] In similar vein is a piece concerning government under the early Ming, which is found to have strictly controlled the activities of officials, and incorporated a fair legal system.[26] The intention of this article would seem to be to dispute previous analyses of this period, and at the same time show that just such features would have to be incorporated into the present regime if corruption and abuse are to be avoided. Slightly more subtle are articles devoted to the Ch'ing emperors Ch'ien-lung and Kang-hsi, and the Han emperor Wu-ti. The first discusses Ch'ien-lung's overweening pride, which led eventually to the penning of a self-criticism, a seeming reference to Mao's statement of his responsibility for many of the calamities of the Great Leap period. Kang-hsi's early pragmatic and scientific attitude which brings China much improvement is contrasted with the fanaticism and ossification of his old age, which renders him 'unable to promote a tremendous development in China's economy during this period'.[27] An apparent elaborate parallelism is developed between the career of the Wu emperor of the Han and Mao, though of course here as elsewhere the latter is not named. He was a man of talent, but by asking too much of his country he brought it close to calamity. Social disorder became rife and such was the divorce between ruler and officials that many members of the state apparatus were imprisoned, and 'some prime ministers did not die a natural death'. It was only after an attempted *coup* by some members of the imperial family that the emperor entrusted political power to a wise subordinate, who managed to re-establish order and a measure of prosperity, by mitigating sentences, strengthening the civil service, developing production, and 'encouraging the free airing of views and inviting able and virtuous scholars to discuss government affairs'.[28] In other words, a discussion which purports to be about real historical issues, and does indeed incorporate historical facts, contains a meaning and purpose which cannot be fully understood without reference to contemporary political events.

Real historical entities are hardly mentioned in recent contributions to a discussion of 'feudalism', one of which begins with the Ch'in and Han, but moves very quickly to the 'feudalistic fascism' of Lin Piao and the Gang of Four. Indeed, according to one author China still carries 'the burden of feudalism' partly for historical reasons, but partly also because of 'incorrect leadership after liberation'.[29]

Many other examples of historical parallelism being used as a source for moral and political instruction could be adduced, but it is now appropriate to consider the fourth feature of traditional, Chinese historiography, its propensity to view history in dynastic terms by way of its employment of the 'dynastic cycle'.

In recent historiography in this area there are similarities of form as well as of content. It is my argument that the former are more noteworthy, but the latter also deserve some attention. From the Marxist point of view it would seem that to employ dynasties as one's primary historical frame of reference would be to display excessive preoccupation with the mere 'superstructure' of history. Not only is it the case, however, that much history writing still incorporates a dynastic referent, but it is also apparent that in some popular examples the dynastic cycle is now presented in Marxist dress. This is manifest in the following conclusions regarding the reform of the early Ming:

Of course it was a bit of an exaggeration to say that 'the officials cherished the people' and 'the people led a happy life'. Yet it was true that the government was free from corruption to a large extent for more than a century during the early Ming Dynasty. Government machinery which was free from corruption was conducive to strengthening the rule, easing the class contradictions and maintaining social order. With the government machinery strengthened and the political situation stabilised, the policy of 'recuperation and rehabilitation' was implemented step by step and the national economy revived and prospered gradually.[30]

Similarly, it is said of the resurgence of China under the successors of Han Wu-ti that

As far as class nature was concerned, this resurgence meant strengthening the dictatorship of the landlord class. This was, of course, at variance with the basic interests of the peasants. However, looking at the problem from a historical point of view, under the conditions at that time, a stable, consolidated feudal government was an essential requirement for developing production. The struggle for production was the ultimate motive force for developing production. As a result of the resurgence during the reigns of [his successors] . . . the people were relieved of their sufferings, the government of the Han Dynasty was consolidated and production was promoted.[31]

In other words the early administrative achievements of the dynasty (in the examples, the Ming and the Han) advanced the productive forces, rather than being a product of the latter's development.

Considering now the similarities of form it could be argued against Levenson that the Marxist scheme of historical periodisation performs in modern Chinese popular history writing the same function as the dynastic cycle in the traditional scholarship since both tend to foreclose scientific analysis in favour of the discussion of data relating to individuals within a relatively fixed framework. This is no more apparent than in the reversal of verdicts on the comparative merits and demerits of Confucianism as compared to legalism. Mention has already been made of the avowed support of legalism by the Gang of Four, and so it is not at all surprising to find recent statements to the effect that legalism stifled intellectual inquiry, and that its policy of requiring the people to learn only from the officials was a retrograde step in education, in culture and in science. Nor are the various progressive features of Confucius and his ideology now discussed – his moral stance, his pedagogy, even his politics and philosophy[32] – to be understood solely in scholarly terms, though no doubt some writers to whom Confucian humanism is attractive are pleased to be able to say as much openly. In tthe old dynastic cyclethee founder of the dynasty was corrruupt. Moreover history wasperceived to be 'running down' over time, since later dynasties could never emulate the greatness of the Chou however much they sought to copy Chou institutions. In the Marxist scheme it may be that history is moving up (through a pre-ordained and inflexible sequence) rather than down, however, it is still the case that key figures at the beginning of an epoch are progressive, whilst those at their end are reactionary. It is no accident therefore that much ink has recently been spilt on the question of when slave society gave way to feudalism. Now it was Kuo Mo-jo's pronouncement on this question which placed Confucius in the ranks of the reactionaries in his attempting to restore and preserve the slave system.[33] The periodisation which is currently favoured puts the transition either long after or long before Confucius's time, that is with the Ch'in and early Han, or with the western Chou. Although a academic debate is now much less regulated than previously, some brave souls even arguing covertly for the applicability of the Asiatic mode of production to ancient or medieval China, it is evident that such reperiodisation renders it meaningless to speak of Confucius as a reactionary figure. Since he is no longer regarded as living at the close of an historical epoch, he cannot be cast as an incorrigible reactionary and defender of an order fast approaching extinction. Again, genuine scholarly interest may be a partial determinant of this work, but its principal thrust must be political in nature. Marxist periodisation, in other words, does provide a rigid framework strikingly akin to that of the dynastic perspective – no real research is necessary into the actual details of history beyond what is necessary in order to fit those details into the framework.

To conclude these remarks on recent popular historiography, then, it has been argued that though more scholarly voices have been raised for the writing of genuinely scientific history, such material as is produced which is given extensive media currency – what has been called here popular history – often conforms to a model of history writing which is both political in nature and closely akin, in form and to a significant extent in content, to what has been defined as 'traditional historiography'. It could be further argued that as there remain such continuities between past and present in this the sphere of ideology greater continuities may well persist in more practical areas, from the activity of the peasantry to the conduct of government. The character of contemporary popular historiography in China, far from supporting Levenson's thesis concerning the break between past and present in Chinese civilisation, may be seen, therefore, to uphold quite a different view.

It has been the argument of this paper that there is much evidence for the view that China has partaken of the post-1789 revolution of western ideology only in a severely circumscribed sense. Western revolutionary ideas have become significantly diluted in the Chinese context, or have failed to make headway against the powerful current of tradition. And the continuance of the past in the present has been recognised by no more unlikely a source than communist historiographers themselves. In the Ming and Ch'ing periods, though the Chinese bureaucracy was a complex and sophisticated organ of government it was ever-reliant upon the character of the emperor and his circle. Powerful eunuchs and court cliques, often of warring advisers or of the relatives of empresses or concubines, could and did paralyse the system the very sophistication of which required firm and consistent guidance from the top. It is striking therefore that those writing for the Chinese regime in the Hua era should themselves attribute its past calamities to the persistence of 'patriarchalism' and 'feudalism', as well as to the maleficence of 'eunuchs' and 'the empresses relatives' (phenomena well documented in Roxane Witke's book on the Maoist court[34]) obstructing the operation of an otherwise rationally organised administrative machine.

NOTES

1. D. C. Price, *Russia and the Roots of the Chinese Revolution, 1896–1911* (Cambridge; Harvard University Press, 1974), p. 91. Here Price refers to the memoirs of Feng Tzu-yu, a close associate of Sun's.

2. Kung-chuan Hsiao, *A Modern China and a New World: K'ang Yu-wei, Reformer and Utopian* (Seattle, University of Washington Press, 1975), pp. 41–96. M. Bernal, *Chinese Socialism to 1907* (Ithaca Cornell University Press, 1976), pp. 18 ff; F. Wakeman, *History and Will: Philosophical Perspectives on Mao Tse-tung's Thought* (Berkeley, University of California Press, 1973), chapter 8.

3. Bernal, *op. cit.*, pp. 22–3; but cf. Kung-chuan Hsiao, *op. cit.*, p. 503.

4. J. R. Levenson, *Confucian China and Its Modern Fate* (Berkeley, University of California Press, 1958–65), I, p. 104.

5. H. Z. Schiffrin, *Sun Yat-sen and the Origins of the Chinese Revolution* (Berkeley, University of California Press, 1968), p. 34ff.

6. M. Gaster, *Chinese Intellectuals and the Revolution of 1911* (Seattle, University of Washington Press, 1969), pp. 106ff; Li Yu-ing, *The Introduction of Socialism into China* (New York, Columbia University Press, 1971), pp. 35ff.

7. Levenson, *op. cit.*, III, p. 26; cf. his *Liang Ch'i-ch'ao and the Mind of Modern China* (Berkeley, University of California Press, 1959), p. 195.

8. Bernal, *op. cit.*, pp. 33ff.

9. R. A. Scalapino and H. schiffrin, 'Early Socialist Currents in the Chinese Revolutionary Movement', *Journal of Asian Studies*, 18 (1958–59), p. 333 n. 16.

10. M. Gasster, *op. cit.*, p. 147 n. 102, quotes the following assessment of the Chinese from George's *Life*:
[The Chinese are] utter heathens, treacherous, sensual, cowardly and

cruel. . . . Their moral standard is as low as their standard of comfort. . . .
No plan for making them tell the truth seems to be effective. . . . The
Chinese seem to be incapable of understanding our religion; but still
less are they capable of understanding our political institutions.

11. R. A. Scalapino and H. Schiffrin, *op. cit.*, pp. 324–6; M. Bernal, *op.
cit.*, pp. 68–9; Sun Yat-sen *San Min Chu I* (Taipei, China Publishing,
n.d.), p. 153.

12. Li Yu-ning, *op. cit.*, pp. 56–9.

13. Chow Tse-tung, *The May Fourth Movement* (Cambridge, Harvard
University Press, 1960); L. Bianco, *Origins of the Chinese Revolution,
1915–1949* (Stanford, Stanford University Press, 1971), chapter 2.

14. S. Schram, *The Political Thought of Mao Tse-tung*, revised edn.
(Harmondsworth, Penguin, 1969), pp. 26–7; Li Jui, *The Early Revol-
utionary Activities of Comrade Mao Tse-tung* (White Plains, M. E.
Sharpe, 1977), pp. 36–40.

15. E. Snow, *Red Star Over China* (London, Gollancz, 1937), pp. 148–50.

16. *Miscellany of Mao Tse-tung Thought* (Springfield, National Technical
Information Service, US Department of Commerce, 1974) part II, pp.
384–96, 397–402, 437–44, 451–5, 469–97. On the Chinese content in
Mao's Marxism, see V. Holubnychy, 'Mao Tse-tung's Materialistic
Dialectics', *China Quarterly* 19 (1964), pp. 3–37.

17. Levenson, *Confucian China*, II, pp. 121ff; I, pp. 104ff; III, pp. 16ff.

18. Kwang-ching Liu, 'World View and Peasant Rebellion: Reflections on
Post-Mao Historiography', *Journal of Asian Studies*, XL (1981), pp.
295–326.

19. R. M. Hartwell, 'Historical Analogism, Public Policy, and Social Science
and Eleventh & Twelfth-Century China', *American Historical Review*,
76 (1971–2), pp. 690–96; E. Balazs, *Chinese Civilization and Bureaucracy*
(New Haven, Yale University Press, 1964), p. 129. On Chinese history
writing, see also C. S. Gardner, *Chinese Traditional Historiography*
(Cambridge, Harvard University Press, 1938); and E. G. Beasley and
E. G. Pulleybank (eds.), Historians of China and Japan (London,
Oxford University Press, 1961).20. Editorial Department, Li-shi yen-
chiu, 'The Vicissitudes of Li-shi yen-chiu and the Plot of the Gang of
Four to use History in Opposing the Party', Li-shi yen-chiu, no. 6 (20
December 1976), Chinese Studies in History, XII (1978–9) no. 2, pp.
49–59. cf. Lin Kanquan, 'On History used for Insinuation to Serve the
Gang', *Hung ch'i*, No. 1 (January 1978): *Joint Publication Research
Series*, 70738 (7 March 1978), pp. 115–26. There are numerous other
examples of this genre.

21. Duan Jingzian, *Guangming ribao* (17 June 1980): *SWB*, FE/6466/B11/
1–4; Pang Paio, *Renmin ribao* (29 January 1980): *SWB*, FE/6349/B11/12.

22. Xinhua–Chinese (5 June 1980), *SWB*, FE/6445/B11/3–5.

23. Wu Weihua, *Guangming ribao* (24 June 1980): *SWB*, FE/6460/B11/11–13; Liu Shuxun, *Guanming ribao* (12 Mar 1980): *SWB*, FE/6413/B11/10–12.

24. Wu Zhao, *Beijing wanbao* (11 September 1980): *SWB*, FE/6542/B11/8; cf. H. Wilhelm 'From Myth to Myth; the Case of Yueh Fei's Biography', in A. F. Wright (ed.), *Confucianism and Chinese Civilization* (Stanford, Stanford University Press, 1975).

25. Shi Yang, *Renmin ribao* (29 July 1980): *SWB*, FE/6487/B11/1–3; Li Shaojun, *Guangming ribao* (5 August, 1980): *SWB*, FE/6500/B11/1–3.

26. Chen Wutong, *Guangming ribao* (16 October 1979): *SWB*, FE/6270/B11/1–6.

27. Ji Gang, *Beijing wanbao* (1 October 1980): *SWB*, FE/6546/B11/1–2; Ji Gang, *Beijing wanbao* (28 August 1980): *SWB*, FE/6539/B11/8–9 (on Ch'ien-lung).

28. Zhang Dake, *Guangming ribao* (2 October 1979): *SWB*, FE/6256/B11/8–14.

29. Zhou Jizhi, *Renmin ribao* (11 July 1980): *SWB*, FE/6480/B11/3–7; Xinhua–Chinese (28 August 1980): *SWB*, FE/6514/B11/1–2.

30. Chen Wutong, *Guangming ribao* (13 November 1979): *SWB*, FE/6270/B11/5.

31. Zhang Dake, *Guangming ribao* (2 October 1979): *SWB*, FE/6256/B11/14.

32. Liu Shuxun, *Guangming ribao* (12 March 1980): *SWB*, FE/6413/B11/10–12; Li Zehou 'A Re-evaluation of Confucius', *Social Sciences in China*, ɪ, no. 2 (June 1980), pp. 99–127.

33. Kuo Mo-jo 'The Question of Dividing Ancient Chinese History into Stages, *Hung ch'i*, no. 7 (January 1972): *Survey of China Mainland Magazines* 73, no. 8 (August, 1972), pp. 70–8.

34. Roxane Witke, *Comrade Chiang Ch'ing* (London, Wiedenfeld & Nicolson, 1977).

IV

REVOLUTION
IN THE
THIRD WORLD

8 Latin America: Laboratory of Revolution

PETER CALVERT

In general, the world press notices only three sorts of events in Latin America. In alphabetical order, they are: earthquakes, hurricanes and military *coups*. Often these military *coups* are referred as 'revolutions', if only for the good and sufficient reason that that is what their promoters want to call them. Sometimes, as in Peru in 1968, we would call them revolutions too. More often, we would regard them as revolutionary incidents without accompanying revolutions;[1] and frequently such incidents are avowedly counter-revolutionary in nature. Even as such, though, they form part of the great revolutionary theme that runs through the history of the national period in Latin America.

This tradition has in several instances given rise to genuine social revolutions; 1979 was the twentieth anniversary of one of them, the Cuban Revolution. It also happened to be a very interesting year for revolutionary events in Latin America, beginning with a civil war in the Central American state of Nicaragua, which attracted considerable foreign support from Panama and Costa Rica, and reaching a climax on 17 July with the flight into exile of General Anastasio Somoza, the third member of his family to have held power in a dynastic succession unique in Latin America. His last act was to try to hand over the shreds of his power to a stand-in, interim president, Dr Francisco Urcuyo, but he, after boldly calling on the victorious forces of the Sandinista National Liberation Front (FSLN) to surrender, found it more prudent to follow his former leader into exile the following day. A five-member interim government, already formed in exile by the FSLN, then assumed power, and set about the task of national reconstruction.[2]

Three months later, the autocratic military ruler of El Salvador, General Humberto Romero, was eased out of power on 16 October in a brief military *coup* led by two colonels, one the commandant of the army cadet school, and the other the officer in charge of the military arsenal. The deposed President had imposed a state of siege in May following rising dissent clumsily met by the army by repressive measures which resulted in, among other incidents, the death of at least eighteen persons shot on the steps of the Cathedral in San Salvador.[3] The new government, after a brief honeymoon period, is now confronting renewed insurgency on a wide scale, and apears to offer little or nothing in the way of reform.

Lastly, on 1 November, a military revolt in Bolivia proclaimed the overthrow of the government of the interim President, Walter Guevara Arze. The President, who had been appointed by Congress early in August as a compromise candidate when the congressional majority refused to sanction the ratification of the election of a civilian, opposition candidate, escaped into hiding, and the troops of General Alberto Natusch Busch, the former head of the Bolivian military college, who had gained control of the principal government buildings, met with determined opposition from loyal troops and civilian demonstrators. They fired on the crowds, and even dive-bombed them from the air, but were unable to break their resistance, while other Latin American states and the United States joined the condemning the action. Eventually, fifteen days after the first abortive *coup*, General Natusch yielded his claim to Congress on condition that the President resigned, and Congress thereupon nominated Sra Lidia Gueiler, President of the Chamber of Deputies, as his successor.[4]

As these incidents bear witness, there are certainly revolutionary forces at work in Latin America, and the events in Nicaragua, especially, taken in conjunction with the contemporary changes of government in the small Caribbean islands of Grenada[5] and Dominica, do indeed demonstrate that they can succeed in obtaining political power for movements seeking a considerable degree of radical social change. But the task of the revolutionaries has certainly not been an easy one, and the violence which in El Salvador and Bolivia has punctuated the political process illustrates that the traditional bases of Latin American politics are very much intact.

Twenty-four years after the first landing of Fidel Castro and his men in Cuba, that country stands out as the only one in the Americas with a communist government – a government which, moreover, claims to be non-aligned, and owes its continuous survival to massive

Russian aid and the acceptance of its existence by the United States. Most of the other governments on the continent have a rather right-wing complexion, though this in itself does not necessarily mean they are not revolutionary. And it appears that, the case of Peru apart, the institution of the military *coup*, far from promoting revolutionary change, acts most effectively as a brake upon it, as in the case of Bolivia and the even more famous case of Chile.[6]

Where widespread social change has occurred, moreover, it has more often than not proceeded incrementally. Nowhere is this more obvious than in the four countries which most readily spring to mind as seats of social revolution – Mexico, Bolivia, Peru and Cuba herself – where change has followed the violent assumption of power, certainly, but it has not itself always been accompanied by violence. The Cubans would say, and have said, that the reason why social revolution has not been more common is the relentless hostility of the repressive force of the United States. Except in the case of a small island like Cuba, only ninety miles off the Florida coast, this is not an explanation which is really very convincing. There is no country in South America on which the armed forces, even of a super-power such as the United States, could act in any effective way, and while in no way seeking to minimise the possible role of the Nixon administration in encouraging the deposition of Allende in Chile, there is a clear lesson from the events of 1924–32 that the Chilean armed forced might resort to force as and when they felt their vital interests threatened.

Nevertheless, the Latin American experience has been very significant in the world history of revolution, and I am going to suggest that it is because Latin America has indeed acted as a laboratory of revolution to the world. Furthermore, I am inclined to regard what has gone on there, and what is going on there, as precisely what one would expect to find in a laboratory. Those of us who are not scientists tend to associate laboratories with brilliant discoveries, remarkable inventions, astonishing feats of ingenuity, dedicated teams of hard-working researchers dedicated to the truth. These things may well all be true. But we do not remember so easily the dry runs, the false starts, the mistakes, the explosions and, above all, repeated failures such as are the lot of the real, workaday scientist. In revolution, as in the history of scientific exploration, we shall find repeatedly that the historical accounts tend to show a higher degree of consistency of approach and depth of forethought than was in fact the case.

Turning to the historical record, therefore, we confront our first problem: where to begin? It is perhaps natural to begin with independence, but it would be a mistake. Leaders of newly-independent countries, then as now, tend to minimise the achievements of their colonial predecessors, especially where, as in the trade of government, they have most surely learnt from them. We know that the history of the national period (since 1810) shows large countries dominated by single individuals with the aid of very small armies. But the striking thing about the Latin Americans' wars of independence is surely how far they resemble the pattern of the conquest of Spain, some three centuries earlier.

If Cortes could capture control of Mexico with a mere 300 men, and Pizarro break the power of the Incas at Cajamarca in Peru in a single battle, a bold surprise attack on the centre of political authority which has been accurately described by one historian as 'a palace revolution',[7] we need scarcely be surprised that it was in the same sort of way that men sought to liberate the conquered territories at the beginning of the nineteenth century. Power once gained could so easily be lost in the same way. It did not take three centuries for the lesson to be learnt – Pizarro himself was assassinated in a palace revolution at Cuzco in 1535, three years before Gonzalo Jimémez de Quesada had achieved the unparalleled, but little known, feat of reaching and founding Bogota in Colombia with the support of only six men. It is the example of Mexica and Peru, with their fabulous wealth, of which all the world heard, which has remained, and with it the lesson of how few men are needed to overthrow great empires. Philip II of Spain for one was under no illusions as to the relevance of the lesson. When Viceroy Franciso de Toledo had the heir to the Inca throne beheaded in 1571, he was reportedly rebuked by his sovereign in the words 'You were sent to Peru to serve kings, not to kill them'.[8]

Nor was the conquest itself merely a change of government, even if at first no doubt it was easily accepted as such by ordinary people. It is true that it took decades – and in some places centuries – for it to bring a substantial change in the condition of individual peasant communities. But the sum total of social change was truly revolutionary and, moreover, dramatically successful.

Today, in Spanish America the vast majority of the population speak Spanish, and in Brazil Portuguese. Indian languages do survive, certainly, and are indeed numerous; there are over 300

Indian languages still spoken in Mexico alone. But with few exceptions they are encapsulated in village communities, isolated from
the mainstream of the community. The dominant culture is Iberian,
so much so that in only one country, Paraguay (the last to be
conquered and the first to become independent) has an Indian
language retained official status into the national period. In June
1975, Peru followed this example by giving official status to
Quechua; and Ecuador too has since followed suit.[9] Elsewhere
Spanish remains supreme.

With the language has come the religion of the conquerors: 95 per
cent of the population of Latin America regard themselves as
Roman Catholic. In Mexico, where there have been years of diligent
persecution of the Church by nineteenth-century liberals and their
socialist successors, the last census recorded 98.8 per cent.[10] And
the customs of the conquerors dominate too, and with them the
international styles of building, eating, working and finding recre-
ation. These things are the evolving product of the conquest, and
there is now no aspect of daily life in the Americas that is not
touched by it in some degree.

In fact, the importance of the Iberian culture is most clearly
shown in the crucial fact that *in toto* it serves to confer high social
status.[11] It is only very recently, and among a few intellectuals, that
the cult of the Indian heritage has assumed the proportions of a
major political force, partly for its own sake, partly because it offers
in identifiable alternative to what many see as the relentless tide of
Americanisation and 'cocacolinisation'.

If the conquest contributed unity to Latin America, independence
has accentuated diversity. The debt of the makers of independence,
and particularly of the greatest of them, to the intellectual contribution of the American and French Revolutions is obvious. The
individual states exist as the product of the first great modern wave
of decolonisation and as an example to later ones. Only Santo
Domingo went back to Spanish rule voluntarily – and then only for a
brief period, – to avoid what seemed to them the far worse alternative
of rule from Haiti.[12] Peninsular-born Spaniards were displaced
from their position as the ruling class throughout Latin America, at
first by the descendants of Spaniards living in the New World, but
very soon by individuals, and groups of mixed Indian or African
racial stocks.

Conspicuous among the attributes of the new states were such plainly classical and European features as republican government, executive power in the hands of a chief magistrate, an elected citizen assembly, and a standing army with national military service. Thereafter diversity set in. Mexico experimented with monarchy, as did Haiti. Uruguay has tried a plural executive, and mistakenly got rid of it again. More recently still Costa Rica has dared to abolish the army.[13] The tendency to diversify, however, set in as soon as it was realised that central authority had already been broken, and that, consequently, there were no logical limitations to the disintegration of the empire; from viceroyalties to kingdoms; from captaincies general or presidencies to provinces, even to districts. What had been one empire became a collection of separate states which varied greatly in size. The importance of this can be exaggerated though: Guatemala is bigger than Portugal, Nicaragua is about the same size as Greece. In other historical circumstances either might have become the seat of a great empire, and, indeed, Guatemala had done so before the Spaniards came, as the Maya ruins bear witness. But they did not do so in modern times, and neither did any of the Spanish-speaking states, in dramatic contrast to the survival of state and empire in Brazil.

Instead, they began to emphasise not what they had in common, but what made them different. New flags, new currencies, new armies, new ceremonials, new anthems – the trappings of nationhood spread inexorably. The rivalry, in the main, occurred in a friendly enough spirit, as between members of the family; but even families may quarrel, and it was done nevertheless; and to this day attempts at reunification characteristically take the existing state structures and boundaries as given, and seek only to transcend them by means of instruments of international co-operation such as the Central American Common Market, LAFTA, the Andean Pact, the United Nations, ECLA, the OAS and the Latin American Economic System.

In this way arose that curious paradox that these states, which have so often been under military rule, have in fact made very little use of their military forces for the purpose for which they were primarily intended – the defence from foreign attack. In the early years, armies had become important because of the fear of reconquest. Spain tried to reconquer Mexico and Peru, took advantage of the American Civil War to reannex the Dominican Republic, and fought for years to keep Cuba.[14] But, in general, the fear of reconquest passed with the collapse of the Spanish monarchy in 1868. Since the end of the period dominated by that fear, there have only been three major wars between the principal Latin American states; and only one of these, the Chaco War (1929–35), has taken place in the twentieth century.

Instead, the military forces have found an alternative role. They had to find an alternative role to justify their existence, and to do this they have gone into politics. They have developed that role of guardians of the Constitution which they assumed in the early days of independence. They have become the political agents of the ruling class of the day, the most important single centre for the socialisation of youth, and the major reservoir of technological and administrative expertise on which governments can draw. In short, they have been able to combine the defence of their own interests with what is, in many ways, a privileged position with the state: the advantages of being at one and the same time the voice of the people and those who listen to it.[15]

This complex role of the military, which in the past was distinctive of Latin American, has made for a strong centre to nationalism, and it is nationalism which has been the most dramatic contribution of Latin America to nineteenth-century thought. By the end of that century the Latin American states constituted the largest single group of independent states which formed no part of one or other of the great empires. And, unlike those states which achieved independence at the same time, in the Balkans, Serbia and Greece, or which later were to be consolidated out of smaller units (e.g. Italy and Germany), they did not (with the exceptions already noted) adopt a monarchy, the then almost universal system of government which was then at the height of its political success. With the only major exception of Brazil, they chose instead the republican form of government, becoming thus the first group of states fully to work out the republican and the dictatorial implications of the French Revolution. This must surely be their most significant contribution, and the most revolutionary one, and it was one to which they were to return. From the emergence of the Second Republic in France in 1849 and the adoption for it of a presidential form of government, we can trace down to our own time the development in modern form of the republicanism which has become almost universal in the twentieth century, and with it, of presidential government. The sweeping away of the great traditional monarchies of China, Turkey,

Russia, Germany and Austro-Hungary in the early years of this century followed naturally from the demonstration they gave that republicanism would work, and in one sense the fall of the monarchy in Brazil in 1889 is, in global terms, the first of that sequence.

When we turn to the Liberal revolutions of the later nineteenth century we have a much less clear picture. In one respect these movements looked back to events that had occurred in Europe as much as 300 years earlier. The liberal movements arose essentially out of a parallel revolt against centralisation and authoritarian government such as had been known under the empire. They came about, however, in a state of affairs that was very different. Central government, with acknowledged authority, had already disappeared. Their clamour for decentralisation, therefore, met with very little resistance, and in certain cases it resulted in schisms within states becoming so pronounced that a return to authoritarian government followed as an almost inevitable consequence, as in Mexico, Colombia and Venezuela and in Guatemala, among others.

The fight against centralisation, however, above all took the form of an ideological struggle against the prime obstacle to change in their eyes, namely the ascendancy of the Church. The degree of their onslaught on the Church depended largely on personalities; hence its depth and degree of effectiveness varied very dramatically from one state to another. In some, such as Ecuador and Paraguay, its effects were hardly felt; in Mexico and Brazil it toppled two empires, and enthroned the secular ideology of positivism in state policy. The consequences of the defeat of the Church as an alternative centre of power and authority were numerous. To begin with there was the effect on the Church itself; one which tended to stifle in Latin America that recognition of the need for change which was felt in Europe. The defeat of the Church also meant in material terms the subordination to the state of the most powerful corporation it contained, one which down to that time, too, had played a major role in the economic system by lending money to those who needed it.[16] Its defeat, therefore, meant the subordination of all other corporations. Economic development, conceived as it was in *étatist* terms, thereafter languished, except where governments gave concessions to foreign or native entrepreneurs. In retrospect, it seems as if the political search for concessions came sometimes to consume more energy than that which would have been required for actual production. And the liberal victories in Latin America did, it seems, act as an example to some Europeans interested in bridling the power of the Church at home. Otherwise how did it happen that Benito Mussolini's father named his son after the hero of Mexican liberalism? From the War of the Reform to the Vatican Concordat of 1929 there are winding roads indeed!

It is an interesting paradox that the liberals, who made the state so powerful, were heirs also to nineteenth-century economic liberalism, which resolved that it should be weak. Hence when they laid the foundations for modern industrialisation they did so in a piecemeal and haphazard manner. But more important was the fact that they established a new relationship with the outside world by bringing in foreign capital to help them, in the first instance, substitute for imported products which were in special demand. In sum, therefore, they set about the planned modernisation of their countries. And it was a modernisation which did not take place easily, as in Europe, by natural transmission across national boundaries, but by the deliberate implantation into developing countries of the technology, money and brains from the developed world necessary for the creation of harbours, ports, railroads, canals, telegraphs, electricity stations, paper mills, textile factories, and so on.

It is fashionable now to deprecate the achievements that were made. But it must be said that in the circumstances of the time, and given the difficulties of geography, resources and the limitations of economic thought, what they succeeded in achieving was of very considerable importance. At independence, for example, only a mule-track joined the capital of Ecuador to its second city. The construction of communications towards the end of the nineteenth century brought about a dramatic increase in the power potential of the state, and with it new responsibilities for the economic and social life of the nation. Indeed, it created the nations to go with the sense of nationalism that already existed.

Recently, the further criticism has been made, more subtly, that these achievements, however considerable, were in fact detrimental, because they were the wrong ones. Latin America, these critics say, suffers in the twentieth century not so much from underdevelopment as from distorted and hence harmful development which hampers the true realisation of the natural productive forces. Development was primarily oriented towards extractive industries and the export market, whether the production took the form of sugar in Cuba, coffee in Brazil, bananas in Honduras, petroleum in Venezuela, or meat in Argentina and Uruguay.[17] It will be many years before the debate over the question of the responsibility of European capital for the development of the nineteenth century produces a resolution of the question of how far economies and political systems were actually subordinate, or how far they created their own problems. Human nature being what it is, it is unlikely it will ever be solved. For those who are most urgent in their criticisms, almost all fail to recognise that just as the Latin Americans themselves were not, so too the states of Europe then were not the states of today. The introduction of capital by private enterprise into Latin America in the nineteenth century did not necessarily bring with it a corresponding interest, or degree of control by, the European states, simply because those states were not interested in that kind of political control in that part of the world, (with some rather minor and specific exceptions, notably the Falkland Islands (1833)).

We must also consider what a desirable degree of development might have been. It can be reasonably argued, and in the last decade there have appeared many who implicitly support such a view, that the development of western Europe and the United States has in fact gone to pathological lengths. What hope would there have been for the twentieth century, still less the twenty-first, if all nations in the last century had industrialised as they are now determined to do? Some of the greatest dangers to the world, for example, pollution and radioactive contamination, come not from the underdevelopment of the poorer nations, but from the overdevelopment of the richer ones. And in the last decade the Caribbean area has begun to suffer from an increasing food crisis, from which neither Mexico nor Cuba is exempt; and it is becoming easier to see what dangers lie in wait for any nation which, like Britain, comes to rely overwhelmingly on its industrial production and hence relies on imports for supplies of foodstuffs. The Latin American states certainly have not got themselves into such a dangerous position; their problems still stem in the main from underutilisation of land, and a maldistribution of population for which, unfortunately, geography itself is at least partly to blame. Hence they can exhibit peasant poverty on the outskirts of cities suffering under an umbrella of smog, and racked by the sound of grinding car gears.

Indeed, Latin America contributed at this period to the social history of Europe in two ways: by taking a substantial proportion of the population of southern Europe who chose to emigrate to the New World, and hence acting as a safety valve for those states; and, by extension, giving an example to the European populations of more spacious life on the other side of the Atlantic which their children might hope to emulate at home. (It is a purely Anglocentric view to think that the United States fulfilled this role for the whole of human kind, important as it undoubtedly was.) For over a century, immigration to Argentina as a proportion to population, ran at over three times the rate to that of the United States.[18]

When, in 1900, the Uruguayan writer José Enrique Rodó published his *Ariel* there were many in Latin America who agreed with his contention that Latin America not only could not, but ought not try to compete with the material values of Europe or the United States. Instead, it should seek to promote spiritual values; what we now would call a better life-style.[19] Clearly this contribution has not reached the rest of the world, at least in the way and to the extent that its author might have hoped. But of its impact on hispanic literature down to our own time there can be no doubt. It is after all a secular version of an old Spanish theme. And it is closely related to the present yearning of many Latin American intellectuals for a form of socialist humanism, morally rather than economically superior. A more legalistic theme was the attempt of the intellectuals in smaller powers, and some of the bigger ones (notably Argentina) to develop a system of international law in which they could be free from the material pressures of the powerful nations.[20] In this more concrete way the Latin Americans made a major contribution to the development of those very organs of international co-operation which in the twentieth century have served to restrain a few of the excesses both of international and internal war. Learning their lesson from the bad example one or two of their number gave to the League of Nations by withdrawing from it, they formed the largest single bloc at the founding of the United Nations, have given it nearly consistent and unanimous support, and to this day wield an influence within it out of proportion to their numbers.[21]

With the advantages of hindsight, however, we can see that the practical impact of intellectual ideas in this period did not match up to its theoretical importance for two reasons, both of which have a continuing relevance to our own time. First is the fact that, although intellectuals talked of revolution, it was military officers who actually practised it, and these men were not then generally as well versed in the practicalities of government as they liked to think. This began to change in the middle of the nineteenth century with the foundation of local military academies. In the twentieth century, a completely different dimension has been added to this system by the foundation for military officers of staff schools which give them both a coherence and an ideological basis which their predecessors lacked.[22] This was but one aspect, in turn, of the general systematisation and expansion of government which gave governments as well as oppositions the chance to learn, as it were, from historical experience. This was of some value to them if only to teach them why the time had come to resign.

But, secondly, although governments acquired the capacity to learn, at the same time neither they, nor the revolutionaries, were immune from the tendency to forget. An interesting example here is the case of Uruguay. Very turbulent and politically unstable in the nineteenth century, it was ruled in the first years of the new century by José Batlle y Ordoñez, who gave it the foundation of a welfare state and constitutional stability, and began a peaceful succession of power and authority which, until two years ago, had been interrupted only briefly in the mid-1930s at the height of the great depression. In time, the new stability of Uruguay came to be associated so overwhelmingly with the intellectual contribution of Batlle that it was generally forgotten on what his power originally had rested, namely, at the beginning of his first term in office, his military defeat of the Nationalist opposition at the Battle of Masoller on 1 September 1904. Batlle himself did not forget. When running for his second term of office in 1911, he took care to pre-empt the opposition's chances of revolt by improving the army's conditions, giving them wireless equipment to maintain communications, and last but not least, corralling the horses and thus depriving them of their basic means of transport.[23]

Scientific certainty among governments, then, bred practical complacency. Confident in the inevitability of progress, they neglected the foundations of power within their societies.

Then, in the twentieth century, came the great social revolutions. They began in Latin America with Mexico (1910), nearly contemporaneous with the fall of the monarchy in Portugal and China, and some seven years before the October Revolution in Russia. The significance of the Mexican Revolution was not just that it was a large-scale conflict, though in fact it was one of the worst ever known in terms of casualities. It was seen in the way that it prefigured other themes of the twentieth century.[24] The Mexicans demonstrated to the rest of the world what could be done to bring good out of the consequences of struggle; to create a state in which both peasants and workers, and, as individuals, the new middle class, could coexist without subordinating one to the other. In particular the peasants benefited, if not as much as they wished or deserved, without losing out to the workers, and not because the workers got nothing. Remembering that the Mexican Revolution began before there was a substantial population of urban workers (and those principally in mining) it is easy to see how easily the Constitution of 1917 could grant them social benefits far in excess of those then available anywhere else.[25]

Secondly, for a brief period, Mexico was again to become the focus of anti-religious feeling, and as such inspired a controversy which was, in the event, to be swallowed up in and contribute powerfully to the outcome of the Spanish Civil War, where the Mexicans became the only power to offer and give support to the Republican side from a Spanish-speaking country, and in return to receive many of its exiles. In turn it is interesting to note that Alberto Bayo, who gained his military training in Spain, trained the followers of Castro in the Sierra before 1959.[26]

Thirdly, it provided a distinctive contribution to the formulation of what is now recognisable as a distinctive Third World position: independence from the great powers without at the same time interference with its neighbours. And it is this third aspect that is of particular interest when we consider the nature of the tool by which in the end it was to begin to lever itself free. In a word it was nationalistion, the economic concomitant of nationalism.

In fact, in 1938 Mexico was just slightly behind Bolivia in becoming the first non-communist state to use nationalisation in a frontal attack on the foreign interests represented by the petroleum corporations. The Bolivians enjoyed the considerable advantages of being remote and land-locked; their poverty, resulting from the scarcity of land which nature had given them, prevented their revolutionary course from becoming a great encompassing movement such as the Mexican. On the other hand, it did not kill very many people, a thing of prime importance to those who were not killed. Instead, revolutionary pressures in the unstable Bolivian political climate led to a sequence of military *coups* from Left and

Right, so that the only substantial degree of coherence given it by a single set of rulers was that imposed by the revolutionary government which seized power in 1952.[27]

Its particular interest lies in its relationship to the third example of social revolution, Cuba, for it was, after all, in Bolivia that the example of the Cuban Revolution, as exemplified by the belief of Che Guevara that a small group could trigger off a continental revolution if applied in the right way, met with a decisive check.[28] Guevara had forgotten that as early as 1952, under cold war conditions, the Bolivian Revolution, partly because of its restricted geographical nature no doubt, but also for idealistic reasons, had received not just the tolerance but the support of the United States. He had not realised that the Bolivian population of the area he chose would identify with their government and army rather than with him and his men; not only had they learnt the wrong language for the area in which they chose to operate, but his Cuban men seemed like bearded descendants of the aristocratic Spanish *conquistadores* in the eyes of the Guarani peasantry. Most seriously, he ignored his own rule, clearly stated in his book *Guerrilla Warfare*, that as long as any other possibility of social change by democratic election existed, armed revolution could not hope to succeed.[29]

Whether or not one thinks that the best future for Latin America can really be to turn it into the scene of 'one-two-three-many Vietnams', and on reflections it seems hard to imagine anything worse, even allowing for rhetorical inappropriateness in the figure of speech,[30] there can be no doubting the very real importance of the Cuban Revolution itself. Born in one of the most advanced countries in Latin America, as measured by any of the usual economic indicators in 1959, and carried to fruition with a distinctive style and individual panache and vivacity with much appeal to aspiring Third World countries, the Cuban Revolution has certainly been popular, at home and abroad, in most of the senses of that world. Not only have the Cubans appealed to the Third World of the non-aligned states, they have even, partly through the force of circumstances of their economic dependence on a Soviet Union which has been slow to realise the value of their appeal to very different traditions, been able to offer a third way within the socialist bloc more attractive than affiliation with any of the two great super-powers of China and the USSR. The use of Cuban troops in Angola highlights their absence of racial identification overseas, their freedom of commitment, and above all their relative smallness as a state. No one can seriously be afraid of conquest by Cuba, and so their most evident weakness has been turned into a position of strength.

Furthermore the Cuban message, reiterated in many languages, is basically a very simple one – that revolution works. They claim that in a small country such as Cuba it is possible to make use of one's own resources, to better one's own people, if not to become a great power in the traditional sense, and to offer a fuller life not in the remote future, but at once.[31] The Cubans came to this theme rather later than they might, after their flirtation with the traditional socialist goal of heavy industrialisation, and they do not emphasise just how much anything more than this simple goal, such as the strategic role as a block to the hegemony of the United States in the Caribbean, depends not on their own resources, but on a unique deployment of economic resources and military assistance from overseas.[32] Such a deployment, as the United States has already demonstrated, is extremely costly even for super-powers, and it would not take very many Cubas to overstrain the resources of the Soviet Union itself. However, only very small amounts of aid could do much in a small Caribbean state such as Jamaica or Grenada.

Since the Cuban Revolution no one has successfully followed their example in Latin America by achieving power through the countryside by popular organisation, in so far as they did do that. In Brazil, in 1964, there began a period of military rule which has undeniably been accompanied by social transformation, only its antecedents are of the Right and not of the Left, and its policies unbendingly pragmatic in the Brazilian positivist tradition.[33] In 1968, the Peruvian military seized power, and until 1980 pursued a left-wing but consistently Third World policy summed up by former President Velasco Alvarado in the phrase: 'Capitalism has failed and communism will not work'.[34] The government of President Allende in Chile, which came to power by election in 1970 in a narrow margin in a three-cornered contest, proceeded to implement an avowedly socialist revolutionary policy, but after a period of increasingly tense polarisation succumbed to a military *coup* in September 1973.[35] And in Nicaragua the greed of the regime had alienated every section of the population except the well-paid National Guard, and it was the withdrawal of support in the urban areas that brought it down.[36] If there is any one factual lesson from all these examples it is that the military remain the most effective political institution in Latin America.

Meanwhile, time is running short in the race for economic development, and Latin America is lagging behind. Indeed, according to some practitioners of the dismal science, no country that has not industrialised already will ever be able to catch up – except China, which for some odd reason they regard as the exception to their own rule. The argument put forward by Gunnar Myrdal and others, and widely accepted, is that in Asia wide ranging social reform can only be brought about through revolution, for in this way only can redistribution of available resources be achieved. The experience of Latin America suggests that this is not necessarily so. There, revolutionary aspirations have constantly acted to strengthen dictatorial governments, and such economic progress as has resulted from political stability has been concentrated in few hands. Cuba is an exception in view of its unique features – its small size and the proximity of the United States as a useful enemy. These have acted together to give it, not just a revolution but a government with broad support – precisely what so many other states lack. It is a government, moreover, which can count on the army, for Raul Castro, the Second Secretary of the Cuban Communist Party, is Minister for the Revolutionary Armed Forces. What both the Cubans and the Mexicans, to say nothing of the Peruvians, mean by revolution, then, is government; orderly government, responsive to popular needs, prepared to strike a balance between the overall needs of national production and the desire to distribute the resulting wealth as equitably as possible. And above all, government unhampered from outside.

What is striking about all Latin American revolutionary programmes, both Left and Right, moreover, is the extent to which they do *not* reject the heritage of the French Revolution. Theirs is a world still dominated by the concept of the state. It is the community of states – whether universal, progressive, or non-aligned – to which, consciously or unconsciously, their leaders give their acceptance. Secondly, far from rejecting the concept of the law as fixed, universal and absolute, radical as well as traditional thinkers have sought to generalise their national experiences in the realm of international law and public affairs. Revolutionary tribunals and revolutionary justice have in Cuba as well as elsewhere given way as the focus of the state system to competitively elected assemblies, party apparatus, and a hierarchically-ordered army with strong and increasing involvement in the political process. Hence though recent radical movements stress the origin of power as their basis of legitimacy, they denounce the way in which it is being used as the criterion of their opponents' illegitimacy.

The lesson of twentieth-century Latin American revolutions to the outside world has been both loud and unambiguous. It is the lesson of the emergence of the Third World, and it is in this sense that it has been received by countries of all political persuasions outside the western hemisphere. It is that these countries can succeed by making use of their own resources, and be successful precisely in proportion to their degree of independence from outside control or influence. If they are large, like Brazil, Mexico or Peru, they may hope to control outside forces, if restricted in influence, and these countries have done just that by the very economic codes of conduct in which the commanding heights of their economies are reserved for state enterprise. If they are small, however, their best, indeed their only hope, lies in association with other small nations for the common maintenance of peace. Lastly, there are other values in the world besides material success, and indeed, in the last quarter of the twentieth century, it may not make much sense to pursue material values at all. Political philosophies are creatures of fashion, and it is not necessary to apply any of them in a manner which is boring, rigid and unimaginative. Because they are expressed in European words they are not necessarily understood within European meanings, and the way in which they are presented lends much to their appeal. Not only have the great powers in the past been guilty of competing primarily in short-term economic inducements, their thinkers as well as politicians have too often said: 'This is how it has to be done; it cannot be done any other way.' With the experience gained from their role as the first new nations of the nineteenth century, the nations, and more particularly individual citizens of Latin America, may in this way continue to hold surprises for us in the twenty-first.

NOTES

1. See Peter Calvert, *A Study of Revolution* (Oxford, Clarendon Press, 1970), p. 4.
2. *The Guardian*, 17–25 July 1979.

3. *The Guardian*, 17 October 1979.
4. *The Daily Telegraph*, 2 November 1979; *The Times* 19 November 1979.
5. *The Guardian*, 14 and 16 March 1979.
6. As argued by inter alia Gary MacEoin, *Chile, the struggle for dignity* (London, Coventure, 1975); and Ian Roxborough, Phil O'Brien and Jackie Roddick, *Chile, the State and Revolution* (London, Macmillan, 1977).
7. Donald M. Dozer, *Latin America, an Interpretative History* (New York, McGraw Hill, 1962), p. 64.
8. Ibid., p. 107.
9. *Prensa Latina* bulletin no. 507.
10. The figures given were 46.38 million Catholics of a total population of 48.23 million. *Statesman's Year Book*, 1979–80, p. 853.
11. William S. Stokes, *Latin American Politics* (New York, Thomas T. Crowell, 1959), pp. 21–2.
12. Dozer, *op. cit.*, p. 343.
13. Charles D. Ameringer, *Don Pepe, A Political Biography of José Figures of Costa Rica* (Albuquerque, University of New Mexico Press, 1978), p. 75.
14. Dozer, *op. cit.*, pp. 343–4.
15. See Peter Calvert, 'The coup, a critical re-statement', *Third World Quarterly*, I, no. 4 (October 1979).
16. M. P. Costeloe, *Church Wealth in Mexico* (Cambridge, Cambridge University Press, 1967), pp. 27–8.
17. André Gunder Frank, *Capitalism & Underdevelopment in Latin America* (Harmondsworth, Penguin, 1969).
18. C. J. Arthur and P. Whitaker, *Argentina* (Englewood NJ, Prentice Hall, 1964), pp. 53–9.
19. José Enrique Rodó, *Ariel* trans. G. Brotherston (Cambridge, Cambridge University Press, 1967).
20. Ibid., pp. 169, 172.
21. Peter Calvert, *Latin America, Internal conflict and International Peace*, (London, Macmillan 1969), p. 108.
22. Alfred Stepan, *The Military and Politics, changing politics in Brazil* (Princeton NJ, Princeton University Press, 1971), pp. 174–6.
23. Dozer, *op. cit.*, p. 445.
24. Peter Calvert, *The Mexican Revolutions, 1910–1914* (Cambridge, Cambridge University Press, 1968), p. 303.
25. Peter Calvert, *Mexico* (London, Benn, 1973), pp. 188–9.
26. Hugh Thomas, *The Spanish Civil War* (Harmondsworth, Penguin, 1965), p. 775.
27. Robert J. Alexander, *The Bolivian National Revolution* (New Brunswick, NJ, Rutgers U.P., 1958). C. J. James Petras, 'Bolivia between Revolutions', *Monthly Review* (June, 1971).

28. Daniel James (ed.), *The Complete Bolivian Diaries of Che Guevara* (London, Allen & Unwin, 1968), pp. 54ff.

29. Ernesto Che Guevara, *Guerilla Warfare* (New York, Monthly Review Press, 1961), p. 15.

30. Cf. Castro's oft-repeated call for 'many Moncadas'. The Moncada barracks incident of 1963 was a failure.

31. Martin Kenner and James Petras (eds.), *Fidel Castro Speaks* (New York, Grove Press, 1969), p. 21.

32. Andrés Sauvez, *Cuba: Castroism and Communism 1959–1966* (Cambridge, Mass, The MIT Press, 1967), p. 241.

33. Stepan, *op. cit.*, p. 263ff.

34. *New York Times*, 31 May 1970.

35. Roxborough, O'Brien and Roddick, *op. cit.*

36. *The Guardian*, Wednesday, 25 July 1979.

9 Revolution in Black Africa

RICHARD JEFFRIES

Most of the societies of Black Africa have, in a sense, undergone a revolutionary transformation during the past century. European colonial rule and the responses to which it gave rise, culminating in the political independence of new nation states, together wrought, formally at least, many of the modernising socio-political changes which extended over four or five centuries in western Europe itself. Short-lived and always somewhat illusory as the parliamentary constitutions of the decolonisation period may in most cases have been, the achievement of political independence did mark the rapid rise to governmental supremacy of indigenous western-educated élites and their secular, instrumental values over traditional forms of rulership. The degree of effective political control exercised by these élites, or the modern institutions of government over wide areas of their societies, may not be very great and is certainly less assured than their rhetoric attempts to suggest. Nations are still largely to be constructed within the official outlines of the new states. But in none of these new ex-colonial states are there feudal or religiously-based regimes, except at the local level, still waiting to be overthrown. It is indicative of the politically modernising impact of European colonial rule that, by 1974, and with the partial exception of the then Portuguese territories, the only African state (outside southern Africa) in which there still could be a revolution in this admittedly limited sense was the only one never to have been colonised by Europeans: Ethiopia.

The reluctance of most Africanists to accord the term 'revolution' to these developments derives not only from their externally generated nature, or from the relatively low levels of political and military mobilisation generally involved in the decolonisation process, or even (and perhaps least) from the failure to institutionalise a system of liberal political democracy. It rather stems from the pervasive influence of neo-Marxist concepts of 'meaningful' revolution. While, prior to the mid-nineteenth century, this might have been construed primarily in socio-political terms, the influence of Marx and his followers – in conjunction, of course, with changing material conditions – has since proven sufficient, if not to have made us all in a sense Marxists, at least to have decisively affected our semantics. The notion, now seemingly central to the paradigm, that a real revolution should effect a marked improvement in the material and other welfare conditions of the mass of the population, is perhaps incontestable enough. What is less clear to this writer is that such progress is only, or is indeed likely, to be attained in Africa by the kind of economic and political strategies for which some neo-Marxists have attempted to purchase a monopoly of revolutionary credentials.

The history of neo-Marxist scholarship in search of revolution in Black Africa reminds one of the Spanish explorers drifting down the Orinoco in search of El Dorado. The African city of gold was at one time envisioned with chimeric clarity as necessarily emerging from the attempts of certain post-colonial governments to break their 'dependency' on western neo-colonial interests. The desirability of such a structural transformations was felt to be so strong that it must, it was argued with a wilful twist of logic, rapidly materialise. The journey down the mainstream of recent African experience has admittedly been such as to make the prospect of arriving at the initial destination at times seem to recede with the distance covered. Yet hope springs anew with the discovery of various tributaries. It is at the end of the most arduous indeed – a protracted peasant-based war – that the politico-economic ideal is now thought most likely to lie.

The neo-Marxist perspective,[1] while subject to slight differences of formulation from one adherent to another, generally sees underdevelopment as the result of a pattern of production and trade – the production of primary products for exchange on the capitalist world market in return for manufactured goods – established during the colonial era and maintained in its essentials by politically and economically dependent neo-colonial regimes. Foreign capitalist investment is seen as hindering rather than contributing to the genuine development of local economies through its large-scale repatriation of profits and drainage of surplus. Indeed, continued exploitation by foreign capital, together with the process of domestic class differentiation to which this supposedly gives rise, is alleged to be the main cause of the decline in living standards which the majority of the population in most African states have undoubtedly suffered since independence. When it comes to the specification of alternative strategies, however, it is necessary to distinguish between what might broadly be termed 'soft' and 'hard' lines. The soft line, with which we are most immediately concerned, and which was highly influential with development economists in the 1960s as well as with several newly independent regimes, such as Nkrumah's in Ghana, argued that genuine economic development (and therefore real revolutionary achievement) required the state's direct participation in the modern sector to the progressive exclusion of foreign capital and the channelling of development resources away from agricultural production for the world market into industrialisation.

The view was, and is, almost entirely empirically mistaken and theoretically misconceived. First, the available evidence suggests that colonial rule significantly improved the material welfare of the mass of the population in the majority of peasant-based economies, if not in those dominated by white settlers. The immense growth in the production of agricultural primary commodities for export was not, at this stage, at the cost of production of foodstuffs for domestic consumption; and the additional wealth gained, if not as great as it might have been within a less oligopolistic marketing system, was relatively widely spread.[2] From a structural point of view, moreover, such agricultural production was the natural growth pole for these societies, given their factor endowments and low level of technological development, quite apart from prevailing world market conditions. The frequently repeated assertion that there has been a secular tendency for the terms of trade of primary commodities as against manufacturers to decline is simply not supported by the evidence.[3] The fact that this has been the case for *some* primary commodities perhaps argues, together with the more general volatility of their world market prices, for diversification into the production of a wider range of commodities, and even for selective industrialisation. There was nothing inherent in the pattern of production and trade established under colonial rule to prevent such diversification after independence. An undiscriminating emphasis on industrialisation, however, especially if through the establishment of para-statals, was bound to lead to severe economic imbalances and even, if not corrected, to economic disaster.

The post-colonial governments in the Ivory Coast and Kenya, frequently condemned by neo-Marxists as paradigm neo-colonial regimes, did not commit this error, and focused their own resources on increasing agricultural production while welcoming foreign investment in manufacturing. These countries have, since independence, been developing their GNP per capita, including both agricultural and manufacturing output, at rates which are extremely impressive by any historically relevant comparison. In the case of the Ivory Coast especially, the growth in manufactured exports during the 1970s was quite phenomenal.[4] Such experiences suggest that the potential complementarity between foreign capital invest-ment and local economic development has been seriously under-estimated in the neo-Marxist perspective, owing partly to an ele-mentary failure to realise that a comparison of onward capital flows with the resulting outward flow of interest and profit ignores how the capital is used in between, so to speak. Many African countries are seriously underdeveloped not because they have been invaded by foreign capital but, on the contrary, because they have been starved of such capital or, to borrow Geoffrey Kay's polemical formulation, because they have not been exploited enough.[5] There is little empirical basis, moreover, for the view that such capitalist-oriented growth inevitably generates greater income inequality; a view which in any case tends to overlook the contribution of income differences to investment, growth and hence a greater potential for mass welfare.[6] Many non-Marxist economists would of course agree that it is desirable to regulate the operation of multi-nationals in developing countries, especially the level of their repatriation of profits. But it is misleading to think that the government of the Ivory Coast has not done so. And it is arguable, more generally, that the governments of African economies which have already developed to a fairly high level by welcoming investment are in a far stronger position to regulate multi-national activities, by virtue of the attractiveness of their expanded markets, and the force of their threat to nationalise foreign assets, than those which are forced to negotiate from a position of extreme underinvestment and under-development.

The economic achievements of the majority of African states, less fortunate in their possession of natural resources or attractive-ness to foreign capital, have not of course been equally impressive. There is probably something to the view that, especially during periods of world economic recession such as we have experienced since the early 1970s, there are fairly strict limits to the number of lesser-developed countries which can realistically hope to develop as rapidly or in the same manner as the Ivory Coast, for example, all at the same time. The huge rise in oil prices during this decade has also hit the economies of non-oil-producing LDCs very savagely. But the important point here is that, where neo-Marxist economic thinking has been taken at all seriously, it has proved positively detrimental. Ghana, for example, was relatively well-endowed to take advantage of favourable world market conditions during the 1960s and early 1970s. Yet Nkrumah's 'socialist' regime, in its determination to achieve rapid industrialisation through state planning and participation, wasted its capital resources on para-statal enterprises which were nearly all unprofitable, often inherently unviable, and largely devoid of stimulating linkages with other sectors of the economy.[7] The milking of the agricultural export sector to finance such 'development' projects in the absence of foreign investment served as a disincentive to production, and thus contributed to growing shortages of foreign exchange, which in turn led to shortages of imported inputs for both agriculture and industry. In combination with an ever-growing overvaluation of the Ghanaian currency, this strategy initiated a process of economic decline which, given the failure to make a radical break in policies, accelerated during the 1970s to produce economic ruin and a catastrophic fall in mass living standards. The increasing worthlessness of the Ghanaian currency and the institution of an extensive system of import controls also resulted in the proliferation of smuggling, black-marketeering and administrative corruption on a scale possibly unrivalled even in African experience. To suggest that Ghana is a less inegalitarian society than, say, the Ivory Coast, quite apart from being inade- quately documented, seems quite fatuous in this context. Nor can the poor planning performance of the Ghanaian state under Nkrumah be properly regarded as an unfortunate aberration of marginal significance for the idea of state planning in African countries in principle. Inefficiency, corrupt decision-making and deliberate overmanning of para-statals to provide jobs for relatives or political clients are endemic to African bureaucracies for socio- logical and structural reasons later to be considered, though their scale and perniciousness are obviously likely to increase with the size of the role accorded to the state in economic regulation and management.

It has sometimes been suggested that the failure of the Nkrumah regime was a failure to go far enough in 'socialising' the economy. The experience of Guinea under Sekou Toure hardly lends much support to this view. Guinea was admittedly at independence much less economically developed than Ghana, but it was (and is) potentially a rich country.

Its well-watered coastal plains could one day feed most of West Africa with rice, its extensive uplands pasture could support vast herds of cattle. The forest area's potential for coffee production has hardly been touched. The country possesses prodigious reserves of high-grade bauxite, iron ore and various other minerals. Many of West Africa's major rivers rise in the Fouta Djalon and, properly tapped, could provide abundant hydro-electric power. The problem – as the French realised only too well – is that very large quantities of skilled manpower and, above all, of capital would have to be mobilised for this potential to be realised.[8]

Scarcely any of this potential has been realised. Production levels of cash crops are today no higher than they were twenty years ago and, in most cases, much lower. There has been a clear fall in the absolute number of most forms of livestock; and, worst of all, Guinea has failed to achieve even self-sufficiency in basic foodstuffs. The main reason is not hard to discern. Sekou Toure's regime has openly espoused Marxist-Leninism, rejected foreign private investment as 'imperialist', and sought to establish a statist economy with a determination and ideological purism that make Nkrumah's efforts seem nerveless by comparison. Admittedly, the industrial sector remains relatively small, but, in addition to the extensive service sector, the state has progressively taken over not only the import-export trade but the country's domestic wholesale and retail trade as well. The state shops and commercial agencies have been characterised by such chronic corruption and inefficiency that severe dislocation and immiseration of the rural economy have resulted. The situation of the peasants would be even worse did they not resort, at the risk of harsh penalties, to smuggling and the use of illegal distribution networks. The sole basis for the regime's economic survival lies in its one major compromise with foreign private capital – the mining of bauxite which, together with its semi-processed product, alumina, accounted by 1975 for over 95 per cent of all exports by value.

The rhetorical tone of Nyerere's regime in Tanzania – liberal, humanitarian, even pious in its socialism – is far removed from the strident hectoring of Sekou Toure. Nyerere's regime is also, in reality, far less of a party-cum-police state. Yet, beneath such (no doubt important) differences, the economic relationship between state and society is not dissimilar. The regime has placed its emphasis on the re-organisation of peasant society and production along supposedly communal lines in 'ujamaa' villages. The 'ujamaa' programme seems to have carried far more appeal, however, for Nordic socialists than for Tanzanian peasants; and, faced with a distinct lack of volunteers, the regime turned to forced villagisation. The intention may have been quite sincere, in part at least, to facilitate the provision of welfare amenities such as schools and health facilities in the rural areas. But bureaucratic implementation has been scarcely less inept here than in the case of Ghana's industrialisation. The new villages were often foolishly sited, and were in any case generally far less efficient bases for agricultural production than the pre-existing scattered patterns of settlement. Administration of communal plots has often also been corrupt, with the distribution of proceeds bearing little relation to the amount of work contributed. For such reasons alone one can hardly be surprised at the fall in production which has resulted. But an additional factor has clearly been the establishment of a state monopoly of crop purchase and the low prices subsequently paid to producers. A large part of the surplus is in this way siphoned off to help pay the salaries of those in the middle and upper ranges of the civil service. The number of such functionaries expanded from 4500 in 1961 to 12,000 in 1971, to well over 20,000 in 1980.[9] Even if their incomes are, officially at least, more modest than those of their counterparts in many African states, they are collectively far more than the Tanzanian economy can possibly afford or than the Tanzanian peasant can reasonably be expected to be happy to pay in return for services rendered.

To the degree that African (or other) regimes use their income from mineral extraction or tax their productive population, in large part their peasantry -- directly, if surreptitiously, through the operations of monopolistic state marketing boards and indirectly through import-export duties - in order to service the wage bill for large numbers of highly paid but essentially parasitic bureaucratic and party or military personnel, they are perhaps most appropriately termed 'kleptocracies'.[10] The term is even more appropriate, of course, to the extent that such functionaries derive additional revenue from various forms of corruption: extortion of bribes in return for services which are supposed to be public rights, for example, or straight forward embezzlement of public monies. Such kleptocracy is, I would argue, the main mode of unproductive exploitation of the peasantry and urban poor in most African states and the main reason, together with population increase, why their living standards have so deteriorated. Capitalist firms of course exploit their workers in a more classical Marxist sense and the world market is far from being a charitable institution. It would take a great deal of ingenuity, and perhaps of ingenuousness, to attempt to calculate the proportion of surplus value respectively appropriated by foreign capital on the one hand, and by local state officials on the other. But foreign capital investment and foreign trade do at least, as Marx himself was concerned to emphasise, have their economically progressive, even productive functions. It is far from clear that kleptocracy does so, while it is all too abundantly clear that it is at its most destructively rampant in some of those regimes which term themselves 'socialist'.

The neo-Marxist reaction to such developments has been, at the most simple level, to look to the leaderships in the ex-colonies of Portugal (Guinea-Bassau, Mozambique and Angola) – leaderships possessed of far more impressive credentials than their Anglo- or Francophonic counterparts as fighters of wars of liberation – to avoid the mistakes of their socialist predecessors. Accompanying this has been a focus on the alleged intensification of class contradictions in non-socialist or pseudo-socialist regimes, Nyerere's now being commonly included, which is expected to give rise to revolutionary upheavals of the peasants and protelarians. Clearly such optimism does not carry much intellectual weight, however, unless it is linked to a realistic assessment of the sources of past failures and to a reasonably persuasive outline of an alternative, suitably progressive strategy. Here the most influential line of thought has developed out of Shivji's characterisation of Tanzania's ruling class (and, by implication, that of other pseudo-socialist regimes) as a 'bureaucratic bourgeoisie', pursuing its own class interests relative to other local classes but mediating and thus furthering the ultimately determinant interests of international capitalism.[11] A recognition of the distinct interests and relative autonomy of the wielders of state power in these societies – relative autonomy from the interests of foreign capital being a *sine qua non* for acknowledging the divergent economic policies they have so obviously pursued – is thus supposedly reconciled with the earlier neo-Marxist position. This may nevertheless be distinguished as a more hard-line position in that the implied (and only true) revolutionary alternative consists in a thorough severance of ties with international capitalism and, therefore, either in economic autarky, or else in much closer ties with (that is to say, dependence on) the communist bloc.

It is, of course, doubtful whether either of these alternatives is seriously on the agenda. The notion of development via economic autarky is something of a red herring even with regard to the historical experiences of the Soviet Union and Communist China; how much more so in the case of countries with so little in the way of the necessary natural resources or indigenous technology and technical manpower. As for the 'Cuban road', it must be doubted whether the Soviet Union, in spite of its increased military interest in certain geo-politically strategic areas of Africa, would be willing to invest similarly huge amounts in such unreliable political environments; or whether, indeed, it possesses the financial capacity to do so. Quite apart from such considerations and the questionable appropriateness of the term 'bureaucratic bourgeosie', however, this interpretation is perversely misleading in its characterisation of African states as inevitably furthering the interests of international capitalism (unless they choose an autarkic or communist path) and in its attribution of the corrupt self-interestedness which undoubtedly characterises many of the office-holders in these states to their links with international capital.

Capitalism is of course by nature expansionist; and certain metropolitan companies have succeeded in establishing profitable niches even in such generally uncongenial political settings as Ghana or Guinea or Tanzania. Equally, the 'socialist' regimes in such countries have been bound to accommodate the capital and technology possessed by multi-national corporations in order effectively to exploit certain of their otherwise unexploitable assets. One cannot reasonably infer from these facts alone that such regimes ultimately 'further' the interests of international capitalism since this implies a relative, 'ex-negative' assessment of what would have been likely to happen if such regimes had not been established. This could not conceivably have been either the establishment of reasonably efficient, certrally-planned economies or a return of 'power to the people'. An assessment, by contrast, of the degree to which such regimes have served the interests of international capitalism must, in principle at least, be very complex and take into account such factors as the need to accommodate local political pressures for change – to a greater degree than colonial governments were able – in order to maintain a fairly stable productive base. Even given the achievements of Toure's and Nyerere's regimes in maintaining a somewhat unusual, though distinctly fragile, kind of political stability, however, one can surely only conclude that their statist economic policies have, on balance, had the effect of hindering rather than aiding international capitalist expansion as well as holding back the development of their societies and inflicting severe damage on their own productive base. Such economic sado-masochism is not of course peculiar to 'socialist' regimes nor entirely a result of their ideological orientation. The quite appalling economic ineptitude of regimes such as Acheampong's in Ghana has created almost equally uncongenial environments in which potential new investors have been unwilling to commit themselves and established companies have felt obliged to withdraw or scale down their operations. The point is rather that state power has often been wielded in these countries, and especially by 'socialist' regimes, in so assertive and irresponsible a manner as to serve no discernible (foreign or domestic) class or even national interest but simply that of incumbent state officials and their clients. From this perspective, the pattern by which certain officials 'facilitate' the awarding of contracts in return for bribes should be seen less as an indication of their dependent, *comprador* status than of their power – a power not only to obstruct foreign capital investment but also to distort its impact on the development of their societies.

The phenomenon of kleptocracy in fact raises two separate, if related, issues: first, why have the state machines in most of these societies expanded so dramatically in size and scope? and secondly, why are they characterised by such chronic inefficiency and corruption? Colonial bureaucraries were, of course, remarkably small; and the agencies of international capitalism have consistently counselled against the kind of inflation which has occurred since independence.[12] The pressure for this expansion has come primarily from the demand of local western-educated and semi-educated people for (preferably white-collar) jobs on a scale that private business has been unable, especially given the often hostile governmental attitude towards it, to provide. The receptivity of governments to this pressure has differed significantly, however, according to their ideological orientation and, more specifically, to the influence of nationalism, dressed up as 'socialism', on their economic policies. The prevalence of bureaucratic corruption in these societies has spawned many explanatory writings, most of which no doubt contain an element of truth, if often an even larger element of tautology.[13] References to the influence of traditional cultural norms and extended family obligations no longer seem very adequate in the face of the transparently self-interested character of much modern corruption. An important facilitating factor for such regular abuse of the official rules, however, would seem to be their phrasing in a language unknown to most of the public together with what amounts to a corporate conspiracy on the part of officials to protect each other against remedial action. The severely limited development of economic opportunities or of articulate, representative political agencies outside the sphere of the state is doubtless also relevant. But the desire and readiness of state officials to enrich themselves at the expense of their publics hardly requires explanation in terms of the specifically corrupting influence of intense exposure to the material standards of the western bourgeosie. The doctrine of original sin will do quite well enough. Corruption is at least as endemic in Sekou Toure's systematically isolated Guinea as in Houphouet-Boigny's 'neo-colonial' Ivory Coast. It is clearly given more sway, moreover, and more scope for ruining the economy in fairly close correlation with the area of bureaucratic discretion in decision-making created by import controls and other mechanisms of state regulation.

The only respect in which the neo-Marxist perspective offers any genuine illumination on this subject lies in the suggestion – and this is far from being peculiar to it – that so scornful an attitude towards the general public (as distinct from members of one's own communal group or political clientele) reflects a lack of commitment of accountability to a truly national public, or to enduring structures of popular representation, of the kind which might be forged during a protracted people's war of liberation. There has been some reason, therefore, to hope that the military and political cadres which fought such wars in the then Portuguese colonies would display (and feel obliged to display) greater rectitude and responsiveness once in power. To some degree, especially in Guinea-Bissau, this has perhaps been so; though, to an even greater extent, we do not as yet really know. But the admittedly limited evidence suggests that such unity of purpose as was developed during these struggles – much less protractedly forged and much less truly national, of course, than in the case of, say, the Chinese or Vietnamese revolutions – has not weathered especially well in the face of the temptations offered by accession to state power and, more particularly, by extensive state regulation of the economy. A recent survey (by a Marxist) of post-war developments in Angola stresses the rapid increase in corruption, black-marketeering and conspicuous consumption, and concludes that, 'In view of the general inefficiency of the greatly expanded state sector, the inflated bureaucracy is largely living off the "windfall profits" of the Gulf Oil Corporation.'[14] It is testimony to the sense of realism of President Machel of Mozambique, and to his genuine concren with the welfare of his people, that, despite his professed Marxist-Leninism, he recently expressed his disenchant-ment with state enterprises 'sick with parasites', authorised the sale of state shops to private trades and invited western business interests to invest.

The basic ideational dynamic of the kind of 'socialist' regime one finds in Black Africa lies, of course, in a certain statist brand of nationalism, combined with a romantic anti-capitalism, rather than in any intellectually tenable developmental rationale. And the neo-Marxist theoretical perspective, however much it tries to distance itself from approval of existing 'socialist' regimes, is deeply imbued with similar preconceptions which are quite misleading as to the real problem. The main cause of growing rural (and increasingly urban) impoverishment is not international capitalism; and a stance of opposition to allegedly dependent involvement in the world capitalist market does not offer even the most partial of solutions. This is not to deny the determined assertion of national independence might represent a certain kind of achievement. But it is very much a political rather than economic achievement; and one which has advertised itself far more persuasively to the western-educated in these countries than to their peasantries, who have good reason to question the degree of benevolence with which such independent power has been wielded.

The peasantries in these states are nevertheless unlikely to become seriously involved in revolutionary wars against their kleptocratic exploiters for a number of reasons. The familiar obstacles to con-certed mobilisation and organisation of the peasantry are com-pounded, in nearly all African states, by the strength of ethnic allegiances and divisions.[15] Moreover, all the major peasant-based revolutions of the twentieth century have been, in an important sense, nationalist wars of liberation: it is, as Julius Nyerere has himself remarked, much more difficult to fight a war of liberation when the oppressors are your own people. Any stirrings of large-scale popular rebellion are in any case virtually bound to be put down by fiercely nationalistic military regimes, which will be less easily dislodged than a pro-Castro Cuban government with one foot already in Florida, or else to be pre-empted by further military *coups*.

We have in fact recently witnessed, in both Liberia and Ghana, 'revolutionary' *coups* led by junior military officers who have expressly identified the cause of their people's suffering and the object of their purgative actions as the intolerable scale of corruption and parasitism on the part of state officials: a kind of lumpen-militariat populism. There is, as should by now be clear, an admirable clear-sightedness in such leaders' identification of their societies' disease. Master-Sergeant Samuel Doe, if not yet as clearly Flt-Lieutenant Jerry Rawlings, would also seem to have developed a hard-headed understanding of the necessarily harsh prerequisites for a cure – the sacking of many state employers, a realistic devaluation of the national currency, and a more general liberalisation of the economy. As has been made abundantly clear by Sekou Toure's forlorn attempts to root out corruption through a Mao-style Cultural Revolution, disciplinary measures and individual replacements are not enough in the absence of a failure to restructure the relationship between state and society. The problem, of course, is that such measures are likely to encounter intense resistance not only from vested economic interests but from the neo-Marxist preconceptions of many of the radical students, trade unionists and intelligentsia to whom these leaders naturally, and somewhat desperately, look for political support. For this reason, the kind of critique developed in this essay is not, certainly should not be, a purely academic business.

NOTES

1. By 'neo-Marxist perspective', I wish to denote that admixture of a Leninist view of imperialism with the theories of 'neo-colonialism' and

'the development of underdevelopment' derived from the Latin American dependency school which one finds in most modern Marxist writings on the political economy of Africa. The theoretical origins of these two schools are, of course, quite different – which partly explains the differences of formulation referred to – but they are most often conjoined in a mode of analysis which, as the late Bill Warren most forcibly argued, needs to be radically distinguished from that of Marx himself. Bill Warren, *Imperialism: Pioneer of Capitalism* (London, NLB, 1980).

2. See, in particular, A. Hopkins, *An Economic History of West Africa* (London, Longman, 1973), pp. 172–86.

3. J. Spraos, 'The Statistical Debate on the Net Barter Terms of Trade Between Primary Commodities and Manufacturers', in *The Economic Journal*, 90 (March 1980).

4. Bastiaan A. den Tuinder, *Ivory Coast: The Challenge of Success* (Baltimore and London, Johns Hopkins University Press, 1978), especially pp. 228–9.

5. G. Kay, *Development and Underdevelopment: A Marxist Analysis* (London, Macmillan, 1975).

6. Warren, *op. cit.*, pp. 179–211.

7. The defects of Nkrumah's economic strategy have been more fully elaborated, amply documented and brilliantly analysed in Tony Killick, *Development Economics in Action* (London, Heinemann, 1978).

8. R. W. Johnson, 'Guinea', in John Dunn (ed.), *West African States: Failure and Promise* (Cambridge, Cambridge University Press, 1978), p. 47. This essay provides by far the most illuminating account yet published of developments in Guinea.

9. W. W. Freund, 'Class Conflict, Political Economy and the Struggle for Socialism in Tanzania', in *African Affairs*, vol. 80, no. 321 (October 1981), pp. 483–99. The literaturre on the impact of villagisation in Tanzania is quite massively voluminous. Arguably the most telling analyses, however, are: Goran Hyden, *Beyond Ujamaa in Tanzania* (London: 1980); Jannik Boesen, 'Tanzania; from Ujamaa to villagization', in B. Mwansasu and C. Pratt (eds)), Towards Socialism in Tanzania (Dar es Salaam and Toronto, University of Toronto Press, 1979); and John Sender, 'The Development of a Capitalist Agriculture in Tanzania: a study with detailed reference to the West Usambaras' (PhD thesis, University of London, 1975).

10. This term is borrowed from S. Andreski, *The African Predicament* (London, Michael Joseph, 1968), p. 92.

11. I. G. Shivji, *Class Struggles in Tanzania* (London and Dar es Salaam, Heinemann, 1976).

12. See, for example, *Accelerated Development in Sub-Saharan Africa: An Agenda for Action* (World Bank, Washington, DC, 1981).

13. For some of the more illuminating examples, see Fred W. Riggs, *Administration in Developing Countries: the theory of prismatic society* (Boston, Houghton Mifflin, 1964); James C. Scott, *Comparative Political Corruption* (Englewood Cliffs, NJ, Prentice-Hall, 1972); M. McMullan, 'A Theory of Corruption', in *The Sociological Review*, ix (June 1961), pp. 181–200.

14. W. G. Clarence-Smith, 'Angola in the 1970s', in *Journal of Southern African Studies*, vol. 7, no. 1 (October 1980), pp. 109–26.

15. See R. D. Jeffries, 'Political Radicalism in Africa: "The Second Independence" ', in *African Affairs*, vol. 77, no. 308, (July 1978).

10 Revolution in the Ottoman Empire and Modern Turkey

C. H. DODD

In the long years of its decline the Ottoman empire was subjected to severe political, economic and intellectual pressure from Europe. But as the Ottoman empire possessed a social and political structure quite alien to that of Europe, the impact of Europe on the Ottoman empire was a matter of great complexity. An important factor in this complexity was that the Ottoman empire was at worst a disguised colony and was never subject to the straightforward imposition of foreign forms of political and social organisation. Consequently, the Ottomans managed to maintain a measure of choice. The Turks largely abandoned their Ottoman political tradition, but it is important that they did so largely of their own volition for to revive a deliberately abandoned tradition is particularly difficult as they have found. Nevertheless, no political tradition is ever completely overthrown and persists in often quite significant ways. The history of revolution and reform in the Ottoman empire and modern Turkey has mainly consisted of undisguised attempts to jettison the antique remains of a crumbling empire, though the process has sometimes necessarily consisted also in attempting to reconcile hardly admitted, but persistent traditions with revolutionary innovation. However, in order to determine what it is of the old that modern Turkey has had to absorb,and reconcile with the new, it is first necessary to delineate the main features of Ottoman social and political organisation.

THE OTTOMAN STATE

The Ottoman state was in origin the creation of warriors, Muslim but Turkish, who ate away at the frontiers of Byzantium until it was finally overthrown in 1453. As the state expanded, however, it needed a regular army and a bureaucracy. These were created partly from subjects of 'slave' status, especially the army. They were young men and boys of Christian parentage converted to Islam and provided with the promise of satisfactory careers.

The pattern for these developments was Muslim, not Turkish. Yet the Ottoman rulers, being Turkish, could not properly claim to head a truly Islamic state in the early fundamentalist sense. They were not in line of descent from the *Quraysh*, the Arab tribe from which Muhammad sprang. They were sultans of the same type as those many who asserted temporal power in the late middle ages in various parts of the Middle East, and who claimed the title of caliph, or successor to the Prophet, to strengthen their claims to legitimacy. The Ottoman sultans like others before them were obeyed the more readily the more they claimed to act in accordance with Islamic Holy Law. Complete obedience to Islamic law is the hallmark of a completely Islamic state. The Ottoman empire is better described as a Muslim state, for the Ottoman sultans did not restrict themselves to Islamic law. Not only was it very difficult to apply to a large and complex state, they were also subject to the influence of a Mongol and Turkish tradition of secular law-making and a Persian tradition of kingly authoritarianism. They developed therefore an extensive power of rule, or law-making which resulted in a corpus of law known as *kanun*. To avoid the problem secular law posed for a Muslim state it could be, and was, claimed that this secular power was really no more than the declaration of customary law and practice (*örf*) allowed by Islam to Muslim rulers. This was pushing interpretation rather far, however, to be comfortable, and did not eliminate the tension which existed between the Islamic religious institution and the temporal power.

In the Ottoman state, Islam was articulated through an extensive and coherent religious institution led by the jurisconsults (*ulema*), among whom the chief jurisconsult, the *Şeyh-ül-Islam* was supreme. He could issue a ruling (*fetva*) to authorise the deposition of the ruler. This on occasion he did, but he could only expect success if he had the armed forces in support. He could be appointed (and dismissed) by the sultan, but he was head of an organisation which exerted influence over important areas of society. In the absence of strongly defined social classes in Ottoman society, the only protection against the government was that provided by the religious institution, often by the religious judges (*kadi's*). The dervish orders also provided solace and practical help to the lowly through their convents. Religion was the countervailing force to government in Ottoman society. However, according to its theorists, at least, Ottoman society possessed a basic harmony. The Ottoman empire was a corporate society composed of different nations (*millet's*) guilds, religious offices, officialdom and the army. It was not a 'civil' society composed of wealthy and powerful classes of nobility and bourgeoisie. In the Ottoman conception, religion provided the norms by which relations were regulated both among the groups and between these corporate groups and government.

It is not at all easy to relate the distinctions between an *activist* and a *limited* style of politics to the Ottoman state.[1] In Europe, it might be claimed, Britain, France and Spain were to some degree established territorial states (before they became nation states) to which patriotic, rather than national, sentiments attached themselves. Then with the French Revolution a new 'universal' nationalistic creed emerged to reject the suffocating restrictions of the state and thus to enable the universal emotions of liberty, fraternity and equality to express themselves through membership of one nation. There is a difficulty applying about this scheme to the Ottoman empire, however, and a considerable one at that. For in its early years the Ottoman empire was not primarily a territorial concept; nor was it primarily an institutional concept in the eye of its subjects. That it was in fact a panoply of institutions, often complex, is beside the point. Essentially it was a fluid expression of the Muslim aim of converting all lands outside the domains of Islam, which were recognised as lands of welfare, into domains submissive to God. The empire's ideology took the form of a universalistic creed designed, if not to liberate barbarians, at least to make them recognise God and submit to Him. It so happened that the Ottomans came realistically to accept that they ruled a territory, but territory was not emotionally important until stressed in the late nineteenth century. It could be argued that the Ottomans were less concerned over gain and loss of territory than were European states. In its prime the Ottoman empire was a movement. It developed into a state in its later years, and much later, after the first world war, into a nation state.

The second feature of the limited state, namely commitment to law as the bond of the community and a defence against arbitrary rule, would appear to apply in full force to the Ottoman empire by virtue of the importance of Islamic law. Certainly, Islam conferred a common legal status on its adherents, whose obligations are laid down unambiguously. This seems an improvement, in fact, on the ancient law of Europe (often a complex of rights, obligations and exemptions) which sometimes preserved liberties, but which the French revolutionaries sought to abolish as an obstacle to man's realising his true nature. Yet in fact Islamic law constituted a very inadequate safeguard against the claims of temporal power. It contained no developed notion of rights rendered sacrosanct through custom, nor did Islam generally recognise that there existed any basis for rights in the nature of things and discernible by reason. Essentially Islamic law is God's command. This induced in Muslims, as mentioned above, a zeal to convert all peoples outside Islam to the faith and to maintain the purity of the Muslim community at home. There was a dynamic or activistic impulse in this, though it should not be exaggerated. Muslims were not required to participate in shared purposes beyond carrying out the quite explicit obligations imposed upon them by religion. They were not mobilised heart and soul in some great human project. They were concerned to do their duty in this world for the sake of salvation in the next.

Finally, the notion that power is suspect, that it was important to *limit* power, not just to legitimise it, could be said to have been the concern of the *ulema* through their concern for Holy Law. Being based in the religious conviction that the Islamic community must live according to the formal requirements of Holy Law, their hostility to the arbitrary use of power was, however, limited. They were not intent on developing the liberties of individuals, groups or classes; the nature of their religious faith did not move them in that direction. The religious institutions sought primarily to exert a legal control over those areas of government to which Holy Law related. Secondly the *ulema* could develop a moral critique of rulers which drew its sustenance from the piety of the early caliphs of Islam. There were no firm precedents in Islam, however, to encourage the creation of political institutions through which this rather veiled opposition to sultanic power could be expressed and developed. The dominant Ottoman pattern is for long periods of calm to be punctured by short sharp bursts of violent political opposition.

ISLAM AND THE MODERNISING STATE

Many Ottomans began to lose confidence in their system in the eighteenth century as they suffered military defeat at the hands of European powers and began to realise that in many ways they had become backward. They suffered a relative and, in some respects, an absolute decline which their necessary involvement in the world market under very adverse conditions did nothing to restrain. By the beginning of the nineteenth century many Ottomans were well aware of the need for rapid change. An important imperial edict of 1839 has been seen by some scholars as encompassing 'many of the ideas contained in the French Declaration of the Rights of the Man and the Citizen of 1789'.[2] It has been more cautiously claimed, however, that this edict and the reforming administration of the time owed most to post-Napoleonic enlightenment, and was intended to produce more efficient, not essentially more liberal, government.[3] The edict provided for security of life, honour and property of all subjects, including the non-Muslims. Trials were to be public, confiscation of property was abolished, fixed taxes were to replace tax farming, fixed salaries were to be paid to officials, conscription was to be better regulated. These measures denoted a new attitude by the sultan's government even if the immediate gains fell mainly to officials, who could now aspire to a secure position, and sometimes to fortune.

In practice, it was the modernising and often quite westernising impulse of the new bureaucrats which was dominant for thirty very formative years between 1839 and 1870. During this period the position of the religious institution was weakened – its revenues were brought under closer scrutiny, its monopoly over education was broken. New codes of law were also imported from the West to provide solutions for problems with which Holy Law could not cope; they had to be manned too, by a new corps of lay lawyers. The direction of the new modernising state was in the hands of the expanding and increasingly better-educated official class. A Muslim bourgeoisie was only just in process of formation, and non-Muslims did not play a significant role in government.[4] Against this official-led modernisation a revolt broke out as the result of an interesting collaboration of western liberalism and Islam, led by a group of largely disaffected younger officials, known as the Young Ottomans, who emerged in 1865.

The young Ottomans developed a critique of Ottoman government which stressed the need for less imitative westernisation, for more freedom and for some reconciliation of the new western trends with Islam, which they rightly perceived as being under dire threat. This was a high-minded critique which in practice meant that the Young Ottomans were intent on attacking autocratic reformers with the help of the *ulema*. Among the Young Ottomans the most distinguished was Namik Kemal (1840–88). He sought to reconcile Islam with the new liberal and democratic ideas then popular and opposed to the nature of Ottoman rule.

Kemal's scheme for effecting a dynamic reconciliation between Islam and liberal democracy failed intellectually on three counts. In the first place there was the well-nigh insuperable problem of establishing a system of individual natural rights since there is no law of nature for a Muslim that is not Islamic law, and a customary law is only sanctioned if it is not inconsistent with the law of Islam.[5] Secondly, since in Islam sovereignty lies in God it cannot be usurped by any form of expression of the popular will. Muhammad and his successors, the Caliphs, only possessed judicial and executive authority. Namik Kemal makes out a partly plausible case for the oath of obedience the Muslim community swears to a newly elected caliph to be viewed as a revocable contract between community and caliph, but conveniently ignores the Islamic theory of trusteeship, which emphasises that the caliph rules the community as trustees to God, not to the community. Thirdly, Namik Kemal believed that the Koranic requirement of consultation by the caliph with some members of the Muslim community justified the creation of an elected assembly, but it is a very large assumption to make and ignores the necessary intermediate stages.

On such a rickety intellectual basis an alliance was formed between liberals and Muslims which had a certain measure of success. Both groups joined in forcing a constitution on the Sultan Abdul Hamid, in 1876. The Constitutional Commission on the 1876 Constitution in fact contained ten members of the *ulema* out of a total membership of twenty-eight. The *ulema* went so far as to advise that Christians might be elected to Parliament.

The constitution restricted the powers of the sultan very little and was soon put into limbo. It was not the Constitution but the short-lived Parliament to which it gave birth which affrighted the sultan. Despite their being hand-picked, the deputies showed themselves to be both spirited in their criticism of the sultan and well-versed in the language of liberalism. Among their members commercial, farming and propertied groups were as prominent as officials.

This was an indication of things to come, but the abrogation of the Constitution was a failure for Islamic modernism. Thereafter Abdul Hamid fostered the pan-Islamic strand in Islam, which led Islam down new fundamentalist and romantic paths which all but killed the desire for reconciliation with western ideas. Islamic sentiment was thus developed by Abdul Hamid to mobilise support for his rule among the general population, but not so intensely as to prevent the development of modern education to the neglect of the Islamic schools. A brave last attempt to reconcile Islam and modernity was made in Young Turk times by Ziya Gökalp (1875–1924). Under the influence of Durkheim, he sought to evade the problem of liberalism by asserting that Islamic law should be subject to constant revision in the dynamic light of changes in the community's consciousness of what constituted its essential inner 'ideal'. This went as far as to raise the social consciousness of the Islamic community to a level with, and even above, the Koran and the tradition of the Prophet as the real fountain of law. This claim could only be based on questionable Koranic evidence, however. Consequently this formulation, by which the community, even a national Muslim community, would have replaced God as the prime source of law, was rejected as unsound by most Muslims. Moderate Muslims had little enough belief in this formulation and the more fundamentalist among them became more stridently so under the leadership of the *Seyh-ül-Islam*, Musa Kâzim Efendi (1858–1919). They believed in strict adherence to the Koran and Holy Law. They were unsympathetic to the Young Turk revolution of 1908, and allying themselves with the sultan, discredited both him and themselves in the counter-*coup* of 1909. These Muslim fundamentalists were rigorously opposed by those Young Turks who were adamant westernizers, like Abdullah Cevdet (1869–1932). Uninterested in Islamic compromises designed to reinvigorate Islam, he claimed that European civilisation had to be imported in its entirety. In an article 'A Very Wakeful Sleep' he describes a vision of a future Turkey:

The Sultan would have one wife and no concubines; the princes would be removed from the care of eunuch and harem servants and given a thorough education, including service in the army; the fez would be abolished, and a new headgear adopted; existing cloth factories would be expanded and new ones opened, and the Sultan, princes, senators, deputies, officers, officials and soldiers made to wear their products; women would dress as they pleased . . . they would be at liberty to choose their husbands . . . ; convents and *tekke's* would be closed . . . ; all *medresse's* would be closed; a consolidated and purified Ottoman Turkish dictionary and grammar would be established . . . ; the Ottomans . . . would by their own efforts and initiative, build roads, bridges, ports, railways, canals, steamships and factories; starting with the land and *Evkaf* laws, the whole legal system would be reformed.[6]

No document of the time, observes Professor Lewis, more accurately foreshadows the subsequent course of events, though not even Abdullah Cevdet prohesied the abolition of sultanate and caliphate. Muslims naturally rejected all this radicalism in favour at best of gradualism. Slow reform was possible, they said, even of religious schools. 'After all', as one journal put it, 'Oxford and the Sorbornne were in their time nothing but a couple of *medresse's*'.[7]

THE MAKING OF THE NATION STATE

By the time of the Young Turk Revolution in 1908, the role played by religion in affairs of state and the management of society had been greatly reduced. For the most part the Young Turk revolutionaries – officers, officials and members of the intelligentsia – were somewhat isolated from their own society and were brought up on a rich diet of western social and political theory, only partly digested. They had little or no time for religion, but were not markedly anti-religious. Consequently after defeating the 1909 counter-revolution, they did not turn on Islam, but on the Sultan-Caliph Abdul Hamid, whom they replaced by the more pliant Mehmed Reşad. The positivist Unionist faction in power continued to chip away at the religious institutions, by amending the law on divorce, for instance, and by removing Şeyh-ül-Islam from the Cabinet. But essentially, they effected a revolution in order to save the empire from external enemies encouraged by Ottoman governmental incapacity. They reintroduced the 1876 Constitution with amendments to restrict the sultan's power, but then clawed back power to use against their liberal opponents, who wanted more individual freedom, greater emphasis on constitutional and democratic procedures and more respect for traditions and religion. In the upshot, after direct intervention by groups of military officers on both sides, the Unionists remained in power. The revolution settled down to the centrally-directed modernising policies of its forebears, if pursued now with more energy and effect.

The Young Turk period saw the development of two ideas of very considerable revolutionary potentiality, namely, nationalism and republicanism. The nationalist appeal in the Ottoman empire expressed itself first, however, as an appeal to Ottomanism (a sentiment for the unity of all Ottoman groups) but also, in sharp contrast, to Turkism, which stressed origins and race. There gradually emerged, however, a feeling of special attachment to the heartland of the empire, namely, Anatolia, which was mainly but not exclusively Turkish. There was, above all, a marked emphasis on a broad view of culture, which was reflected in Ziya Gökalp. 'The Nation', he said, 'is a group composed of men and women who have undergone the same education, who have received the same acquisitions in language, religion, morality and aesthetics.'[8] Culture essentially, it seems, consisted in the latent values of society found among ordinary folk. Yet the territory of Anatolia, the homeland itself, had a special appeal. The 'Turkish Poems' of Mehmed Emin, (1869–1944) reflected the very mixed character of Turkish nationalism, but stressed the Turkish environment. 'If you continue in this line of poetry', he was told, 'and describe the mosques and the monuments of our towns and villages, you may be sure that the public will hasten to follow you and accept you.'[9] This appeal to Turkish nationalism was in part forced upon the Turks by the self-assertion of other national groups in the empire, and finally by the loss of the Arab provinces. Consequently, the Turkish component was stressed over the religious. The tempting conclusion is that during the war of liberation led by Kemal Atatürk against the allied occupying powers (1919–22) the Turks responded as Turks, conscious of their common Turkish cultural bonds, and fought a war of *national* liberation. Certainly there were appeals to the nation (*millet*), but the world *millet* was used in Ottoman times to refer to any community, including the Muslim community. In fact, in 1920 when clerical deputies in the National Assembly voted to agree with Atatürk that sovereignty lay in the nation they almost certainly had the Muslim community in mind.[10] Only the intelligentsia comprehended a cultural conception of the nation based on a Turkish identity. Indeed, when the Atatürkist government sought to effect a cultural revolution, most of whose measures were directed against religion, cultural nationalism could have little appeal. The abolition of the caliphate, the religious schools, Holy Law, religious courts and the mystic orders, the assertion of direct state control over religious affairs, and the change from the Arabic to the Latin alphabet were momentous changes – even if they were the culmination of a century of increasing restriction of Islam. However, this revolution was not achieved through the support of a populace mobilised behind the new nation. It was in fact pushed through against the latent opposition of the masses. Its success depended partly on forceful leadership, but partly on the traditional habits of obedience long enjoined upon Ottoman subjects. Mustafa Kemal Atatürk was not an upstart but a pasha, a victorious general to whom the historic Islamic title of *gazi* (warrior for the faith) was popularly accorded. What mattered most for the peasants was the closing of dervish convents and the consequent decline in provision for popular religion, and this did not altogether disappear overnight. To them the larger affairs of religion and state were not really comprehensible.[11] With a successful military leader as president–a *gazi* easily to be confused with a sultan in the popular mind – what had changed? Even as late as 1962 surveys of peasant attitudes did not suggest that nationalism had much hold, and in these and other studies the continuing importance of religion for the ordinary people is evident.[12]

The revolutionary doctrine of republicanism which derived from the legacy of the French Revolution was used by the Ottoman intelligentsia as a warrant for limiting the sultan's power. It was not, however, until after the 1908 revolution, which first appeared as a festival of freedom, that the sultan was actually required to swear fidelity to the nation. It was not until 1921 that sovereignty of the people was given full recognition in a constitutional document. This was a significant departure. The deputies in the National Assembly were subsequently not backward in asserting that they were the real representatives of the people, 'We . . . the real representatives of the nation are absolutely determined that the Sultanate will never return.'[13] Against this vigorous assertion of republican principle, the suggestion that the constitutionally weak President Mustafa Kemal Atatürk should be allowed the important power of dissolving the National Assembly had to be abandoned. The democratic fervour shown by the deputies in 1924 (or their distrust of Mustafa Kemal) was circumvented by the domination of the National Assembly by means of the People's Party in the single party regime which soon emerged, and which a system of indirect election made easier to operate. During the Atatürkist regime to all intents and purposes no real expression of the national will was allowed. It was assumed that it was represented by Mustafa Kemal Atatürk and the Republican People's Party. However, there was very little ideological indoctrination and little attempt was made to build a personality cult around Kemal Atatürk. Nor was it the case that leading members of party and government reached their positions through dedication to the party. There were no purges of those who had deviated from the right way; there were no agonising guilt-ridden reappraisals of party policy, and there was no all-embracing ideology with which all citizens were to identify if they were to be considered true citizens. In short, it was not a totalitarian regime. In this regard, then, it was not revolutionary. The regime did not vigorously mobilise the populace behind some totally absorbing ideal. Instead it preached the virtues of modern civilised living, in which Atatürk sincerely believed, to a limited audience. The Atatürk regime was didactic, reformist, purposeful but not revolutionary if by that is meant the adoption of a completely activist stance. It was an autocratic, but tutelary regime which would have liked to have been more liberal and democratic, but was in part prevented from movement in this direction by the unpreparedness of Turkish society for such a venture. Conscious of the potential rifts in society, between the religious and the secularists, and between the developing social classes, the Atatürkist regime adopted a solidarist attitude which denied the possibility of inter-group and inter-class conflict. This had a wide appeal in a society accustomed to the Ottoman tradition of harmonious social and economic interaction in which the state played a large part.

The Liberal and Democratic Revolution

It has been argued that the Atatürkist period witnessed a real development of individualism in Turkey. The limitations on the influence of religion, it is claimed, helped break the Islamic 'neighbourhood' mentality so unconducive to individual creativity.[14] If this is so, then this was a step towards the liberal and democratic revolution which occurred after the second world war and continued until 1980, when the military intervened in the third attempt since 1950 to save democracy, but one which may turn out to be its death blow. In 1946 the ruling Republican People's Party decided to abandon its monopoly of power and to allow a multi-party system to operate. In 1950 a new direct electoral system was introduced. The result was the emergence of a number of parties of which the Democrat Party was the most prominent and which swept to power in 1950. Since the leaders of the new dominant party had been former and quite senior members of the Republican People's Party, it was not a change stemming directly from new forces in society. Yet there were many in society who were disaffected with the didactic, secularising and highly centralised rule of the People's Party and only too eager for change. Not least among them were the growing numbers of industrialists and businessmen who wanted more economic freedom. The People's Party had now to follow the Democrat Party in actively seeking popular support at the polls. For the first time the ordinary Turk was invited to participate. For many sections of society it was a real gain for freedom if often at the expense of the power and prestige of the political, bureaucratic and military élites. It is difficult to say that this was more activist, if that is the hallmark of true revolution, than the tutelary regime it replaced. It was, if anything, less so. The Democrat Party government was less inclined to undertake grand strategies and mobilise the populace behind it than its predecessors had been. Its style was to lead the populace in a paternalistic but sympathetic way. It was not long before concessions were made on the popular side of religion, though countenance was not given to any substantial revival of the institutions or law of Islam. The Democrat Party did come, however, to believe that it had a special penchant for representing the actual will of the people (not some ideal will) and stressed its legitimacy by reference to the strength of its popular support. On these grounds it began to meddle with the political and legal apparatus, and proscribe its opponents. It claimed that existing legal and political restrictions were an illegitimate hindrance to the expression of the popular will and were designed to suit the aims of its opponents. The constitution inherited a political structure from the Atatürkist regime which allowed for few checks and balances and concentrated power in the single elected Assembly. This stregthened the Democrat Party's sense of its own legitimacy as the creator of economic prosperity for all (or nearly all) classes of society.

The military intervention of 1960–1 resulted in a constitution which created checks and balances and led also to the adoption of a system of proportional representation. This prevented any party from asserting a greater claim to legitimacy on the basis of Assembly seats than its overall vote warranted (as had happened with the Democrat Party government). This was not necessarily intended to be a return to limited government in the sense of imposing limits on the area of governmental activity. Indeed, the Republican People's Party, which confidently expected to be voted into power, showed much interest in overall social and economic planning. Government was to take on more than it had under the Democrat Party. But the intention was to limit the intrusion of politics into justice, administration, communications and education (particularly the universities), the trade unions and even the military. This attempt to limit or contain politics has not worked, however, and principally for two interconnected reasons. In the first place, since 1961 strong political movements have developed of revolutionary potential partly inside, but mainly outside, the confines of the now delimited political system. A markedly socialist Turkish Workers' Party was closed down in 1971 by the military, their first substantial intervention after 1960–1, but the solidarist, nationalistic, and anti-communist Nationalist Action Party had a small number of seats inside Parliament in the 1970s as well as commandos outside. The Islamic National Salvation Party also obtained a small number of seats inside Parliament and like the Nationalist Action Party found supporters in various parts of the administration. Supporters of the defunct Turkish Workers' Party and of clandestine organisations of the further Left developed support in the universities in particular, and also, it seems, in some of the trade unions; in both areas they encountered the often violent opposition of adherents of the Nationalist Action Party. The institutions firmly placed outside the arena of legitimate politics by the constitution became politicised. The second reason for this wide politicisation was that the two major parties, alternating in power, have not been able to clamp down on extremism. One reason is that save for a period in the 1960s neither party has been able (thanks partly to proportional representation) to govern without taking in minor parties or leaning in their direction. The Republican People's Party, declaring itself left of centre, sought to absorb supporters of the further Left. The Justice Party had to enter into deliberate coalitions with the Islamic and rightist parties. This increased the antagonism of the two major parties to each other, which for historical and personal reasons was already severe.[15] In conditions of uncontrollable violence in society, deadlock between the major political parties and economic chaos, the military intervened in September 1980, and seems intent on establishing a constitution much less liberal than that of 1961.

The Turkish liberal and democratic revolution has therefore come to grief for the time being. Since the military's intervention firm but positive government has effected improvements in many fields. It is apparent that in the Turkish context large measures of freedom encourage anti-systemic groups to emerge. This happens in all liberal and democratic systems to some degree, but in Turkey there is less than the necessary consensus on the value of liberal and democratic institutions. The reasons for this are partly contemporary: if Turkey could have overcome her economic and social problems the liberal and democratic system would have attracted more support. But they are also in part historical. The Ottoman tradition is for authoritarian government open to some religious (or generally moral) criticism but unsympathetic to opposition generally. The tradition also stresses social harmony with which Atatürkist solidarism was in accord. The secular revolution which Atatürk brought to dramatic completion freed government from a measure of control, but still left the populace obedient to its rulers, even to the secular Atatürkists, partly out of a traditional deference and habit. In one major sense the Atatürk revolution failed. Its 'disestablishment' of religion did not lead to a sudden surge in activity. Religion was perhaps not the dead-hand on progress which the secularists claimed to be the case. When with the Democrat Party governments of the 1950s, economic development got under way there was at least as much entrepreneurship in evidence among the religious as among the lay. And in the 1970s the Islamic National Salvation Party was foremost in urging the need for technological development. The Atatürk revolution eventually had some success, however, in transmuting a shared religious into a shared national feeling, or in blurring the line between the two. This popular support for the political system, whether based on deference, habit or national unity, has now begun to break down however. Secular education, the ideas of liberalism and democracy, and the dislocating effects of patchy economic and social change have been mainly responsible, and the liberal and democratic institutions which have aided these processes have not yet attracted a loyalty to enable them to withstand the shock. In a society in which so much change seems to be needed conservatism is not a strong trend, and especially, if when it appears it takes on a traditionalist Islamic tinge.

The Ottoman modernising revolution which began in the early nineteenth century paid some attention to the establishment of rules guaranteeing a range of personal freedoms, usually at the instigation of the European powers. Ottoman reforming statesmen followed in the main, however, an authoritarian line, which resulted in the modernisation of the machinery of government and the reduction of the influence of Islam in state and society. Attempts to reconcile Islam with the liberal and positivist ideas absorbed by the intelligentsia from Europe failed; the Ottoman Constitution of 1876 also failed against the force of modernising authoritarianism which was becoming increasingly secularist at home despite some promotion of the Pan-Islamic movement abroad. The Young Turk revolution of 1908 further developed secularist policies brushing aside both Islamic reaction and their own liberal wing, but they asserted the primacy of popular sovereignty for the first time and overthrew Sultan Abdul Hamid. During this period a cultural and territorial version of Turkish nationalism developed as a dominant strain in a powerful movement within the intelligentsia, some of whom advocated an enlightened Ottoman patriotism, whilst others adhered to a romantic and dangerous Pan-Turkish or Turanian movement. It was on the basis of this cultural and territorial nationalism that the new nation state was formally created by Mustafa Kemal Atatürk. Sovereignty was finally claimed for the nation; the elected National Assembly sought to exercise this sovereign power, but, in fact, power rested with Atatürk and the Republican People's Party, with party and state closely interwined for a long period. Led from the centre, with variable degrees of intensity, the people lagged behind, confusing president of the republic with sultan, and nationalism with religion. Nor was there a social revolution; Atatürkist solidarism recreated Ottoman social harmony and the new intelligentsia of the towns shared power with the paternalistic proprietors in the countryside. Not until 1946 did Turkey begin to experience revolution which drastically affected the lives of the populace. In part stemming from, and in part instigating dynamic processes of economic and social change, this democratic revolution perhaps constitutes the greatest of the upheavals which Turkey has seen, and the one with which the country has been least able to cope.

The strengths and weaknesses of this problematic Turkish democracy are not unrelated to the course of Turkish revolutionary history. The Atatürkist revolution may not have had an impressive immediate cultural impact. Nor may it have done more than put the coping stone on an existing movement towards the creation of the nation state. Yet the actual abolition of the sultanate and caliphate was vital, as was the elimination of the Muslim clergy and the dervish orders. There remained no dynasty and, more important no religious authority and organisation to provide legitimacy for any counter-revolutionary movement, and this is important today when the liberal and democratic revolution is under threat. Moreover, whilst liberal democracy formed no official part of the ideology of the Atatürkist ideology, and single partyism was supreme, Kemal Atatürk did foster an experiment with a second party in 1930.[16] He also later introduced controlled discussion into the Assembly and tried to keep the party in touch with the needs of the populace. The experiment with a measure of democracy was unsuccessful because conservative and reactionary elements saw it as an opportunity to attack the new republic. There were as yet no substantial business and industrial middle classes to provide support; the promotion of democracy was primarily the function of a section of the intellectual élite. Most of the élite, including those in the bureaucracy, however, were intent on modernising Turkey in tutelary fashion. With their People's Party convictions they were not sympathetic to Democrat Party governments after the war. When in principle favourably disposed towards democracy, higher officials often did not care much for its actual manifestations. This was then a dubious legacy from the revolutionary past. Nor has it helped the fortunes of democracy that politically divided though the élite has now become, each group or faction has not altogether lost the conviction that as an élite it has a right and duty to play a dominant role, an attitude which helps make inter-élite relations acutely difficult. Meanwhile, at the other end of the social scale, the populace has learned through the democratic revolution that its vote can be made to count, particularly by influencing politicians to obtain concrete local benefits from government. Just as important is the fact that with economic and social development employer, employee, and other organisations, have grown in size and are now used to much freedom of action, let alone expression.

Opposed to extremes of Left and Right, educated in the prime Atatürkist values of populism, secularism and republicanism, the military command now in power seems bound to operate under the terms of the Atatürkist or democratic formulae, or by reference to both. Of late years it has shown an increasing capacity to work with the new professional and economic bourgeoisie, classes which, having appeared late on the scene of the Turkish revolution, have not sufficiently understood and nurtured the political institutions that were rather easily created in a period of post-war democratic euphoria.

NOTES

1. The distinction made and elaborated by Dr Noel O'Sullivan, above pp. 9–12.
2. S. J. and E. K. Shaw, *History of the Ottoman Empire and Modern Turkey, Vol. II Reform, Revolution and Republic: the Rise of Modern Turkey, 1808–1975* (Cambridge, 1977), p. 61.
3. See Şerif Mardin, *The Genesis of Young Ottoman Thought: a Study in the Modernisation of Turkish Political Ideas* (Princeton, 1964), pp. 169–95.
4. Commercial activities in coastal towns were still in the hands of non-Muslims, but in the interior, and even in Istanbul and Salonica, Muslim entrepreneurial groups were on the rise. See Kemal Karpat, 'The Transformation of the Ottoman State, 1789–1908', *International Journal of Middle Eastern Studies*, III, (1972), pp. 243–81.
5. For full discussion of Namik Kemal's thought, see Mardin, *Genesis*, pp. 283–336.
6. Quoted in B. Lewis, *The Emergence of Modern Turkey*, 2nd edn. (London, 1968), p. 236.
7. Ibid., p. 237.
8. Trans. in N. Berkes (ed.), *Turkish Nationalism and Western Civilization* (New York, 1959), pp. 134–8.
9. D. Kushner, *The Rise of Turkish Nationalism, 1876–1908* (London, 1977), p. 155.
10. See Şerif Mardin, 'Religion and Secularism in Turkey', in Ali Kazancigil and Ergun Özbudun (eds.), *Atatürk, Founder of a Modern State* (London, 1981), p. 209.
11. Ibid., p. 202, where illuminating responses by first world war soldiers to questions about religion are given which reveal ignorance and elementary misconceptions about the nature of Islam.
12. See my *Democracy and Development in Turkey* (Beverley, 1979), pp. 71–76, for information on various surveys made.

13. Suna Kili, *Turkish Constitutional Developments and Assembly Debates on the Constitutions of 1924 and 1961* (Istanbul, 1971), p. 43.

14. Ş. Mardin, 'Religion and Secularism in Turkey', in Kazanciğil and Özbudun, *Atatürk*, pp. 212–17.

15. Members of the Justice Party, heir to the defunct Democrat Party, had attributed the military intervention of 1960 to collusion between the People's Republican Party and the military.

16. See W. F. Weiker, *Political Tutelage and Democracy in Turkey: the Free Party and its Aftermath* (Leiden, 1973), p. 65, where evidence for Atatürk's initiative in forming a new party is presented.

11 Revolution in Iran 1979: Religion as Political Ideology

HAMID ENAYAT

It is always hazardous to write about a phenomenon which is still in the process of formation. The Iranian Revolution has not yet run its full course, and is adopting different forms and directions all the time. This is sometimes baffling even for specialised observers. But the uncertainties attendant upon studying a moving scene should not deter political scientists from making observations and reaching conclusions, provided, of course, that these are treated as tentative. My observations in this paper relate mainly to certain basic features of the Revolution in its early stages, which roughly cover the year 1979. The fact that since then many ideas and trends associated with the Revolution have changed in character, and have even taken a course diametrically opposed to their initial direction, should not detract from any validity that the views presented here may have.

The first question that must be briefly discussed is whether the term revolution can be applied at all to the events of 1979. There are some people, both inside and outside Iran, who would answer this question in the negative, claiming that what happened was merely a transfer of power from one group of people to another, without bringing about a radical transformation in the social and economic structure of a country. This view is forcefully expressed by some left-wing writers,[1] not all of them necessarily Marxist, who prefer at best the term 'uprising' (*qiyam*) or at worst 'sedition' (*fitnah*) in describing the process leading to the overthrow of the monarchy. I think otherwise: there is no doubt that some important and far-reaching changes have occurred in Iran, at the political as well as economic and cultural levels, which cannot possibly be defined by any term other than revolution, with all the good or evil notions associated with it. It is true that much of the economic framework of the old regime, together with its accompanying social attitudes, cultural norms and administrative institutions, have remained intact.

In some cases one might even say that these have been reinforced: for instance, the exploitative techniques of property-owning classes, especially the tradesmen, and a widespread, uncritical acceptance of authority and submission to force, without this giving rise to any effective regimentation or uniformity, as in the case of the Russian and Cuban Revolutions.

Nevertheless, the changes that *have* taken place are real and highly significant. Not only have the ruling cliques of the old regime been replaced by completely new people with a completely new mentality and new values; successive purges have made sure that even the lower echelons of the bureaucracy are affected. On the economic plane, there has been large-scale nationalisation of firms, banks and insurance companies, both domestic and foreign, as well as the confiscation of huge fortunes belonging to persons rightly or wrongly accused of various wrong-doings in the period before the Revolution. Perhaps more important has been the change in the whole cultural and moral climate of the land. The Revolution definitely marks the end of an era of westernisation as an un-challenged goal in Iran's cultural, educational and social life. Traces of this rejection had appeared among the intellectuals long before, and were reflected even in the official rhetoric of the Shah's regime, which at times tended to rebut the charges of its subservience to the West by overindulgence in verbal anti-westernism. Hence the many contradictions between its ideological pretensions and its practical stance. The essentially Islamic ideology of the movement that over-threw the Shah resolved these contradictions, although only tem-porarily, by posing as the antithesis of all the cultural innovations and adaptations implicit in any scheme of modernisation. I say only temporarily, because this rejectionist posture may be followed later on by a backlash in favour of the West, if it is not bolstered by a coherent strategy to make Iran fairly self-reliant in the crucial sectors of her national life. In the People's Republic of China, too, the Cultural Revolution proved to be a rather short-lived affair, although the machinery and methods employed by the communist leadership were far more sophisticated than those available to the Islamic Republic.

Independence from the West found its most vivid – and perhaps sole-expression in the realm of foreign relations. Post-Pahlavi Iran found herself, notwithstanding the chaos in every area of her col-lective administration, firmly in the camp of the non-aligned, anti-imperialist, anti-Zionist forces in the world. This again may have been based on a shallow or fleeting commitment, liable to falter or even undergo a metamorphosis into its opposite, as happened in the case of Egypt. But it nevertheless arose from a deeply-held conviction, shared by all shades of opinion inside the revolutionary camp, ranging from the moderate, liberal Nationalist Front to the extremist, militant *Hizbullahis* (adherents of a non-party or one-party system regulated exclusively by Khomeini's vision of Islam), all subscribing to the slogan 'Neither the East nor the West'.

Closely related to the cultural reorientation was a revised ordering of social values. There was markedly less preoccupation with wealth and income as an index to the social status or merit of the individual. There was much less of a spirit of 'oneupmanship' and 'Keeping Up with the Jones's', which was responsible for a great deal of extravagance and corruption under the old regime. A positive manifestation of the same development was the attitude of the lower strata of the population. These people had suffered for decades, despite repeated measures taken at the top, not only on account of their social and economic deprivations but also because of an almost total lack of access to decision-makers. But they were now, for the first time, holding their heads high, and were insisting on their rights in a new mood of self-assertiveness. Moreover, although they still did not have much say in the running of affairs, they could at least meet, and sometimes take to task, men who were making vital decisions on their behalf. Of all the changes these very consequences should prove the opposite, as I know of no other revolution which has not given rise to similar results, or conversely has succeeded in establishing a firm order within a short period.

Throughout history, the causes of revolutions seem to have remained surprisingly limited in range, and more or less the same as those explained with such dubious simplicity in Aristotle's *Politics*.[2] In this sense, allowing for cultural nuances and the altered circumstances of time and place, no claim can be made about the uniqueness or even singularity of the Iranian Revolution. This should be reassuring to political scientists and those historians who relish repetitiveness in history, or similarities between crucial events in different times and places. The case of Iran certainly corroborates a number of propositions current among most theorists of revolution. One of these is that revolutions do not take place as a result of decline or acute social and political crisis or economic misery alone, that they do not occur merely in consequence of popular discontent erupting into violent mass demonstrations following periods of suppression and tyranny. There should be some positive elements in its background as well – in the form not only of economic and social development and cultural awakening, but even of some degree of democracy, or pretension to it.[3] The more the general picture of the society looks like one of overwhelming darkness, the less the likelihood of a revolution. Only when there is an uneasy comingling of all these mutually contradictory elements can a revolutionary situation arise.

This proposition has now once again been proved by the Iranian Revolution, showing that every revolution is preceded not only by social and economic inequities, but also by some form of social and economic development. The violent overthrow of the Iranian monarchy was foreshadowed by a situation full of the most improbable paradoxes, combining progress and decline, enlightenment and obscurantism, modernisation and atavistic tendencies, cultivation of Sassanian, pre-Islamic symbols and professions of faith in Shi'ite Islam, autocratic methods of government and formalistic adherence to democratic procedures, mass mobilisation and stulifying political control. It was the presence of all these contradictions in the body politic of Iran during the decade immediately preceding the Revolution which both signalled an impending doom and fostered an overweaning confidence in the resilience of the imperial regime – depending on one's standpoint in the political spectrum. Throughout that period, there were some people who constantly depicted the regime as tottering on the verge of collapse, while there were others who were equally confident of its ultimate ability to weather any crisis. Setting aside their perfunctory exaggerations, both groups were in a sense right, because they were referring to two different sets of circumstances. As suggested, it was a situation full of contradictions, and here one realises how simplistic and superficial most of the judgements on the Shah's regime are. It is unrealistic to describe it as totally evil or dictatorial, just as it is absurd to praise it as enlightened and benevolent. Both descriptions hold a grain of truth, without being invalidated by the fact that, as time went by, and especially after the spectacular increase in Iran's oil income following the 1973 energy crisis, the Shah's style of government became increasingly despotic, and his entourage more corrupt.

Another aspect in which the Iranian Revolution conforms to the familiar pattern of revolutions is the way in which the politial landscape underwent rapid changes during 1979. At first the country was engulfed by an unprecedented mood of harmony and mutual compassion nourished by a sweeping but vague consensus on common goals. Then, perhaps because of the same vagueness as well as the sudden and stupendous rhythm with which the old regime was overthrown, it was replaced by creeping divisions and tensions, followed by lurches to the right and the left, and bitter disillusionment.

Western sociological concepts, whether Marxist or non-Marxist, have been freely used to explain both the background, and the rapid collapse of the imperial order.[4] Most of these fall wide of the mark. Neither the theory of class struggle, nor the analysis of the growth of the urban middle classes or the migrant poor, nor any account of the stresses and strains to which the Iranian society was subjected as a result of the forced modernisation, can convincingly answer the cardinal question in this debate: how did the elaborate machinery, developed over the years to deal with the regime's opponents through a variety of methods ranging from heavy-handed suppression through manipulation to gratification or co-option, so utterly break down in less than a year? The question becomes all the more pressing when one remembers that the breakdown happened at a time when the regime, with all its malaise at the cultural, social, economic and political levels, was certainly not going through the kind of crisis which could be even remotely comparable to, for instance, the strains imposed on the French monarchy between 1787 and 1789, or to the plight of a war-stricken Tsarist Russia on the eve of the October Revolution. Perhaps the final answer to this question must await the revelation of all the relevant facts concerning the last years of the Shah's reign, and especially his relations with the United States. More knowledge is needed too about the Shah's own mental wanderings during his last months, at a time of fatal sickness and failure of willpower, in the face of not only a popular uprising but also of American pressure.

But one sociological notion which may serve as the summation of all the complicated, non-material causes of the aforementioned breakdown, and can therefore be helpful in our analysis, is *anomy*: the Revolution was undoubtedly preceded by a decline in the traditional modes of authority and the criteria of assessing one's social standing. This was not entirely the result of the Shah's drive for modernisation; it was not therefore unavoidable. Evidently, the weakening of the extended family, the migration of rural groups to towns, the habits and mores inseparable from industrialisation, the imbalance between defective or superficial modernity and traditional values and attitudes, could to a considerable extent account for its breakdown. People were torn away from their cultural and moral roots. The sense of individual identity, of group solidarity, and of corporate loyalty was placed under intolerable strain. But what exacerbated the institutional causes of these defects was some of the personal wayward features of the high political leadership. One example was the campaign against gerontocracy, apparently launched in the wake of the Shah's brainwave that all the ills of the country were the fault of the old people in positions of leadership and management. The campaign started at the end of the 1960s, and resulted in the appointment of scores of highly-educated and motivated youth to crucial positions in the bureaucratic, industrial and academic fields. The enterprise proved to be disastrous for the simple reason that the new appointees, however technically competent, never enjoyed the same degree of acceptability as did the senior members of the 'old guard'. The upshot was the further loosening of the chain of authority, whether in the office, factory, school or university. The damaging effects of this policy, which undermined the cohesion of the regime itself, accumulated as the popular struggle sharpened. By the time the opposition seemd poised to capture power, most of the veteran politicians had either abandoned the ruling clique, or were discredited, or reduced to silence.

The larger cultural backcloth to the developing sense of anomy was a feeling of inferiority in the face of the West, so well-known in most countries of the Third World. It was a feeling shared by vast groups of people of all classes, rich and poor. But among the educated élite, it was buttressed by a conviction that one of the main causes of the slow pace of progress in the country was its attachment to traditional values and beliefs, of which Shi'ite Islam was the most important source. The mass of the people, however, remained loyal to Islam beneath their apparent attraction to western modes of entertainment and fashions – an anomaly which misled many Iranian and foreign intellectuals into thinking that religion was on the decline. A revealing example of this dichotomy in the nation's moral life was provided by the annual festivals of Shiraz, in which a privileged minority exhibited its infatuation with the latest, ultramodern products of western arts, sometimes in public places before the eyes of bemused Shirazis.

The mention of religion raises a different issue. So far, this paper has been concerned mainly with those features of the Iranian Revolution which make it more or less similar to most other revolutions. But as was noted before, the Revolution took place against the background of a heightened religious consciousness which merely brought the underlying loyalty to Shi'ism into the open. And it is by virtue of Shi'ism that the Revolution acquired certain characteristics giving it a particular, if not unique, place among the revolutions of our age. This emphasis on religion is bound to provoke a refutation by those writers who see the Revolution as nothing but the outcome of purely social and economic processes. If by revolution is meant the complex of long-term factors which gradually undermined the Pahlavi regime, their refutation is justified. But if what is meant is the crucial and final stage of the popular uprising which acted as the catalyst of those factors, I insist on the role of religion as the principal element in the whole equation. This cannot be fully appreciated unless one remembers that there were two distinct phases in the Revolution. In the first, starting in 1977 with the appearance of the first signs of social tension in the country, until the first riots in the holy city of Qum in January 1978, the secular intellectuals of moderate left-wing or liberal leanings played the dominant part, by issuing petitions and broadsheets, holding 'poetry evenings' and appealing to international bodies for the defence of human rights and civil liberties. This period coincided with the campaign by the Carter Administration in the United States for the same aims, a coincidence which was seized upon by some of the more militant leftists and religionalists as evidence of an American 'plot' behind the intellectuals' strivings. The radical attacks on the intellectual opposition, together with the refusal of the regime to accede to its demands, prepared the ground for the religious ascendency in the second period, as a result of which Shi'ism became the ideology of the anti- regime movement *par excellence*.

Shi'ism could not have played this part had it not gone through a major political transformation since the end of the last century, if not earlier. In a sense, the Revolution of 1979 was a repetition of four earlier episodes: the 'Tobacco rebellion' of 1892, the Constitutional Revolution of 1906, the oil nationalisation movement of

1951–3, and the abortive uprising of 1963 led by Ayatollah Khomeini. In terms of social and political causes, there were important differences between these episodes: the first was a movement against foreign domination, but restricted to a specific issue – the abolition of a concession granted to a British company; the second represented the first effort by Iranians in modern times to establish a democratic system of government; the third again was an instance of the anti-imperialist struggle, but of a much wider scope than the first; and the fourth highlighted the attempt of the Ulama to stand up to a fresh drive for the secularisation of the state masquerading under the guise of the Shah's 'White Revolution'.

Despite these differences, the four episodes shared a number of features in common, of which two are worth mentioning: first, each of them witnessed an alliance of varying duration between the three main social and political forces in the country: the Ulama, the indigenous bourgeoisie, and (especially in the case of the last two) the secular, or semi-secular liberal nationalists. (The leftists, whether socialist or communists, made their appearance as an active force only in the 1950s.) Secondly, in each case, the great mass of the people participated in the movement only at the instance of the religious leaders; or to put it conversely, without the active encouragement of the religious leaders, the agitation for these various causes would not have enjoyed the support of the vast majority of the people. One could also cite a third common feature which applies only to the first three: the popular movement succeeded only *initially* in fulfilling its goals, whether it was the cancellation of the concession (1892), or adoption of fundamental law (1906), or the nationalisation of oil (1951), with the religious leaders emerging as the immediate beneficiaries. (This did not happen in the case of the 1963 uprising because the intransigent, anti-royalist stand of Ayatollah Khomeini created, from the start, a gulf between him and the more conservative Ulama, thereby dividing the religious leadership.) But on each occasion, while the religious leaders emerged as the *immediate* beneficiaries, on each occasion too, either the government or the semi-secular nationalists soon managed to gain the upper hand, and excluded their religious partners from power. Soon after 1892, the government granted new banking and mining concessions to the British, Russian and other western powers without encountering any effective opposition; the constitutional regime eventually resulted in the establishment of Rida Shah's fierce 'anticlericalism'; and by the time the oil nationalisation movement was crushed in the *coup* of 1953, the nationalist forces led by Dr Musaddiq had succeeded in discrediting the religious camp led by Ayatollah Kashani as allies of the British and the royalists. Accordingly, the Ulama drew three lessons from these precedents: (i) whenever they genuinely set their hearts on a political campaign, there is nothing which can stand in the way of their immediate success; (ii) in order to ensure the consummation of their success, they should not trust, or share power with, their secular or semi-secular rivals; and (iii) the defeat of 1963 showed that the religious leadership cannot have any hope of even initial success unless it manages to have a degree of internal unity: for this purpose, it has to adopt positions which would appeal to all shades of opinion among the Ulama, ranging from the liberal to the radical.

Armed with this political experience, the Ulama launched the popular movement of 1979. From the outset, their militant wing was determined not to allow itself to be outwitted by the assortment of liberal and radical forces which had taken part in the incipient phase of the movement, as described before. One of their leading thinkers, Murtada Mutahhari, wrote a few months before the actual overthrow of the monarchy:

The history of Islamic movements during the last hundred years reveals one unfortunate defect in its leadership: it has continued the struggle under its leadership [only] up to the moment of victory, but has refused to carry it on further [preferring instead] to go after its own business and allow others to usurp the result of its efforts. . . . The clergy brought the Constitutional movement [of 1906] to fruition, but refused to continue it and benefit from it: hence a harsh dictatorship soon came to power, leaving nothing but a mere name of Constitutionalism, and fostering the misconception among the people that despotism in principle is better than a constitutional regime, and that constitutionalism is a sin.[5]

This new resolve to ensure the continued mastery of not only the popular movement but also the fruits of its achievement stemmed from a complex of political factors, relating to the Ulama's experience in recent history as well as to their evolving political outlook. One can designate the totality of these factors as 'revivalism', to discern it from any reformism or renaissance, which, in its true sense, is yet to materialise in both Shi'ism or Sunnism. Political revivalism in Shi'ism is of fairly recent origin, although one might trace its roots back to the intellectual and theological trends in the eighteenth and nineteenth centuries. It revolves essentially around a reinterpretation of a number of central concepts of Shi'ism in the direction of political activism, and a positive stand in the face of injustice. Without this reinterpretation, Shi'ism could not have played the part it did in the events of 1978 and 1979.

In its classical version, Islamic political thought, whether of Sunni or Shi'ite persuasion, does not have a theory of revolution. The closest approximation of it is a timid admission of the right to revolt against unjust rulers. This in practice is of little value, because the only people who can ascertain whether a ruler is just or unjust are the Ulama, namely the very men who have nearly always endorsed the legitimacy of even the most tyrannical of regimes. Consequently, both sects in practice obeyed unjust rulers. Their only difference on this score lay in the reasons which each of them adduced to justify obedience. Most of the prominent jurists among the Sunnis pre-scribed obedience to the rulers, even the unjust, on the basis of the general Koranic injunction that God, the Prophet and the 'Holders of Authority' (*ulu'l-amr*) should be obeyed, and that in any case even an unjust regime is preferable to anarchy. The Shi'ites adopted the same attitude, but for a different reason: the preservation and survival of their community as a minority under the Sunni rule. This is what is known as *diquiyyah*, which has often been translated in English as 'expedient dissimulation', but in recent Shi'ite literature is interpreted less as a negative stance, and more as another form of clandestine struggle against tyranny.

Apart from the latter reformulation, there are two doctrines and one historical precedent which can be potential antecedents for a theory of revolution. First is the doctrine of *ghayb'ah*, or occultation of the Imam, stating that the twelfth descendant of the Imam, known as the Mahdi, disappeared in 893 to return at the end of time to 'fill the world with justice'. Ordinary Shi'ites understood this to mean that between these two dates there can be no real justice in the world. This notion, which has been behind the famous, theoretical denial by *some* leading jurists of the legitimacy of temporal power, is potentially revolutionary. But in fact it has not been so until recently. The reason is not far to see. By maintaining that all existing authorities in the world are illegitimate, and the truly legitimate rule will only appear at the end of the universe, most Shi'ites throughout history, instead of revolting against their gov-ernments, chose to settle into a serene indifference to politics. Any millenarian, chiliastic doctrine promising an ideal state in the future, as does Twelver Shi'ism, is politically a double-edged sword: it can exhort its adherents to resort to militancy, but it can also predispose them to quietism and submissiveness.

This becomes particularly clear in the case of the second doctrine– the millenarian anticipation (*intizar*) of the return of the twelfth Imam, which is a corollary to the first doctrine. The illegitimacy of temporal rulers is not an open-ended concept: it entails the expectation that a legitimate ruler is destined to appear at a future time. But this expectation also is liable to produce either of two contradictory political attitudes: it can generate a historicist conviction in the final triumph of the right, thereby promoting militancy; but it can also lead to fatalism, and a passive acceptance of the *given*, in the hope that real salvation is to come later. Finally, the historical precedent is the memory of the Karbala tragedy, the uprising of the third Imam, Husayn Ibn Ali, which was crushed in blood in 680. Again, for the best part of their history, the Shi'ites commemorated Husayn's martyrdom simply as an occasion for mourning and weeping, and nothing more. They rarely tried to deduce from it any political lesson in the fight against the established order. It was thus that the whole 'Husayniah myth' became a symbol for sacrificial acting out of martyrdom for the sake of martyrdom, or a masochistic endurance of suffering as sign of piety.

During the last hundred years, the Shi'ite understanding of all these issues has been slowly transformed, partly by dint of the general awakening of Iranians, partly in response to changing social and political conditions, and partly through a natural evolution of the Shi'ite mind, brought on occasionally by its inherent mechanism for change as represented by the institution of *ijtihad* or individual judgement. The result invariably has been the discarding of the quietist interpretation of each issue in favour of a militant one.[6] This is what in the context of Muslim thought in other countries has been called the politicisation, or secularisation or de-sacralisation of some key Islamic precepts.[7] But in the Iranian case it is perhaps more accurately described as a new tide of realism which was initially intended to replace the paralysing idealism of the past. This was most apparent at the time of Constitutional Revolution of 1906, when by their stand for legal constraints on the powers of the monarch, the Ulama were in fact declaring that Shi'ites should not put off positive political action for the betterment of their conditions until the return of the Imam, and that the creation of a just system of government was within their reach. This was not an entirely new position on their part, since examples of it could be found in the earlier stages of judicial and theological thought in Shi'ism. What was new was the recognition of the need for modern legal arrangements in the form of a fundamental law and parliament to ensure just rule.

This process of realistic thought was interrupted by Rida Shah's dictatorship (1925–41). It re-emerged in the post-war period, clearly with a reduced momentum, only to be suppressed again by the re-establishment of a dictatorship after the *coup* of 1953. The next phase of its revival was gradual and almost imperceptible, starting in the early 1960s amidst a new political crisis, and reaching its climax on the eve of the Revolution of 1979. The ideological principles of the new phase can be found in the writings of a host of religious authors mostly brought up in the traditional centres of Shi'ite education in Iran and Iraq. Again, one example from the works of Mutahhari should be enough to convey the mental climate of the new generation of the militant Ulamma. It concerns the redefinition of the concept of anticipation, which, as he says, is of two kinds:

[first] an anticipation which is constructive, protective, and productive of strength and dynamism, thus being of kind which can be counted as a worship and adulation of right; [second] an anticipation which is sinful, destructive, enslaving, and paralysing, and should therefore be considered as a form of anarchism [or permissiveness, *Ibahigari*]. These two kinds of anticipation are the results of two kinds of interpretation of the majestic reappearance of the Mahdi. In their turn, they lead to two perceptions of historical change and revolution.[8]

The concept of the Mahdi is of Koranic origin. It is the Koran which emphatically promises the final victory of the Islamic faith and of the pious and the righteous. . . . Mahdism involves above everything else an optimism towards the universal order of nature and the evolutionary course of history, and confidence in future. . . . the principle of anticipation also emanates from another Koranic and Islamic precept, which is the 'prohibition of despondency in the Spirit of God' [*ruhullah*]. Those who believe in the divine providence never give up hope.[9]

What is most noticeable in this activist, optimistic and revolutionary vision is a return to the pristine idealism of Shi'ism – something which the earlier generation of the Ulama had tried to modify in the interest of a compromise with the powers that be, and more important, with the political institutions imported from the West. When those powers and the westernised institutions – the parliament, the constitutional monarchy, the political parties and the press – proved to be corrupt and corrupting, the Ulama's tendency was either to withdraw from politics, or, as happened during the Revolution, opt for militant idealism. Those who like Ayatollah Shariatmadari chose the middle course, became the target of virulent attack from both sides.

It was just mentioned that the Shi'ite attempts during the last hundred years at redefining traditional concepts were occasioned by motley political and ideological changes in their universe. This applies also to the new Shi'ite militant idealism. But here mention may be made of one sociological cause as well, which incidentally emphasises the fact that, contrary to the impression gained by some outsiders, the Ulama are no more monolithic than other social groups in Iran. In the past, the Ulama were preponderantly dependent for their financial revenues on the populace, from whom they received various donations, either as the obligatory *khums* (fifth), *zakat* (alms tax), or the voluntary *sadaqat* and *nuzur* (vows); a minority of them were also in the pay of the state. Religious students (*talabah*) who formed the immediate 'constituency' of each of the Ulama, and sometimes acted as their private armies, often belonged to the deprived classes. An important development which seems to have taken place since the second world war, and especially with the expansion of the state, and availability of more varied financial resources, has been the emergence of a new stratum of religionists, both teachers and students, who were neither totally dependant on popular donations, nor on direct state support. Thanks to a variety of fresh job opportunities – teaching in non-religious institutions, schools and universities, journalism, publishing, etc. – they were able to earn enough to be independant of both the patriarchal Ulama and the state if they wanted to – although in terms of religious dogma they were inevitably affiliated to one or the other of the Ulama. This brought them nearer to other groups of educated people – teachers, lecturers, writers and intellectuals in general – with all that it meant in terms of exposure to radicalising currents, and response to social and political strains. Much of, but by no means all, the ideological and organisational work which consciously or unconsciously prepared the ground for the religious leadership of the Revolution, especially the political use of the mosques, was done by this group. They, of course, overlapped with or were joined by other disgruntled religious elements: those who genuinely strove to vindicate Islamic values irrespective of the constitutional form of the state (republican or monarchy), those who were damaged by the state control over the endowments, those who wanted to synthesize Islam with socialism or Marxism, and those who sought nothing but the *vilayat-i faqih* (guardianship or rulership of the jurisconsul). The conjunction of all these ideological, political and social causes of dissent explains the sudden upsurge of oppositional politics among the religious community, even those conservative circles long known to the allies of the monarchy, in 1979. It also partly explains why the uprising of 1963 resulted in defeat, while that of 1979 triumphed: in the former, the conservative Ulama were alienated by the militants, whereas in the latter they had common grounds with them.

Because the Revolution was so deeply animated by religion, there were many sceptics who from the outset feared that it would throw up a retrogressive and ruthless regime, cut off from the realities of the modern world, and unable to produce a clear and consistent blue-print for the future. Subsequent excesses by the revolutionaries confirmed some of these fears, substantiating the claim, mentioned at the beginning of this paper, that what happened in 1979 was not a revolution, but an upheaval unleashed by a shaky alliance of confused radicals and hidebound fundamentalists, with no promise of establishing a humane and democratic order. It may be too late for politicians to judge the truth of this claim; but it is certainly too early for historians to do so. Hence the pleadings by some of the more stoic advocates of the Revolution to avoid rash condemnation of what is taking place in Iran, on the grounds that all the glaring aberrations that one can observe are the normal side-effects of any and every revolution, to be soon superseded by a rational or moderate and equitable system.

One point is clear: the mere immersion in religious symbols, and the dominant urge to go back fourteen centuries in an effort to restore the model-state created by the Prophet Muhammad or Imam Ali, should not by itself give cause for describing the Iranian Revolution as a retrogressive anomaly. The hankering after a past Golden Age, as has been noted by Hannah Arendt, inspired many revolutions in the West too. 'The fact', she writes that the word 'revolution' meant originally restoration, hence something which to us is its very opposite, is not a mere oddity of semantics. The revolutions of the seventeenth and eighteenth centuries, which to us appear to show all evidence of a new spirit, the spirit of the modern age, were intended to be restorations. It is true, the civil wars in England foreshadowed a great many tendencies which we have come to associate with what was essentially new in the revolutions of the eighteenth century. . . . Yet the fact is that the short-lived victory of this first modern revolution was officially understood as a restoration, namely as 'freedom by God's blessing restored', as the inscription runs on the great seal of 1651. . . . [T]he French and the American Revolutions . . . were played in their initial stages by men who were firmly convinced that they would do no more than restore an older order of things that had been disturbed and violated by the despotism of absolute monarchy or the abuses of colonial government. They pleaded in all sincerity that they wanted to revolve back to old times when things were as they ought to be.[10]

To sum up Shi'ite Islam was the prime source for the mobilising myth and the organisational framework of the Revolution. As such, it may account for a number of other features which make the Revolution in Iran dissimilar from the normal type of revolutions in our time, thus acting as the root of both its weaknesses and strengths: its highly personalised leadership represented by the charisma of Ayatollah Khomeini; its relative ability during the months before the overthrow of the monarchy to shun unnecessary and widespread violence, and instead to rely on persuasion or threats of violence in winning over individuals or groups to its side; its initial appeal to many social groups which were in fact benefiting from the pre-revolutionary conditions: most of the middle classes, many merchants, civil servants, etc. whose material or political grievances against the old regime were not, by themselves, enough to spur them to rebellious acts; and, finally, the ease with which the Revolution could get the majority of the people to agree on a small number of simple and general slogans – 'freedom, independence, Islamic republic' – without facing the necessity of much intellectual or ideological hair-splitting over the meaning of these terms.

NOTES

1. For an Iranian example of this view, see *Naqsh-i ruhaniyyun dar guzar-i qudrat* ('The Role of the Clergy in the Transfer of Power', published by the Organisation of Communist Unity) (Tehran, 1357 (1978–79)).
2. Aristotle, *Politics*, trans. Benjamin Jowett (Oxford, 1908), Book v.
3. Jeffry Kapler, *New Perspectives On the French Revolution: Readings in Historical Sociology* (London, 1965), p. 17.
4. See Muhammad Ja'far and Azar Tabari, 'Iran: Islam and the Struggle for Socialism', in *Khamsin*, Journal of Revolutionary Socialists of the Middle East, 8 (1981), pp. 83–104; Fred Halliday, *Iran: Dictatorship and Development* (London, 1979), pp. 285–303. On the role of the migrant poor in the Revolution, see Farhad Kazemi, *Poverty and Revolution in Iran: The Migrant Poor, Urban Marginality and Politics* (New York University Press, 1980).
5. Murtada Mutahhari, *Nahdat-ha-yi Islami dar sad salih-yi akhir* ('Islamic Movements During the Last Hundred Years') (Qum, 1358 (1978)), pp. 95–6.
6. For full details of these reinterpretations, see the present author's *Modern Islamic Political Thought* (Macmillan, forthcoming), Chapter 5.
7. Cf. Clifford Geertz, *Islam Observed* (Yale University Press 1968), pp. 90ff.
8. Murtada Mutahhari, *Qiyam va inqilab-i Mahdi az did-gah-i falsafih-i tarikh* ('The Mahdi's Uprising and Revolution from the Standpoint of the Philosophy of History') (Tehran, 1398 (1978)), pp. 7–8.
9. Ibid. pp. 5–6.
10. Hannah Arendt, *On Revolution* (New York, 1963), pp. 36–7.

Index